Prophets and Patriots

Prophets and Patriots

FAITH IN DEMOCRACY ACROSS THE
POLITICAL DIVIDE

Ruth Braunstein

UNIVERSITY OF CALIFORNIA PRESS

University of California Press, one of the most distinguished university presses in the United States, enriches lives around the world by advancing scholarship in the humanities, social sciences, and natural sciences. Its activities are supported by the UC Press Foundation and by philanthropic contributions from individuals and institutions. For more information, visit www.ucpress.edu.

University of California Press
Oakland, California

Library of Congress Cataloging-in-Publication Data

Names: Braunstein, Ruth, 1981- author.
Title: Prophets and patriots : faith in democracy across the political divide/ Ruth Braunstein.
Description: Oakland, California : University of California Press, [2017] | Includes bibliographical references and index.
Identifiers: LCCN 2016036911 (print) | LCCN 2016039686 (ebook) | ISBN 9780520293649 (cloth : alk. paper) | ISBN 9780520293656 (pbk. : alk. paper) | ISBN 9780520966888 (ebook)
Subjects: LCSH: Political participation—United States. | Democracy—United States. | Tea Party movement—United States. | Religion and politics—United States. | Social movements—United States.
Classification: LCC JK1764 .B74 2017 (print) | LCC JK1764 (ebook) | DDC 323/.0420973—dc23
LC record available at https://lccn.loc.gov/2016036911

26 25 24 23 22 21 20 19 18 17
10 9 8 7 6 5 4 3 2 1

For Jan and Richard Braunstein and Tim Sullivan

Contents

List of Figures and Table

Acknowledgments

Few pieces of writing are the product of a single mind, and this book is no exception. My largest debt of gratitude is owed to the men and women I met during the research for this project. Thank you for your patience, your candor, your humor, and most of all, your trust. Special thanks go to the women I call Linda and Nora, who opened the doors to the two groups in which I conducted fieldwork, answered countless questions, and remained supportive of this research even when they were uncomfortable with my observations and long after I surely wore out my welcome. While I was not able to include more than a fraction of the experiences I shared with these groups or of the stories that individuals shared with me, my wish is that they see in this book a sketch of their efforts that feels true.

While completing this project, I was privileged to receive mentorship, advice, and moral support from colleagues at New York University's Sociology Department and Institute for Public Knowledge and at the University of Connecticut's Sociology Department and Humanities Institute. At NYU, I received invaluable feedback and encouragement from Hillary Angelo, Melissa Aronczyk, Kathleen Gerson, Jeff Goodwin, Jennifer Heerwig, Colin Jerolmack, Jane Jones, Eric Klinenberg, Issa Kohler-Hausmann, Amy LeClair, Steven Lukes, Brian McCabe, Michael McQuarrie,

Tey Meadow, Ashley Mears, Richard Sennett, Harel Shapira, Anna Skarpelis, Owen Whooley, and Grace Yukich. At UConn, I received generous feedback and support during the latter stages of writing this book from Claudio Benzecry, Mary Bernstein, Andrew Deener, Manisha Desai, Susan Herbst, Michael Lynch, Christin Munsch, Jeremy Pais, Bandana Purkayastha, Daisy Reyes, and Daniel Winchester.

Over the years, this book also benefited significantly because of feedback from and conversations with a wider community of scholars, including Jeffrey Alexander, Gianpaolo Baiocchi, Amy Binder, David Buckley, Hana Brown, Todd Nicholas Fuist, Brad Fulton, Philip Gorski, Neil Gross, Jeffrey Guhin, David Grazian, Drew Halfmann, Arlie Hochschild, Caroline Lee, Paul Lichterman, Myra Marx Ferree, Thomas Medvetz, Rory McVeigh, David Meyer, Ziad Munson, John O'Brien, Andrew Perrin, Rebecca Sager, David Smilde, David Snow, Erika Summers-Effler, Nella Van Dyke, Jonathan VanAntwerpen, Rhys Williams, Nicholas Wilson, and Richard Wood.

Special thanks go to three mentors and conversation partners, who played an integral role in this project from its inception. From our first conversations about this project, Jeff Manza pushed me to consider both how the larger political context was shaping what I observed within these groups and why this research should matter to people beyond any single scholarly subfield. If this book provides satisfying answers to either of those questions, it is thanks to Jeff's honest critiques and to the stacks of books he lent me each time we met. Courtney Bender was an invaluable sounding board as I navigated the everyday complexities of ethnographic research; she also understood from the beginning that there was an interesting story to tell about the role religion played in these groups, even as I struggled to explain precisely what was "religious" about them. Our meetings over the years were like booster shots, invariably leaving me refocused and reenergized. Finally, I feel enormously privileged to have developed my ideas about this project, and about being a sociologist, through conversations with Craig Calhoun. His unique way of seeing the world, and his incisive comments on countless pieces of my writing—often sent from far-flung locales at all hours of the day and night—have encouraged me to complicate and clarify the stories I am trying to tell. I can never thank him enough for his generosity, enthusiasm, and confidence.

Over the years, I was invited to present the developing arguments of this book in a number of venues, including Colby College's Sociology Department Colloquium; Columbia University's Religion and Politics in American Public Life Lecture Series; the Craft of Ethnography Workshop at NYU; Lehigh University's Humanities Center; the NYLON workshop in politics, culture, and social theory at NYU; the University of Pennsylvania's Urban Ethnography Workshop; Yale University's Center for Comparative Research; Yale's Center for Cultural Sociology; Yale's MacMillan Center Initiative on Religion, Politics and Society; and the Young Scholars in Social Movements Mini-Conference at the University of Notre Dame's Center for the Study of Social Movements. I also presented aspects of this work at the annual meetings of the American Sociological Association, the Association for the Sociology of Religion, the Eastern Sociological Society, the Social Science History Association, and the Society for the Scientific Study of Religion. Overall, the generous feedback I received from these individuals and audiences significantly strengthened this research. To the extent that this book contains any remaining errors or weaknesses, the fault is entirely my own.

During the writing of this book, I benefited from the time and support afforded to me as an American Fellow of AAUW and a Public Discourse Project Faculty Fellow at the UConn Humanities Institute. I also gratefully acknowledge the generous support for this research from the NYU Sociology Department and the UConn College of Liberal Arts and Sciences (CLAS) and CLAS Book Support Committee. Additional thanks go to Debbie Ivens Lewites for her transcription services. I am also deeply indebted to Naomi Schneider at the University of California Press for her support for this project. Thanks, too, to the outside reviewers whose detailed feedback pushed me to sharpen the arguments in the book, as well as to the entire UC Press team who guided me through the production process.

I wish to acknowledge that portions of this book were adapted from the following previously published works: "Who Are 'We the People'?" in *Contexts* (2011); "Who Are 'We the People'? Multidimensional Identity Work in the Tea Party," in *Understanding the Tea Party Movement*, edited by Nella Van Dyke and David S. Meyer (Ashgate, 2014); and "The Role of Bridging Cultural Practices in Racially and Socioeconomically Diverse

Civic Organizations" (with Brad R. Fulton and Richard L. Wood), in *American Sociological Review* (2014).

Finally, for the much needed encouragement and distractions over the years, thank you to my friends and family, especially my parents, Jan and Richard Braunstein; my siblings, Julie and Jake Braunstein; and my in-laws, Seth Gyselinck and Colleen, Vin, and Kevin Sullivan. Thanks, too, to Beatrice, the tiny puppy who joined our family during the year I completed this book; and to our baby boy, Charlie, who arrived just as it went to press. Their complete disregard for this project was a helpful reminder that there were more important things in the world than work. Above all, thank you to my partner in all things, Tim Sullivan—I am the luckiest.

1 Introduction

"I went to college," said Javier, who sat to my right, his arms wrapped around his squirmy one-year-old son.[1] "But I am still having trouble finding a good job, one where I can buy a house and take care of my family." He was especially frustrated by the "myth," as he called it, that if you followed a certain "linear path" that included college, then you would succeed. He repeated the word *linear*, as if this were the most frustrating part. He, like many other people in that room, had found that path to be anything but straight or predictable. And in recent years, it had felt more like a trap—leading them in circles and tightening around them all the time.

Javier was one of approximately one hundred men and women who had gathered that afternoon in the auditorium of a Lutheran church in the northeastern city where they lived. This Lutheran congregation was a core member of Interfaith, a progressive, faith-based community-organizing coalition that I had been studying for over a year. Interfaith was affiliated with the PICO National Network—short for "People Improving Communities through Organizing"—one of a handful of faith-based community-organizing (FBCO) networks operating throughout the United States.[2] Like other FBCO

1

coalitions nationwide, Interfaith was a coalition of multiple member organizations—in their case a diverse set of religious congregations—that came together to address local quality-of-life issues like public safety, health care, education, and housing in their communities. In so doing, they aspired to develop leaders capable of exerting power at all levels of public life.

Interfaith drew its members primarily from two neighborhoods located on opposite sides of the city where it operated. One neighborhood was predominantly white and middle class; the other was racially and ethnically diverse and lower income, having welcomed successive waves of immigrants over the past several decades. By organizing in a diverse set of religious congregations across these neighborhoods, the group sought to build a coalition that reflected the diversity of their city as a whole. This, they believed, provided them with the political legitimacy they needed to fight for programs and policies that promoted social justice, economic inclusion, human dignity, and the common good.

As I looked around the room that afternoon, the diversity of the coalition was on display. The men and women crowded around round tables and standing along the edges of the room were black, white, Latino, and Arab; Protestant, Catholic, Jewish, and Muslim; middle-class and low-income. It was a Sunday afternoon, but most of the people present were not members of this Lutheran congregation; they worshipped in churches, synagogues, and mosques all over the city. They had traveled here not to worship together but rather to discuss how they could work together to confront the economic challenges that Americans around the country still faced in the wake of the Great Recession. Or as the pastor of the church put it before leading an opening prayer: "How do we live together as a nation under these circumstances?"

Before we broke off into the small group where Javier shared his story, Gabriel, one of the organizers running the event, polled the group. "How many of you—raise your hand—know somebody that has lost their job in the last couple of years?" Despite the fact that people came from a wide range of backgrounds, nearly every hand in the room went up. "Look around the room, everybody. Turn around, those of you in front." People nodded knowingly as they saw the sea of hands.

"All right, put your hands down," he told them. "How many of you know somebody who is underwater in their mortgage or is having trouble paying their bills?" Again, almost everybody raised a hand. "All right," Gabriel responded, on a roll now. "How many of you know somebody—raise your hand again—that doesn't have health insurance or lacks adequate resources for health care? Almost everybody." He paused for effect. "Folks, it didn't always used to be this way in our country."

Looking around the room that day, I could not help but think of another group of men and women I had met during the previous year. I had concurrently been conducting fieldwork with the Patriots, a group of Tea Party activists who had mobilized in the suburban and rural communities that lay approximately one to two hours north of this urban church. The Patriots' membership was primarily white and middle class, with an active base of small business owners, veterans, religious conservatives, and libertarian-leaning independents. As a group, they sought to empower ordinary citizens to hold government accountable and advance what they viewed as the core principles of the United States Constitution—limited federal government, personal responsibility, and individual liberty. They had mobilized in the wake of President Barack Obama's election and debates about "Obamacare," a policy that they felt represented everything wrong with American politics today.[3]

On the surface, the groups could not have been more different. But during my first year of fieldwork, as I shuttled back and forth between them, I became increasingly struck by their similarities. It would take another year of intensive fieldwork and several more years of analysis and observation from afar to understand more precisely what these similarities meant and how they could be reconciled with the ways in which the groups' cultures and practices also diverged significantly. But on that Sunday afternoon with Interfaith, as I heard Javier's distressed admission, as I saw the crowd's hands go up in a signal of shared anxiety, as I heard Gabriel's sober commentary about the current state of the country, I felt a flutter of familiarity. I flashed back to an event I had attended with the Patriots about a year earlier.

I had arrived late at a Comfort Inn in a rural hamlet north of the city and was directed down a back stairwell to a basement conference room. It was early in my fieldwork, and I was not sure what to expect from this "candidate meet and greet" that local Tea Party groups had organized. The room was packed with between seventy-five and one hundred people, and the hotel staff was setting up additional chairs as I arrived. Someone motioned for me to sit in one of the new chairs, and I tried to quietly settle in as one of the candidates addressed the lively crowd.

After a few minutes, he handed the microphone to the main attraction, a feisty candidate for governor who had parlayed a successful career in business into a freewheeling campaign on behalf of overburdened "taxpayers." He had also become a lightning rod for controversy, even among Tea Partiers.

He had been stuck in traffic and looked exhausted after a long day of campaigning. But his weariness lent authenticity to his remarks that night. Before speaking, he paused and looked around the room. "Everywhere I go, the faces are different," he told them, quietly. "But the look is the same. It's the look of hope. Hope and frustration at the same time. People want to believe they can believe in their government."

"Everyone here has played by the rules," he said to the group, gaining a bit of steam. "And the people in D.C. are trying to change the rules." This has left us "ungrounded," he explained. "We don't feel the government is serving us, and we can't move forward."

"What do we teach our kids?" he asked, as the audience nodded. "We have taught them family values, respect, to go out there and earn it. But when our kids follow those rules, and then they find they can't find a job in their community, and they have to move to another state to find work, that is not what we prepared for."

Again there were nods; murmurs of agreement rippled through the room as if people had been privately struggling with this dilemma and now were reminded they were not the only ones. Hammering this point home, he offered a hopeful rallying cry. "They hear our rumblings coming down the road. I've seen you all over the state. You are not alone!"

During the question-and-answer period that followed, a woman shared her personal experience with this issue. Her voice quivered as she explained that her sons went to excellent colleges but could not find jobs. "They followed all the rules and made plans," she said angrily, leaning forward and clenching her fists, "and now nothing is as they planned." She was close to tears as she sat back down. A moment later, someone mentioned that people they knew were leaving the state to find jobs, to which someone else added, "We all want to move!" Another voice piled on: "But we can't sell our houses!" A few people shouted, "Yeah!"

I began my fieldwork with both Interfaith and the Patriots in 2010, two years after the financial crisis hit Wall Street like a tidal wave. Although the immediate danger had receded and the financial markets were slowly showing signs of recovery, the painful aftereffects of the ensuing Great Recession were still being felt on "Main Street." Unemployment remained high, especially for new college graduates who were starting their adult lives with record high levels of debt. Families struggled to pay their mortgages. Health-care bills mounted. Between 2010 and 2012, as I crisscrossed the state attending town hall meetings, public hearings, events with public officials and political candidates, protests, rallies, and smaller, less public gatherings of these groups, I watched as people came to terms with a changed world.

In suburban community centers and urban church auditoriums—those specific locales that comprise "Main Street"—I heard a similar refrain: "I worked hard and followed the rules my whole life, and now I have nothing to show for it. What do I do now?" If there was ever a time when working- and middle-class Americans could come together in shared grief, I thought, it seemed that this was the time. And indeed, a wide swath of Americans had mobilized, their fear and frustration solidifying into an increasingly sharp critique of how the government was handling the fallout from the crisis.

Of course, much of this frustration had been simmering just below the surface since before 2008, reflecting mounting perceptions of government unresponsiveness to ordinary citizens, and unease that the increasing complexity of public policies made it impossible for ordinary people to participate in debates about issues that affected their lives.[4] For decades, the key mechanisms underlying representative democracy—trust, responsiveness, and accountability—had been showing signs of strain. The crisis stretched these already tenuous bonds to their limits. For many Americans, this not only threatened the political legitimacy of the system but also cast its moral legitimacy into question.

Local Tea Party groups like the Patriots were among the first to respond, to great media fanfare. The Occupy movement soon followed, billed by many as the Left's answer to the Tea Party. Meanwhile, faith-based

media cov. diff. b/w P & I

community-organizing coalitions like Interfaith had been operating below the media's radar all along, voicing many of the same concerns about disparities between elites and ordinary Americans that were suddenly the focus of mainstream debates.

All of these groups shared similar populist concerns: the economy seemed to serve a few at the expense of the many; it was increasingly difficult for ordinary Americans to live the productive, healthy, and comfortable lives they had once enjoyed (or dreamed of); and ordinary people were not being included in decisions about how to chart a course back to the world they had been promised. Amid debates about how to stabilize and regulate the economy, these groups' impassioned reactions refocused attention on programs and policies intended to serve ordinary Americans.

WAKING UP, STANDING UP, SPEAKING UP

To be sure, there are myriad differences between the people who joined Tea Party groups like the Patriots, and the people who joined faith-based community-organizing coalitions like Interfaith. In addition to having demographic differences, the two groups lined up on opposite sides of nearly every national policy issue they confronted: while the Patriots vehemently opposed Obamacare, Interfaith members worked to support its passage and implementation; while Interfaith members took measures to improve conditions for their undocumented neighbors and called for a path to citizenship, the Patriots worried about the negative impacts of "illegals" on their communities and opposed most immigration reform proposals; the list goes on and on. Moreover, although both groups were formally nonpartisan, most members of the Patriots identified as and supported Republicans, and most members of Interfaith identified as and supported Democrats.

On this level, these groups could easily be situated in the context of rising partisan polarization, and their moral and political disagreements interpreted as evidence of a new front in the "culture war."[5] This kind of analysis would not be entirely wrong, but it would not tell the whole story. Moreover, this is the part of the story that everyone already knows—that when it comes to policy preferences, conservative and progressive activists hold starkly different positions on most issues. But focusing only on differences in their policy goals obscures more basic similarities between them that should not be overlooked.

These similarities are the untold story of these groups. Seeing these similarities requires that we shift our focus from the ends these groups seek—the policy demands that are often the most visible aspect of their efforts—to the *means* through which they make these demands.[6] It also requires that we shift our focus from their specific policy preferences to their concerns about the *political process* itself. When we focus on these aspects of their work, we can see that the groups share a surprising number of common features.

Most of the men and women who participated in these groups did not consider themselves activists; but in the face of rising anxiety and frustration, they had decided to act. They stopped feeling ashamed and started sharing their pain with others. They stopped worrying alone, yelling at the TV set, or setting aside the newspaper with a feeling of dread. They did not know how to solve the vast problems facing the country, but they shared a growing suspicion that they could not simply defer to political elites or trust that either political party would automatically serve their interests. Rather, they suspected that any durable solution to the country's problems would require higher levels of active participation by ordinary people like them, whose lives were most affected. If they wished to have a government "of the people, by the people," they would need to develop the knowledge and skills necessary to participate in these complex debates.

They flocked to these local citizens groups, where they worked alongside their neighbors to become better informed, more vigilant, and well organized—to become, in short, what I came to call *active citizens*. Once they were there, they learned as they went along. The woman who stood to speak about her unemployed sons at the candidate meet and greet told me later that she had been volunteering for a candidate for the state senate who was rising in popularity among local Tea Partiers. She also planned to attend the upcoming Restoring Honor Rally in Washington, D.C., hosted by the popular Fox News host Glenn Beck.[7] While volunteering for a political candidate is a somewhat conventional way to get involved in politics, Beck's rally promoted an alternative vision of active citizenship. America, he said that day in Washington, D.C., needed to turn back to God. For Beck and for many of the Patriots, active citizenship fused political vigilance with personal virtue.

At the same candidate meet and greet, I also ran into Gilbert, a core leader of the Patriots, who told me that he was heading to Washington, D.C., that weekend for an activist training class run by the national organization FreedomWorks. "I know how to run my business during the day," he explained, and then, motioning to the crowd of people milling around after the event, added, "but I'm excited to learn how to turn things like this into lasting electoral and legislative gains." Knowing my politics were to the left of his, he smiled as he noted that groups on the left have been much better at organizing and activism than groups on the right. "But I'm excited to learn more!"

Meanwhile, Interfaith members were also learning how to become better organizers and activists. Early members of the group had gravitated toward a model of "community organizing" that was "faith-based"—meaning they organized people through religious congregations and then worked together on the basis of their shared values as people of faith, such as their commitment to justice and human dignity. These values were not viewed simply as powerful sources of shared motivation to act: by linking them to American values, Interfaith also sought to project them outward into public debates about how to achieve the common good.

In terms of their more practical tactics, Interfaith's approach to building power in their communities can be traced to Saul Alinsky, considered by many to be the founder of contemporary community organizing. Alinsky—who wrote in his 1946 call to action: "The power of the people is transmitted through the gears of their own organizations, and democracy moves forward"—believed that citizens needed to develop enduring local organizations in which they could develop the knowledge, skills, and sense of empowerment necessary to exercise their "people power."[8]

At events like the one where I met Javier, Interfaith members gathered to do just this. They learned how to have intentional "one-to-one" conversations with their neighbors in order to surface the concerns that no one was talking about; how to conduct research and educate others about these problems; how to organize public actions (this was their term, *actions*) that pressure public officials to work with them to solve these problems; and then how to evaluate this long process, learn from their mistakes, and start again.

While this basic model of community organizing is typically associated with groups on the political left, Gilbert was introduced to many of these same basic tactics when he attended FreedomWorks' activist training. This is because conservatives have increasingly seen in Alinsky's writings a set of practical strategies that can be powerfully applied to various political ends. Although Alinsky has developed a reputation in recent years—most notably among viewers of Glenn Beck—as a dangerous left-wing radical, FreedomWorks' leaders and employees studied Alinsky closely and were known to spread "the Alinsky gospel," in the words of one reporter, as they provided early support to emerging local Tea Party groups, including the Patriots.[9]

All of the activities in which the Patriots and Interfaith engaged required a tremendous commitment of time and energy, as I discovered when I began participating in both groups and saw the little free time I had shrink to zero. Active citizenship is like a double shift, requiring people to attend meetings in the evenings after a full day at work and on weekends, when others are relaxing with friends or family. It requires them to spend more time every day reading the news and doing research on issues outside of their area of expertise. It requires them to put their relationships with friends, family members, and neighbors on the line by sharing stories and information about topics that are often viewed as too touchy or personal to discuss openly.

Their choice to pursue active citizenship thus sets these men and women apart from most of their fellow Americans. Of course, not everyone is equally capable of making this kind of time commitment— the demands of work or family life may not leave any free time for active political involvement; and the myriad social, cultural, and political barriers to participation are harder to overcome the fewer resources one has.[10] It is perhaps unsurprising in light of this that the most active members of Interfaith and the Patriots were retirees, stay-at-home mothers, parents of grown children, the self-employed, and the underemployed. In different ways, each of these groups had control over their time that most people lacked—in the words of the sociologist Doug McAdam, they were "biographically available" to participate in this kind of political action.[11]

In contrast, whether because of a lack of availability or of motivation, most Americans remain relatively inactive politically. Based on one of the most elementary measures of political engagement, voter turnout, the United States trails far behind most other developed countries.[12] Amid rising anxieties about their future, most Americans still choose distraction over action. Meanwhile, even those Americans who do pursue political engagement of some kind rarely take the active approach pursued by Interfaith and the Patriots. Their efforts are instead channeled to more passive activities (like signing on to advocacy organizations' mailing lists) or activities that do not address problems with the political system itself (like charity work). Active citizenship is one choice among many, and it is one of the more difficult and time-consuming choices. The fact that participants in both Interfaith and the Patriots chose it is noteworthy.

This is not to say that these groups were the same; it is to suggest that aspects of their work were homologous—as we will see, their efforts had shared historical roots, developed in response to shared political challenges, and as a result shared certain structural features in common. But while the groups' efforts *converged* at this level, the more specific ways in which they imagined what it meant for them to be active citizens in a democracy, and then worked together to enact these ideal visions, *diverged* significantly.

KEY ARGUMENTS AND CONTRIBUTIONS OF THIS BOOK

By shifting our focus from the groups' ends to their means, and from their concerns about policy to their concerns about the political process itself, this book highlights similarities between these groups that are typically not acknowledged. At the same time, it also traces more subtle differences between them that typically go unrecognized. In so doing, it challenges some of our prevailing understandings of what divides groups on opposite sides of the political spectrum, of the role of religion in public life, of the cultural underpinnings of democratic practice, and of the contested nature of American democracy and citizenship. Here, I briefly preview the key arguments and contributions of this research, which are discussed in more detail in chapter 7.

First, the stories recounted in this book destabilize prevailing understandings of how conservative and progressive groups engage in political life. For example, contentious grassroots approaches to exerting power are typically associated with groups on the political Left, economically disadvantaged groups, and groups who lack other forms of political influence. Meanwhile, it is assumed that groups on the political Right and economically advantaged groups pursue more elite channels of influence. Yet both Interfaith and the Patriots engaged in grassroots organizing and protest. This similarity calls attention not only to the strategic value of these practices for a wide range of groups but also to the varied ways that groups across the political divide infuse these practices with meaning.

Similarly, both groups asserted that religion offers values, lessons, and notions of "the good" that can help solve the country's most pressing problems—a claim typically associated with groups on the political right. By chronicling efforts to put faith into action at both ends of the political spectrum, this book disrupts popular accounts of a culture war between religious conservatives and liberal secularists. A careful parsing of the similarities and differences between these groups thus forces us to reconsider long-standing assumptions about the role of religion in American political life and enables us to develop a fuller and more nuanced picture of the contemporary political landscape as a whole.

Second, by tracing how these groups' styles nonetheless diverged in practice, this book deepens our understanding of the cultural underpinnings of democratic life. Just as a single beam of light can, upon hitting some surfaces, split into two separate beams of light, so too did the groups' shared vision of active citizenship, when put into practice, result in two different styles of active citizenship. But this split did not happen randomly or automatically. Rather, this book calls attention to two cultural processes that channeled the groups toward different ways of enacting their roles as active citizens. First, each group drew selectively from American culture and history to develop a group-level narrative of active citizenship that helped them cultivate a shared *democratic imaginary*—an understanding of how democracy ought to work and the role of active citizens (like them) within it. Second, group negotiations about what kinds of practices were most *appropriate* for "groups like them" led each group to embrace practices that were consistent with its ideal model of democracy and citizenship, even when these were not necessarily the most effective ways of achieving the group's immediate political goals. Attention to these cultural dynamics is necessary in order to understand the relationship between how political actors imagine and enact their roles in democratic public life.

These findings also offer more practical insights into the possibilities of overcoming political disagreement. Namely, they suggest that even groups who share certain broad goals and ideals will face significant cultural barriers to cooperation. Although "strange bedfellows"—groups who partner on some issues while disagreeing on others—abound in American political life, such partnering may not be possible for groups who have significantly different democratic imaginaries. By filtering groups' perceptions of what kinds of practices are appropriate and meaningful in any given situation, divergent imaginaries lead groups to view alternative choices not only as inappropriate but also as undemocratic and even un-American. The notion that groups would be able to overcome these differences in order to pursue shared goals underestimates the moral salience of these distinctions.

Yet these differences need not be interpreted as threats to American democracy itself. This is the final takeaway of this book. Indeed, although these groups developed competing styles of active citizenship rooted in divergent democratic imaginaries, members of the two groups acknowledged the high stakes of the fight in which they were engaged. They shared an abiding faith in the American democratic project itself. This finding underscores the observation by the historian Stephen Prothero that "the nation rests not on agreement about its core ideas and values, but on a willingness to continue to debate them." And this debate is never settled. Indeed, he states, "in every generation the nation must be imagined anew."[13] Although Interfaith and the Patriots are only two of countless groups involved in the continual work of reimagining the nation, their stories offer insights that can help us understand this crucial (albeit messy and often painful) aspect of political life.

STUDYING ACTIVE CITIZENSHIP

While there are many possible ways to study groups like Interfaith and the Patriots, the story recounted in this book is the result of three choices.

First, this book situates the groups in the historical context of both the rise of active citizenship and the declining public authority of religion, rather than in the more common context of contemporary political polarization. This broader lens reveals important convergences between the groups' ideas and practices that may otherwise be obscured.

Second, this book provides detailed analyses of how the groups talked, acted, and interacted with others, across public and internal group settings. This on-the-ground and behind-the-scenes approach reveals details about these groups that would be missed by focusing on their public rhetoric alone. Namely, it illuminates the cultural processes through which their shared commitment to active citizenship manifested practically in two distinct styles of action, which reflected divergent ways of imagining how American democracy works and the role of active citizens in it.

Finally, this book is the product of a particular research method— multisite comparative ethnography—and a research design that juxtaposed two groups across the political divide. This approach draws our attention to unexpected parallels between the groups while also casting subtle differences between them into clearer relief.

Convergence: Active Citizenship in Historical Context

THE RISE OF ACTIVE CITIZENSHIP

Active citizenship bears much in common with what the sociologist Michael Schudson calls "informed citizenship," one of a handful of models of good citizenship that have developed over the course of American history.[14] As Schudson chronicles in his rich history of changes in Americans' conceptions of how citizens should behave, the ideal of informed citizenship emerged only recently, during the late nineteenth and early twentieth centuries. Although informed citizenship has come to be viewed as a standard, albeit difficult, way of becoming politically engaged, it represented a significant departure from previous ideas about the proper role of ordinary citizens in political life.

Most immediately, it was a reaction against the party-dominated system that emerged in the early 1800s, in which citizens' primary role was to fall in line with one of the mass-based political parties. Theoretically, citizens chose the party that best represented their interests, but in reality this decision was typically based on a combination of ethnic tribalism and the potential for immediate economic gain—it was "a politics of affilia- tion," in Schudson's words.[15] Moreover, rooted as it was in saloon culture, this system was not only unruly but also deeply corrupt. Reformers were understandably concerned about the shortcomings of blind partisanship for democracy, but they did not wish to return to the previous system either. Before the rise of mass-based parties, American politics since the colonial era had been dominated by an elite-driven "politics of assent," in which citizens' primary role had been to politely defer to the judgment of recognized social elites within their communities.

Finding both of these models wanting, reformers imagined a new kind of politics and, by extension, a new kind of citizen, who would take a much more active role in political life than ever before in the country's history. Creating the context for this new model of active citizenship would involve significant changes to the political system itself. As Schudson recounts, "The period 1890 to 1920 brought a flock of important reforms, not matched anywhere else in the world, to assault party control and the enthusiastic mode of civic participation that it fostered. State-printed bal- lots replaced party-printed tickets; nonpartisan municipal elections in many cities supplanted party-based elections; the initiative, the referen- dum, and the direct election of senators sidestepped party machinery; and the growth of an independent commercial press replaced party-directed newspapers. All of these changes provided the institutional groundwork for an ideal of an informed, rather than blindly partisan, citizen."[16] In this new system, citizens were expected to become knowledgeable about issues, develop informed opinions and positions, and support or reject political candidates on these bases. They were also expected to advocate the policy changes they sought, often joining with others to form advocacy organizations that would have been viewed as dangerous only a century earlier. Although these organizations gained credibility by distancing themselves from the impurity of party politics, the parties began to change, too. Responding to reformers' pressures, parties adopted a more "infor- mational style of campaigning, moving from parades to pamphlets."[17]

These changes also pushed the boundaries of who could officially par- ticipate in political life. Each new model of good citizenship incorporated a wider swath of Americans, expanding from propertied white males to include white males who lacked property and, eventually, to include women and nonwhites (albeit conditionally).[18] Embedded in this vision of active and informed citizenship, then, is the notion that everyone has the right and the responsibility to participate, regardless of race, gender, social class, or status. It is rooted, in principle if not in practice, in a populist-minded ideal of mass empowerment.

For Americans during this time of transition, taking on a more active and informed role in political life was viewed not only as a more meaningful and democratic form of citizenship but also as a necessary duty—the only means of preventing their fragile democracy from slipping back into elitism or corruption. Avoiding this slippage would require the vigilant efforts of millions of citizens; this would be hard work, they reasoned, but it was a price all Americans should be willing to pay for their democracy.

Despite the reformers' democratic intentions, however, they unintentionally made it "more difficult and less interesting" for ordinary Americans to engage in the political process.[19] Suggesting that good citizens were obliged to develop basic knowledge of how the system works, of what alternative candidates believe, and of the benefits and drawbacks of various policy proposals significantly raised the barrier to entry into political life. Reformers sought to create a system that was "more democratic, inclusive, and dedicated to public, collective goals."[20] Yet by elevating intelligence over loyalty as a condition for engagement, reformers effectively limited the share of Americans who were capable of participating in politics. Meanwhile, reformers also made the process "less politically engaging" than the party-driven competition and camaraderie of the previous era.[21] In the decades following this wave of reforms, citizens "began a retreat from political activity [and] voter turnout dropped precipitously."[22]

Nonetheless, Schudson shows that active and informed citizenship became the dominant model of good citizenship at the time and, indeed, "remains the most cherished ideal" in American political life today.[23] That said, it did not replace the previous models of citizenship entirely, and newer models of good citizenship have continued to emerge during the past century, including a model that focuses on defending citizens' rights in the courtroom rather than at the ballot box, in the press, or in the streets. In short, Americans today have access to multiple models of good citizenship. Active citizenship is one option among many—to embrace this form is also to reject other alternatives, from complacency to deference to blind partisanship.

This history of changes in Americans' ideals of good citizenship provides a necessary backdrop for understanding how Interfaith's and the Patriots' choice to become active citizens sets them apart from many of their fellow Americans, past and present. But this is not the only context that is necessary in order to understand the distinctiveness of their activities. Their efforts must also be embedded in the history of changes in the role of religion in the public life of a diverse democracy.

THE DECLINING PUBLIC AUTHORITY OF RELIGION

Over the past century, the American religious landscape has been redefined by a number of major changes. The country has become more religiously diverse at the same time that record numbers of Americans are disavowing religion. Meanwhile, religion's public authority has declined even as it has become increasingly politicized. Together, these forces have transformed the ways in which most Americans interact with religious others, as well as the ways in which they imagine religion's place in public life. Most relevant to my purposes here, these changes have prompted a decline in the role religious values play in public debates about many issues of common concern, particularly those related to the economy and the political process. When Interfaith and the Patriots participate in these debates, they do so against the backdrop of this complex religious landscape.

Perhaps the most significant background factor shaping these changes is a long-term historical shift in which modern societies like the United States have become secularized. We are now living, in the words of the philosopher Charles Taylor, in a "secular age." This does not mean that religion has disappeared, but rather that "belief in God is . . . understood to be one option among others, and frequently not the easiest to embrace."[24] This shift has also involved the differentiation of society into specialized spheres of activity, from science and medicine to law and government. As a result, the public authority and relevance of religion within society as a whole has declined.[25]

Most members of society have either welcomed these changes or viewed them as inevitable. But they have been met with hostility by some religious elites and communities who benefited from the previous social order and feel threatened by the secularized order that replaced it. This sense of threat has been compounded by the rising religious diversity of American society. Whereas mid-twentieth-century America was marked by relatively predictable (if not always positive) relations between Protestants, Catholics, and Jews, sweeping changes in immigration policy, beginning in 1965, brought newcomers hailing from nations in which Christianity was not the majority religion.[26] Although nearly three-quarters of Americans still affiliate with Christianity or Judaism, the presence of Islam, Hinduism, and Buddhism, as well as new variants of global Christianity, has infused American religious culture with new traditions and practices and reshaped the context in which Americans experience and navigate religious diversity.[27]

Complicating this story of rising religious diversity, however, is the fact that a growing number of Americans no longer identify with *any* religious tradition. According to recent estimates, nearly one-fourth of the overall population and more than one-third of adults under thirty now fall into this camp.[28] Despite significant differences within this group between atheists, agnostics, and "spiritual but not religious" seekers, they are united by a desire to distance themselves from organized religion. And while researchers are far from fully understanding this emerging trend, one factor that appears to be driving it is concern about religious conservatives' role in politics, which is viewed by many as exclusionary, majoritarian, and generally antidemocratic.[29]

Taking these various trends into account, the picture that emerges resembles influential accounts of a culture war between two irreconcilable camps.[30] According to this narrative, religious conservatives resisting societal secularization and rising religious diversity face off against liberal secularists, who responded to conservatives' lack of concern for the rights of religious minorities by both disengaging from religious life and promoting a stricter separation of church and state. While there is much about this narrative that is accurate, it is incomplete.

Namely, it underestimates the extent to which a wide array of religiously motivated groups engage in public life and infuse public discourse with moral concern, and especially the role of progressive religious actors like Interfaith. There are reasonable explanations for why these actors have been overlooked. Most notably, since the 1970s, conservative religious

[handwritten margin notes: "lib. vs. conserv'ed. groups"]

groups (known collectively as the Christian Right or the religious Right) have been far more visible and politically influential than their liberal counterparts. Although liberal religious groups were working below the radar all along, their voices have been eclipsed by these more strident conservative religious voices. Liberal religious groups have also struggled to gain prominence within the Democratic Party and progressive political coalitions that are dominated by secular (and secularist) voices and interests.[31]

As a result, when most members of the public think about the role religion plays in public debates, they picture conservative religious actors promoting conservative (and primarily Christian) values in the context of a relatively narrow set of debates about gender and sexual politics. Furthermore, many view these efforts as a threat to the fragile balance that the United States seeks to preserve between protecting each individual's right to freely exercise his or her faith and ensuring that no religious group is able to impose its beliefs on others, especially through the law. The association of *all* public religion with the religious Right has thus led to widespread efforts to limit the role of religion in public policy debates.

In addition to active efforts to expunge religion from public life, other factors, too, have led to the declining relevance of religious values to public debates. As American society has become increasingly religiously diverse and nonreligious, references to sectarian religious language have become less accessible and persuasive to wide swaths of the population. Meanwhile, scientific, technical, and ethical languages have grown increasingly persuasive, not only to members of the public, but also to political insiders. Together, these developments have produced a context in which religious values are no longer central to public debates about most issues of common concern, and especially those related to the economy and the political process.

While this could be viewed as a positive, even democratic, development, observers across the political divide have also raised concerns about potentially antidemocratic implications of this shift. In his influential 1984 book, *The Naked Public Square*, the conservative Catholic writer Richard John Neuhaus argued that American democracy cannot survive if widely held religious values are excluded from public debates. More recent debates among liberal political theorists have echoed this concern, arguing that when religious citizens are sent the message that it is inappropriate, insensitive, or ineffective to publicly express their views in religious terms, this can limit their capacity to engage in public debates.[32]

This is because religion is not only a set of abstract values and beliefs but also, as sociologists of religion have shown, a widely accessible *language* through which ordinary people are able to express their views about how society should work.[33] And as much recent research has demonstrated, religious citizens continue to infuse public debates with moral significance, drawing on their faith values and traditions to offer critiques of policies and institutions that fail to take moral considerations into account.[34] It follows that without these religious voices a historically significant check on modern institutions would be lost.

Members of Interfaith and the Patriots echoed these concerns. They worried that American society would lose its footing if it lost sight of the broadly shared values that most Americans' faith traditions taught. And they suggested that any solution to the country's problems must involve bringing these values, and the ordinary people of faith who live them out everyday, back into public discussions about how to pursue the public good. In this way, both groups rejected the liberal secularist notion that there is no place for religion, or God, in the public life of a diverse democratic society. Thus, for these groups, active citizenship not only involved becoming more informed about and engaged in the political process but also involved publicly projecting their values into public debates.

Divergence: Active Citizenship in Action and Interaction

Despite these convergences in their broad ideals and goals, however, when the groups set out to enact their roles as active citizens—by working to hold government accountable and putting their faith into action—their practical choices about how to act and interact with others reflected markedly different "group styles" of active citizenship.[35] Understanding how the groups' styles diverged in this way is the second main goal of this book. It is tempting to conclude that the groups' divergent styles, like their policy preferences, simply reflect opposing political ideologies. But the organizational, cultural, and tactical choices they made were not clearly conservative or progressive. Consider the above anecdote about FreedomWorks' adoption of "Alinsky-style" community-organizing tactics, or the fact that

Interfaith adopted a faith-based approach more typically associated with conservatism. To make sense of these choices, it is necessary to keep in mind that although some tactics and styles may be more closely associated at any given time with the political Left or Right, a broader historical and comparative lens reveals that they have often been used by groups across the political divide.

The question thus becomes whether there is some other pattern in the ways that groups make these kinds of organizational, cultural, and tactical choices. Answering this question requires a close look at the internal cultures of both groups. Culturally oriented sociologists of civic life have increasingly found that the ways in which political actors act and interact with others is fundamentally shaped by the cultures of the groups in which they are embedded. This is because group members develop shared ways of understanding political issues and their relationships to other political actors. As they confront new situations, their interpretations of those situations and their decisions about how to act are filtered through these shared understandings.[36]

By examining how Interfaith and the Patriots talked, acted, and interacted with others, across public and internal group settings, this book illuminates aspects of these groups' efforts that would not be visible through an analysis of their public rhetoric alone. Not only does this approach provide a more complex portrait of how these groups imagined and enacted their roles as active citizens, but it also allows for careful specification of the cultural processes through which the groups' shared commitment to active citizenship manifested practically in two distinct styles of action.

This kind of analysis is possible only because I had access to both the public and the internal worlds of these groups and was able to observe how they reacted to events in real time. To study this complex process, I carried out what sociologists call ethnographic research. Between 2010 and 2012, I systematically observed the activities of both organizations at public events and internal meetings, interviewed participants, and participated in both groups, albeit in relatively limited ways, in order to better understand the experience of engaging in this kind of activity. I also conducted follow-up observations and conversations during the three years after this period of intensive fieldwork ended. (The appendix presents more specific details about my fieldwork with each group.)

It is rare for researchers to conduct ethnographic research simultaneously within groups on the left and the right. As discussed in more detail in the appendix, this kind of research can be challenging. But viewing the groups' activities in comparative perspective illuminated aspects of the two groups that researchers have not previously recognized.

Juxtaposition: Active Citizenship in Comparative Perspective

The method of multisite comparative ethnography—when one conducts ethnographic research in two or more groups for the purposes of comparison—provides a lens through which to notice details about each of these groups that may not seem important without contrast to the other.[37] It highlights surprising parallels across the groups while also casting subtle differences between the groups into clearer relief. Taken together, this allows us to discern both general similarities and general differences between the groups.[38]

Because local Tea Party groups and faith-based community-organizing coalitions have not previously been systematically compared to one another, observers have tended to overlook several aspects of these groups that are highlighted in this book. Our existing knowledge about groups like Interfaith and the Patriots, while incredibly rich and valuable, has largely been based on in-depth studies of *either* faith-based community organizing or the Tea Party movement, respectively. When FBCOs have been compared to other movements, these comparison cases have typically shared their progressive political goals.[39] Similarly, when the Tea Party has been compared to other movements, it has typically been to other conservative and right-wing movements.[40] These choices have rendered certain aspects of these groups visible while obscuring others.

One exception has been the effort to compare the Tea Party to the Occupy movement. Occupy, which emerged in 2011, was quickly hailed by journalists and academic observers as the Tea Party's progressive counterpart.[41] At the level of national discourse, this comparison has merit—together Tea Partiers and Occupiers were populist barbs in political elites' (right and left) sides, at least for a time. But organizationally, the comparison between the two movements becomes more fraught. While both movements mobilized large numbers of Americans quickly and engaged in highly visible public protest activities, Tea Partiers also sought to develop a network of local chapters that would endure beyond this initial movement-like activity.

Although the jury is still out on what will become of the Tea Party movement in the future, it is evident that in a short period of time it spawned hundreds of these local groups across the country.[42] Despite claims that much of the movement's influence can be attributed to national organizations (like the Tea Party Patriots or FreedomWorks) and high profile donors (like the Koch brothers), this network of local Tea Party groups, which is largely independent from these national actors, should not be overlooked.[43]

When we shift our focus to these local groups, the Tea Party bears a closer resemblance to the growing field of faith-based community-organizing coalitions than to Occupy.[44] Yet the FBCO field is rarely cited as an appropriate comparison case. This is likely because the FBCO field has gone largely unrecognized by scholars and the media alike, despite the widespread presence of these coalitions in urban (and increasingly suburban) communities across the country.[45] This low profile makes sense in light of the field's localized focus. Although local coalitions have scaled up in recent years by joining together to intervene in selected state and national policy debates, their activities still rarely attract national media attention.[46]

This organizational field may also be overlooked because FBCO coalitions are not easily categorized as either social movements or civic organizations.[47] Like local Tea Party groups, community organizations around the country have been linked to episodic movement-like activity around single issues or themes (including Occupy). But Tea Partiers and community organizers both focus on building a different kind of grassroots citizen power, rooted in enduring citizens organizations. As networks of local groups around the country, which receive some combination of training, infrastructure, and coordinating assistance from national organizations, the Tea Party movement and the FBCO field both resemble some of the most influential mass civic organizations in American history.[48] And over the past several years, Tea Party activism and faith-based community organizing have been two of the most widely used platforms through which ordinary citizens have come together to build enduring power in their communities and across the country as a whole.

That these two prominent forms of citizen engagement have not been systematically compared to one another reflects a more general reticence by sociologists to compare groups across the political spectrum.[49] While there are some notable exceptions, this trend has had two problematic effects: first, it has led to oversimplified understandings of the differences between groups like these (e.g., conservatives are religious and progressives are secular; groups on the left are contentious, while groups on the right pursue elite influence); second, it has prevented us from seeing similarities between them.[50]

I have sought to avoid these assumptions, not only by comparing these two groups, but also by employing a symmetrical approach that is increasingly being used by researchers engaged in multisite comparative ethnography.[51] In practice, this meant suspending judgment about what motivated participants in each group, how they defined themselves and understood their actions, and how they situated their efforts in relation to others'. It also meant applying the same basic analytic strategy to both groups while making every effort not to squeeze both cases into an explanatory framework that fit one better than the other. (See the appendix for more details.)

While I do not expect members of Interfaith or the Patriots to agree with every aspect of the analysis in this book, I hope they view this approach as evidence of the seriousness with which I took the responsibility to be open-minded and evenhanded. Ideally, it has allowed for a careful analysis of similarities and differences between the groups while providing textured insights into how they positioned and pursued their respective democratic visions.

OVERVIEW OF THE BOOK

Building on the foundation provided in this chapter, the following chapters trace how members of Interfaith and the Patriots imagined and enacted their roles as active citizens. Chapter 2 focuses on the parallel ways in which members of these groups described their choice to become more active. For members of the two groups, this involved waking up, standing up, and speaking up—acts that were described as political and sacred responsibilities alike. In justifying their choices and distinguishing them from alternatives, participants in both of these groups drew loosely on a *civil discourse* that valorized the qualities associated with active citizenship, while critiquing or distancing themselves from fellow citizens who chose not to pursue this path.[52] In the process, they also drew on a *civil religious discourse* that infused active citizenship and American democracy itself with sacred significance.[53]

Chapters 3–5 trace how this shared commitment to the ideal of active citizenship generated two different styles of active citizenship. Chapter 3 identifies one key process through which the groups developed different ways of imagining what it meant to be an active citizen in practice. Both Interfaith and the Patriots drew from American culture and history to develop narratives of active citizenship. Yet the groups' narratives highlighted different combinations of characters, events, and plotlines that coalesced into different ideal-typical models of active citizenship—the prophet and the patriot. The fact that they told such different stories about the origins and development of the American democratic project reveals profoundly different democratic imaginaries—ways of understanding how democracy works and the proper role of active citizens in it. Consequently, when these narratives were referenced in the course of the groups' efforts, they offered different blueprints for their action.

Chapters 4 and 5 demonstrate how members of the groups subsequently enacted their roles as active citizens by putting their faith into action and holding government accountable. Chapter 4 shows that although both groups asserted a public role for religion in a diverse democratic society, they differed in their understandings of how this should work in practice. Efforts by members of Interfaith to put their faith into action were driven by concerns about religious inclusion, while the Patriots were driven by concerns about religious liberty. Participants in the groups thus emphasized subtly different religious values, developed different ways of engaging with religious others, and engaged in different kinds of religious (and civil religious) practices.

Chapter 5 shows that although holding government accountable was a central component of both groups' efforts, the ways in which they organized their neighbors, developed skills and knowledge, and interacted with public officials differed in significant ways. Interfaith's efforts to work alongside government to solve shared problems were grounded in a vision of a covenantal relationship between moral communities and political authorities. Meanwhile, the Patriots' confrontational relationship with government reflected a contractual model of citizenship that framed their individual God-given rights as perpetually threatened by government control.

In both cases, the groups' practical choices about how to enact their active citizenship can be traced to differences in their democratic imaginaries. While chapters 4 and 5 demonstrate a clear relationship between the groups' imaginaries and their respective styles, chapter 6 specifies a key mechanism through which these ways of imagining what it means to be an active citizen influenced how the groups actually practiced active citizenship. Close attention is paid to moments of disagreement and conflict within each group: over whether to be civil or confrontational in interactions with public officials; whether to pursue self-interest or the common good; whether to speak with a collective voice or as individuals; and whether to attempt to replace or persuade elected officials who did not represent the groups' interests. In each case, the choices both groups made were shaped by collective considerations of what kinds of actions were most *appropriate* for "groups like them" in light of their ideal visions of how active citizens should behave. As the groups embraced practices that felt appropriate and rejected others that seemed inappropriate, they were channeled toward different styles of active citizenship. Finally, chapter 7 summarizes the key findings, takeaways, and contributions of the book. The appendix supplies additional details about how the research for this book was conducted.

In the end, this is a story about how a handful of real people dedicated their time and energy to making a difference in their communities and in their country. Readers may find that this story destabilizes some of their assumptions about how citizens across the political divide engage in political life—conducting this research certainly had that effect on me. But this story is not intended to merely be provocative. Rather, I undertook this project out of a desire to improve public and scholarly understandings of two groups who are, in one case overexposed and thus caricatured, and in the other case relatively unseen and thus dismissed.

Although our images of these groups have led us to believe they share nothing in common, the closer vantage point these portraits provide reveals surprising convergences in their concerns, their critiques of government, and their goals. Meanwhile, juxtaposing these portraits also provides the context necessary to understand how the choices they each made were meaningful to them, and how their practices ultimately diverged in the ways that they did. Overall, the book reveals how different ways of understanding what it means to be part of the American people can shape the ways in which people practice citizenship.

A NOTE ON TERMINOLOGY

Throughout this book, I frequently use the terms *citizen* and *citizenship*. As I write these words, I am cognizant that members of Interfaith would likely point out that they sought to mobilize their undocumented neighbors alongside born and naturalized citizens. As a result, I want to be clear that I do not use these terms to refer to one's official status as a legal citizen of the United States. When I use the term *citizen*, I refer to a *role* that all individuals can play when they engage in the public life of their community, at the local, national, or global level. Regardless of one's legal status, playing this role involves a particular moral orientation toward other members of one's political community and toward political authorities—as fellow citizens and cocreators of a shared society.[54] Playing this role also requires a basic understanding of the rules and norms of the political "game" one is playing—in this case, of the American political system, which comprises both its formal institutions and its more informal political culture.

Throughout this book, I refer to this political system as a *democracy* or a *democratic project*. As I write these words, I am also cognizant that members of the Patriots would likely note that this is not in fact accurate—they often pointed out that the United States is technically not a democracy but rather a federal republic, a constitutional republic, or a representative democracy. They were correct to distinguish these forms of government from a direct democracy, which the United States is not. Yet they also acknowledged that the United States is "the greatest experiment in democracy and liberty in the whole of human history," as their founder and leader once wrote. When I refer to American democracy, I am referencing this more general meaning of the term, which conveys the basic principles and spirit undergirding the social and political system as a whole.[55]

As will become clear in the chapters that follow, there are many ways in which individuals can play the role of citizen and various visions of what it means for a society to be democratic. These meanings have not only changed significantly over time but also have been contested during each era. Debates over how these terms should be defined have informed American political culture since the country's founding and will likely continue to do so for the foreseeable future. An in-depth look at Interfaith and the Patriots not only reveals how members of these groups understand what it means to be a citizen in a democracy but also offers insights into these broader debates over the meaning and practice of American citizenship.

2 Becoming Active Citizens

WAKING UP, THE AHA MOMENT, AND
THE *INFORMED CITIZEN*

It was six o'clock in the morning when two middle-aged white men strode toward me across the empty train station parking lot. They were both wearing khaki pants and button-down shirts and carrying stacks of paper under each arm. *Business casual* was the term Gilbert had used to describe how I should dress this morning to distribute copies of their newspaper, the *Informed Citizen,* to commuters as they boarded their trains.

"This is just the type of activism the Patriots look for," he had written in his email the day before. "For me the days of yelling at the TV are over!" He said that after we finished handing out the papers, he would also be happy to talk to me about how he got involved in the group. "We call it the aha moment!" As they approached, it was clear which one of them was Gilbert; his greeting, like his email, was punctuated by exclamation points. "There she is!"

He introduced me to the other man, Jamie, and ran into the train station coffee shop to buy a large coffee, which he sipped even as drops of sweat dripped from his forehead, forcing him to wipe them away with the back of his hand every few minutes during the next two hours. It was over eighty degrees and humid. They chatted about how they should approach the station, and whether Jamie should take some of the papers and hit another station down the street soon. They agreed he should and kept looking around for someone named Phil.

Without finding him we headed upstairs to the covered area riders must pass through between the parking lot and the tracks. We situated ourselves at the top of the stairs. They explained that they had selected this spot so they were not in the way but were still able to catch most people. They had not had any trouble with the staff for passing out the newspapers, and they assumed that as long as they were not bothering anyone they would be fine there.

Jamie mentioned having had only one run-in so far. Truth be told, he seemed a bit excited to have this war story to tell (and I subsequently heard him recount it on another occasion). He said that he had seen the same man twice while handing out the papers. He knew it was the same person, he explained, because the man had called him a racist both times. As he delivered this punch line, they both lowered their eyes and shook their heads, noting it was unfortunate for someone to make a snap judgment such as this.

They showed me the stacks of a few hundred "newspapers" that they were each holding, which were photocopied and stapled a bit crookedly along the sides. Gilbert explained that because the group was composed of many small business owners—including him and Jamie—they were able to pool their skills and resources to write and produce these papers themselves. A month later, when I ran into him at the candidate meet and greet described in chapter 1, he showed me the new edition of the *Informed Citizen.* It had evolved into a professional-quality newspaper printed on newsprint. "Have you seen the new edition?" he asked me as he rushed around the information table he was manning to dig a copy out of a box. He showed me all of the improvements they had made to the layout and explained that in the next issue they were planning to add bylines.[1] They were also thinking of hiring interns, billing it as an opportunity for young people to learn about politics and produce a newspaper. They were learning quickly.

Gilbert and his wife, Rebecca (also an active Patriot), owned a small business that was tied to the real estate market and had suffered in recent years. They had made a number of difficult decisions, including laying off some of their employees and liquidating their retirement savings accounts, in order to keep their business afloat. Although they had never been politically active before, they started paying attention to politics because they believed that the requirements imposed on small businesses by Obamacare and other forms of government regulation would mean the end of their livelihoods. They often said that government should be required to make the same kinds of sacrifices that small business owners and households had to make during tough times. They became involved in a few Tea Party groups in the area and, despite having a young child, made time to attend multiple events each week.

For Gilbert, Rebecca, and many of the other Patriots, the problem was not just that they perceived Obamacare as bad policy. They also worried about what it signified—the quiet destruction of a country that valued thrift, autonomy, and entrepreneurialism, a country where middle-class taxpayers and small businesses were celebrated rather than crushed by overtaxation and overregulation.

As a small business owner himself, Jamie agreed with these sentiments. But he also made a point of prefacing any criticism of the government with an acknowledgement that *the people* had failed to uphold their end of the bargain, too. The group's resident economic expert and a self-proclaimed "capitalist," Jamie was also a "reformed hippie," in Gilbert's words. Jamie told me on that first day we met that the protestors of the 1960s (himself included) did a lot of work to keep the government in check. But then everything started going well and people got comfortable going to work every day and driving big cars and living in big houses, and they stopped paying attention to the government. Now everything had gotten out of control again, he explained, and it was up to those same citizens to push back to preserve everything they had worked for. That the Tea Party was an older, wiser, and wealthier incarnation of 1960s protest movements was not, for him, a contradiction in terms.

Similarly, Linda, the Patriots' founder and leader, once insisted to me in an interview: "It's no longer a right-left thing." Rather, she explained, it was about being informed and engaged. During that same conversation, she compared the dilemma facing Americans to that facing the hero of the movie *The Matrix*. She had started writing the issue of her daily news digest, the *Must Know News,* that would appear the following morning, and she gave me a preview of the question she planned to pose to the group:

> Morpheus, the leader of a small but growing movement (today's equivalent to the Tea Party) seeks to challenge the contemporary power structure (our government). Neo is believed to be "the chosen one" who will lead humans out of captivity (That's us individually). Early in the film Morpheus gives Neo a choice between a red pill and a blue pill. If he takes the red pill he can see the world as it truly is. If he takes the blue pill he will wake up at home, remember nothing, and continue to live in a mirage. As you read the following, I ask you just one question—which pill will you take—the blue or the red?

The Patriots, she explained to me, chose "to have our eyes wide open. And then there's 50 percent of Americans that are taking the other pill and they don't want to know anything. They say, 'The government's got it, you know, we're good and we're busy raising our kids, and we don't have time for this.' It's a choice."

Linda's journey to this choice was similar to that of many other Tea Partiers I had met. Addressing a local taxpayers' watchdog group, Linda recounted the story of her conversion from a stay-at-home mom to, as she put it, a "politically crazed woman": "I was busy living the American dream. I am sorry for that, because I wasn't paying attention." She cited the debate over Obamacare as the moment when she sat up and took notice. This bill's passage was concrete proof that President Obama was willing to legislate against the will of the people. But more generally, the bill was a symbol. It signaled a seismic shift: the world was shifting beneath her feet; the country was hurtling toward socialism. Although she used to be in the U.S. Navy, where she was taught not to question the president, she knew she needed to stand up and demand to be heard now, because her children's futures were at stake.

Others told similar tales of awakening from decades of complacency and setting out to become active and informed citizens. While some joined the Patriots through ties to local Republican networks or community groups, others showed up alone (and often in defiance of liberal friends and family members). Although some had previous political experience, many truly were novices. Linda, for example, had served on her local board of education, but others had privately honed their political chops for years—on Internet message boards and around the dinner table—before joining others in public.

Some were small business owners concerned about overregulation; some were religious conservatives concerned that God was being shoved out of public life; and some were libertarian-leaning independents concerned about the erosion of individual liberty. Despite their many differences, they all sought to become the kinds of citizens who could keep the government in check. They had long felt marginalized within a society obsessed with political correctness, maligned by a media biased toward the Left, and ignored by political elites obsessed with their own power. They had been a "silent majority," they said, but not for long; they were about to become "we the people."

This new identity empowered the Patriots to claim their voices as active citizens. They were fed up with "politics as usual" and blamed both the Republican and the Democratic parties for failing to represent the American people. By shedding their partisan affiliations and rallying around a unifying populist identity as "we the people," they asserted the rightful authority of all ordinary citizens. Through this lens, many of the Patriots viewed the Tea Party as the vanguard of a potentially broad-based populist movement against government and elite domination, a movement that had the potential to one day include *all* of "the people." After all, they insisted, they were not demanding anything controversial: they wanted only to safeguard those values that made America the greatest country on earth, which the founders enshrined in the Constitution, and which the military sacrificed time and again to protect. With their eyes wide open, the Patriots were working to scratch the surface of an opaque political process, peer inside, and report back what they saw. They were confident that if only their neighbors, friends, and family took the time to listen to them, they would join their efforts.

On the back of a one-page description of the Patriots' "Mission Statement and Core Values," which they handed out at their meetings and public events, they had written in large bold text: "Government goes to those who show up." Jamie typically ended his emails with this mantra, and others repeated it when the group gathered, attributing it to FreedomWorks' president, Matt Kibbe.[2] "Showing up" was an animating premise of their activities—the burdensome yet necessary complement to "waking up." And they wanted *everyone* to show up. The one-pager continued:

> We invite everyone in [the community] to join us, receive our e-mails and participate in group activities. . . . It is necessary that we reach out to others in order to bring this country back to the founding principles that made us the great nation we are. Everyone has a skill, passion and ability they can bring to the group. Staying home and yelling at the TV is no longer an option. We have to make our voice heard to let elected officials and other voting citizens know, we cannot spend our way to prosperity and sacrifice our rights to a government who thinks they can take care of us better than we can.

In their own ways, members of the group contributed to this outreach effort. An early member of the group, Josephine, produced homemade pamphlets that she printed at her own expense and dropped off at businesses in her town to be distributed to their customers. The glossy pamphlets featured a clipart image of an American flag rippling in the wind. Underneath the flag was the title, *Seeds of Liberty,* followed by a list of three "seeds":

Faith
In the Lord God Our Creator

Knowledge
Of the History of the United States
and the World Around Us

Courage
To Speak Out and Fight to Defend
The Founding Fathers' Gift to Us . . .
The Constitution of These United States.

She also regularly submitted letters to the editor of her local newspaper and posted to a blog on the group's website. In the blog posts, she acknowledged that she was overwhelmed by the task ahead of them. After all, she reasoned, the Patriots and other Tea Party groups could only do so much without the rest of their fellow citizens lending a hand. She once wrote, "There is so much to pay attention to if WE THE PEOPLE want to protect Our Country, Our Constitution, Our Liberty. . . . WE ARE IN TROUBLE[;]

and right now, I'm not sure those of us who have been tirelessly on top of it all can continue without a majority of the country helping. In the words of Abraham Lincoln . . . 'America will never be destroyed from the outside. If we falter and lose our freedoms, it will be because we destroyed ourselves.'"

This same sense of urgency sent Linda to her computer at five-thirty every morning to write the *Must Know News*, the lengthy news digest that she sent to the growing list of people who added their names to her email list. When I first met Linda, the list included around a thousand people; it eventually exceeded five thousand names. The *Must Know News* was part commentary, part news clippings, and part calendar of events, and it served as a hub linking Tea Party groups in the area. Although it began as a daily email, Linda later began posting it on a blog, enabling her to embed more videos and images. Each edition was crafted with the input of group members who contacted Linda about their concerns each day. She often quoted them at length or linked to commentaries on their blogs and Facebook pages, where discussions continued in the comment sections and on their "walls."

At the end of each email was a list of events of interest to Tea Partiers in the area: group meetings, reading groups, public rallies, and candidate meet and greets and fund-raisers. While the most active among the Patriots attended several of these events each week during busy periods, some of her subscribers never attended face-to-face events. Still, the constant flow of online communication helped keep all of these participants connected to one another. This proved especially useful during periods in which there were few face-to-face activities scheduled in the area. Indeed, although meetings and rallies were sparse during the first half of 2012, Linda reported one summer morning that she had received 6,318 emails in response to her previous day's email, in which she had asked: "Is ANY-ONE paying attention?" This, she announced, was "a[n] inbox record for me. . . . I am thrilled to know so many Patriots!"

For many of the Patriots, engagement in this online community was a form of action unto itself. It encouraged them to read more widely—and particularly to look beyond the mainstream media for their news—and to develop opinions about complex issues. As the name of Linda's daily newsletter suggested, this was information that any good citizen "must know." The urgency they felt was palpable as they consumed, debated, and spread this information with voracious energy.

It was in this same spirit that Jamie and Gilbert volunteered to distribute newspapers at the train station hours before their long workdays began and, later, traveled to Washington, D.C., for FreedomWorks' activist training sessions during rare free weekends. Although they would eventually develop a more technical vocabulary for talking about how to organize their neighbors and get out their message, their interactions with passersby in the early days appeared to be structured by a simple desire to connect with people.

As Gilbert and I stood on the train platform that first morning, it was clear why he was chosen to take on this task. Charming and quick to smile, he did not fit the caricatures of enraged reactionaries that many people associated with the Tea Party. He was above-average friendly to everyone who passed. Careful not to seem pushy, he extended a newspaper to each person, saying, "Just a little something put together by a group of concerned citizens in the area."

He identified the Patriots each time as concerned citizens, not as business owners or conservative citizens or members of the Tea Party (although the newspaper identified them clearly as such). Just concerned citizens, a broad identity that was accurate and likely shared by many people who passed. While each person's concerns were surely different, it was as if those differences were less relevant that morning than the need for all of them to come together, inform themselves, and become the kind of citizenry that could hold government accountable to its constitutional mandate.

As he struggled to balance the newspapers and his coffee, he chuckled and offered self-deprecating jokes to the people who reached for the sweaty papers. In the midst of this balancing act, he asked if I was there to help or just observe. His smile and friendly tone suggested he would accept either answer. I wavered—it was still early in my fieldwork, and I had not yet decided how extensively I would participate in the group's activities, or whether I would mostly observe. But watching him struggle, I took the stack of newspapers and held them while he passed them out. Most people took them without looking. Some flatly refused. Others scanned the front to determine what it was all about before waving him off.

One man lingered at the top of the nearby stairs as he read the front page. When he finished reading, he looked up at me and shook his head. I flushed, feeling for the first time how Gilbert and Jamie must have felt when their neighbors looked at them like they were doing something troubling and wrong. Saying nothing, he handed the newspaper back to Gilbert and descended the stairs. The man named Phil eventually arrived, and Jamie left with him to tackle another station down the road. Gilbert commented that this was just the sort of thing he loved about working with these guys—no one had to tell them to do anything; they just wanted to get stuff done.

The significance of the newspaper distribution was confirmed when I discovered that this was one of the activities that the Patriots highlighted when a local reporter profiled the group. Months later, upon reading in the local paper his description of Jamie and Gilbert distributing their newspapers, I was struck by the similarities to my own experience. They had brought the reporter to the same train station where I had met them, and they had explained why they were doing this, in much the same way that they had explained it to me. The quotes the reporter ran could have been copied from my own field notes.

On one level, their practiced repetition suggested this was a performance they had staged: for my benefit, for the reporter, and for the broader publics they imagined as their audiences and potential recruits. But this activity was not *only* about promoting a careful public image of their group. They had gone to the train station to hand out newspapers before the reporter or I arrived, and they had continued going after. They handed the newspapers out at rallies and information booths, posted it on their website, and left it in the vestibules of local shops and restaurants. Josephine and others followed suit in their own ways, barely aware that anyone might be watching. These practices were as meaningful for participants in the group as they were central to the image they projected beyond the group.

Sitting in a tiny diner near her home months later, Linda told me that of all the things the group had done together, the newspaper was what she was most proud of. I had expected her to point to recent electoral victories by the candidates they had supported or the increase in the size of the group. But she explained that it was the newspaper, "because we got it into people's hands that were not part of the Tea Party. The Tea Party—you're preaching to the choir.... They're the ones already doing their homework." She told me, "Everybody that handed out that newspaper came back with at least two conversations, where people had read it, had already gotten it, and were saying, 'I didn't know this, or I didn't know that.'"

She recalled that I had helped with the newspaper distribution and asked if I was there the day they had "gotten their heads handed to them," referencing the man who had called them racists. I said I had heard about it. She nodded and shrugged, saying, "Yeah, but they read it. It doesn't matter what they outwardly said. They left with it. They read it." The waitress interrupted us. "You want more coffee?" As the waitress refilled my cup, Linda remarked, "I don't need to be right. I just need people to think, and know. That's my thing. I hope I'm wrong.... I swear to God I hope I'm wrong!"

STANDING UP, THE ART OF LISTENING, AND PROPHETIC VOICE

Jon, a Lutheran pastor with shoulder-length brown hair who appeared to be in his early forties, pulled an easel with a large white pad to the front of the auditorium. This pad was a constant fixture in Interfaith's meetings, and its blank pages were filled quickly during participatory exercises like the one Jon was about to lead. He looked out at the diverse crowd and asked people to list some of the changes they were still experiencing in the wake of the economic recession. Someone in the back of the room called out, "Unemployment," and Jon recorded this with a thick marker on the blank page. A Mexican woman across the table from me raised her hand and offered, "Immigration problems, education problems." He wrote these down, too, and nodded, saying, "Yes, yes." Another voice called out, "Stress on families." Probing for more responses, he reflected, "Our congregations, our whole societies, are going through major changes. Many things we took as obvious and relied on are not there any more." People nodded, and he asked what areas of people's lives had been affected most. Within a couple of minutes, the large blank page was covered with a range of concerns.

This exercise was the centerpiece of Interfaith's quarterly leadership meeting. It was Sunday afternoon, and we were sitting around tables in the large auditorium of a 150-year-old Baptist church whose congregation had recently become involved in Interfaith's work. This church was a symbolically salient place for Interfaith members to gather that day—not only was it located about halfway between the two neighborhoods where most of Interfaith's organizing work was concentrated, but it also attracted both black and white members, a rarity among congregations in the United States today. This church represented the kind of bridge across the city's divided communities that Interfaith hoped to become.

Although much of Interfaith's work was driven by small teams of lay "leaders"—this was how Interfaith referred to their individual members, as "leaders"—within each of its member congregations, coalition-wide meetings like this one were important opportunities for leaders from multiple congregations to gather and consider some of the bigger themes driving Interfaith's collective work. These were also crucial opportunities to teach new members about what it meant to engage in community organizing, as opposed to other forms of social action with which they may have been more familiar.

Indeed, organizing was still new to many people in this group; and even those with some organizing experience were not necessarily familiar with the specific organizing model they had adopted when they became affiliated with the PICO National Network. Interfaith had formed a few years earlier out of a merger between two smaller organizations in very different neighborhoods on opposite sides of the city, Riverside and Westside. These organizations had not previously been affiliated with any of the national organizing networks, and one of them had only recently begun thinking about community organizing as the framework for their social action.

Robert, the founder of the group that was newer to organizing, once explained what prompted him to form a social justice committee at his Catholic church in the predominantly white middle-class neighborhood of Riverside:

> At my church, we were very good at charity, and not that strong on justice, and so I wanted something that was going to address the systemic changes that are necessary to effect the long-term change. . . . Charity's nice, and it's neces-

sary, but I want you to not just eat for today, but eat for tomorrow. The old story, "Gimme a fish, I eat today; teach me to fish, I eat for a lifetime." So you develop the leaders and develop self-sufficiency for people, particularly people who have a lower amount of income. That was something I wanted to do.

Across town in Westside—a lower-income neighborhood that is racially and ethnically more diverse than Riverside—a Haitian priest was doing something similar in his own congregation. It was not long before a staff member at the Catholic Campaign for Human Development put them in touch with one another and the merger was set in motion.

Robert explained, "[We agreed] it would be great to sort of merge these groups, particularly because of the racial divide. I felt that both of us could help each other—a mainly white group and a mainly black group, coming from two different parts of [the city]." Although decades have passed since Martin Luther King Jr. lamented that churches are the most segregated places in America on Sunday mornings, most religious congregations are still racially and ethnically divided.[3] Interfaith members did not imagine that their efforts would heal these long-standing racial divides; but as a Lutheran pastor who worked with the group once told me, "We were trying to do something different—to unsplinter the sections of [the city]. A small way, you know?"

But cultivating diversity was about more than just prefiguring the kind of society that most Interfaith members sought. They also believed that their racial, ethnic, socioeconomic, and religious diversity gave them the credibility to speak on behalf of the city's faith community as a whole.[4] As part of this diverse faith community—and by extension as part of PICO's national network of faith-based community organizations—each individual participant multiplied his or her power (at least in principle) many times over.

When Robert explained why he was drawn to organizing, he described it as a means of cultivating this kind of broad-based power, which would be necessary in order to, in his words, "address the systemic changes that are necessary to effect the long-term change." In pursuing this kind of social change, Robert made an intentional move away from charity, the standard form of social action within his middle-class parish.

His congregation was already relatively "progressive," he noted. That had been part of what originally drew him to it—members were encouraged to go beyond the church walls and deal with problems existing in society. But they did this mainly through charity. And charity, he explained, "is always easier than justice." He spoke of people writing large checks—"twenty thousand dollars, fifty thousand dollars, two hundred thousand dollars, some of them ten million dollars. . . . But you know, it doesn't affect [the giver's] life. It doesn't change his life. You know? Because it doesn't threaten the way he lives."

A commitment to justice, on the other hand, requires rethinking the established order, including one's own place in it. Robert found people were not always comfortable with the broader implications of this: "I remember talking to someone who was a dyed-in-the-wool capitalist, about some of the things I was doing. And he said, . . . 'This threatens the established order.' I said, 'I know.'"

He laughed as he recounted this conversation to me, clearly aware of the irony—we were sitting in a fast-food Mexican restaurant at the foot of the city's financial district, blocks from an Occupy movement encampment and in the shadow of the big banks they were protesting. Interfaith had declared solidarity with the Occupiers, and several leaders in the group had been participating in protest activities. Meanwhile, Robert had recently been rehired by one of these large financial firms, after downsizing a few years back had left him underemployed during most of the time I had known him.

On first glance Robert might have resembled his "dyed-in-the-wool capitalist" friend as he walked down the street in his suit each morning, wire-rimmed glasses perched on his nose. But he did not want to play the role of the well-intentioned middle-class white liberal who swooped in with his checkbook to help those poor people across town. He wanted to work alongside the people who bore the brunt of the city's problems and, along with them, become empowered enough to demand solutions to the problems they all faced, as neighbors and as fellow citizens. As he put it, his self-interest was just as much at stake in the fight for justice as theirs— he had a personal interest in creating a better world.

Robert traced this interest back to his faith. "I believe very much in the core value of the Catholic social teaching," he told me, "which is that every human being is imbued with basic human dignity that *no* person has the right to take away from them." But everywhere he looked, he saw politics dividing people, excluding people, saying that this group was more important than that group, that this person counts but that person doesn't. "And what are you doing?" he asked me rhetorically. "You're really saying: That person is not worth as much as you are."

Like many of the leaders he now worked alongside, Robert had found in community organizing—and later in the faith-based model of community organizing developed by PICO—a way of bringing people together rather than dividing them, and of empowering people to work for the common good of their community as a whole. Community organizing, he explained, is "not the only way. But it's a more *active* role." For Robert, part of what had been missing was this *active* part—he wanted to *do* something, to change the way we all *do* politics. But this required a fundamental shift away from partisan politics and away from charity, and toward a model rooted in developing more active and informed citizens.

The quarterly leadership meeting where Jon led the white-notepad exercise was geared toward this end. The theme of the meeting, "prophetic voice," urged participants to go beyond the church walls, stand up, and speak up. At the beginning of the meeting, the senior pastor of Jon's Lutheran church, Rev. Fischer, explained why the concept of "prophetic voice" was so important. Rev. Fischer was an energetic man in his sixties, and his silver mustache, goatee, and glasses were among the few visible signs of his age. Although the clergy typically stood back and let Interfaith's lay leaders run the show, he participated fully in the daily life of the organization and served for a time as vice chair of its board. Before most meetings, one could find him hanging signs or setting up audiovisual equipment, pausing to greet people with a warm smile and a closely whispered "glad you could come" before scurrying off to complete another task. In more extended conversations, he alternated between the calmness of a poet and the indignation of a firebrand preacher.

That afternoon, Rev. Fischer tended more toward the latter, his voice echoing above the shuffling of a hundred bodies settling in. He reminded the group of one quality that all of their traditions shared—a commitment to a "ministry of justice." He insisted that at its root their work together was about standing up alongside and on behalf of "people with their backs against the wall." Of course, this included many people in that room, who were being squeezed by the economic instability that had roiled the nation and their city for the past several years. They were standing up for themselves, as much as for their neighbors in need.

With Rev. Fischer's reflection fresh in everyone's minds, Jon had easily filled the blank page of the oversized white pad with a list of problems that people in the room reported they were facing. With the heavily marked page behind him, Jon stood quietly for a moment and allowed the room to quiet down. He asked people what emotions helped them to deal with change, and one by one people called out an emotion or feeling: pain, fear, regret, anger, disappointment, frustration, tension, excitement, opportunity, hopefulness, hopelessness, resistance, thinking, challenge, courage, a feeling of being overwhelmed. As Jon recorded them on the white notepad, he remarked that these emotions were "all over the spectrum."

He then flipped to a new page where he had already drawn a two-by-two table. Within each of the four boxes was a single word describing a representative type of response to change. The top left was *denial.* The top right was *blame.* These, he said, are "not helpful, and just create more problems." The bottom left was *self-blame,* which he noted was unfortunately common among leaders like them, who have a "gift for self-analysis and [self-]criticism." The bottom right was *problem solving.* This, he said, was "what we want to work toward."

He explained that problem solving, unlike the other potential responses to change, "connects us to our community around us" and requires that we channel our emotions into a set of questions concerning the best way to deal with change. The handout listed several questions associated with a problem-solving response, including: "What exactly will be our goal? How can we work together? What other information do we need here?" He suggested that people begin this process through "one-to-one" conversations (or "one-to-ones") with people in their communities and "research actions" (information-gathering sessions) with people whose interests are at stake in the issues they seek to address. At root, each of these practices involves asking questions, sharing stories, and most importantly, listening. Together, these practices formed the heart of the faith-based community-organizing model that Interfaith used.

These practices were viewed as crucial because they helped group members tap into the fears, anxieties, and concerns that often lurked beneath the surface of their communities. One of PICO's national consultants, Jack, once conveyed this idea during another coalition-wide training session by showing an image of an iceberg. Only the tip was visible above the water; its vast underside was submerged. This, Jack said, pointing to the image, was how most of us have conversations with one another. We skim the surface. When we see people at church, he explained, we usually just wave from afar and say, "Hey, how's it going? How's the family? See you next week. Okay. Gotta run!" He acted it out as the group laughed and murmured and nodded in recognition. "That is not real," he said bluntly.

Beneath the surface, Jack explained, "is all of the stuff in our lives that really is the real stuff." The first level of this gets into questions about "our families, our work experiences . . . the community that we live in." Then, deeper down "are the real deep things of faith and fear and hope and dreams and what we want to leave behind after we're gone." Demonstrating what this deeper conversation would look like, he said, "Tell me about your experience of living in this community. What would you like to change if you could? What do you want to leave for your children?"

"These are *sacred* conversations when we get to those lower levels," he explained. And it was only by going beneath the surface in this way that we could "move from private pain to public action." People often got stuck, he stated: "They're afraid. They're paralyzed. They don't know what to do." Yet, he explained, when "you come along, and you invite people to talk about what's happening for them, and you begin to create the opportunity for them to band together with other people and do something about it . . . they get unstuck. And things can begin to happen."

When everyone in a community is doing one-to-ones, Jack remarked, this "get[s] a community-wide conversation started about what people care the most about, about their self-interest, about the things . . . that they care so deeply about, that they're going to get up off the couch, . . . they're going to get up from in front of the television, and . . . they're going to go out and come to a public meeting. And they're going to get *woken up!*"

"You are a *fire starter!*" he told them, his voice louder and more forceful now, clearly trying to shake his audience up. "You want to let them know they're not alone. There is some hope. And together we can do something, and you are developing a network of people that can demonstrate power."

Most of the people in the group had gotten involved in Interfaith after having one-to-one conversations like these—with organizers, clergy, or other lay leaders. In some cases, they had not been fully aware of what was happening, but had shown up when they were subsequently invited to attend a meeting of their congregation's social justice committee. There, they were encouraged to find their voice—to transform their private pain into public action.

For example, Raquel, an active and outspoken participant in Interfaith's economic justice work, once explained that although she had been quite shy as a young woman, finding her voice had been a gift. "Being able to combine that with connecting people in the community, and just living life, creating life as we want it to be," was what drove her to become more deeply involved in Interfaith's work.

At some point, these newcomers were invited to attend a coalition-wide training session like the quarterly leadership meeting, where Jon led the exercise about dealing with change. For many people, this was the first time they were formally introduced to the ideas driving Interfaith's work. Before the meeting had begun, I caught up with one of these newcomers, Louise. Robert had met Louise, a sixtyish white woman who attended his Catholic church, a few weeks earlier. Through a one-to-one conversation, he learned she suffered from a longtime chronic illness and was following the health-care reform debates closely out of self-interest. But she was also thinking about the bigger moral issues at stake and had always been interested in "humanistic causes," as she put it.

He invited her to join Interfaith's health-care working group, in which I had become a regular participant. On her first day participating in the group, she attended a research action—a meeting focused on learning more about an issue—with a local state senator. In some organizations, it might have seemed premature to bring a new member to a meeting with an elected official, but here they encouraged people to learn by doing.

Before the quarterly leadership meeting had begun, Louise told me that she had never been involved in anything like this before, although she had grown up watching her father, the head of a postal workers' union, travel around the country organizing postal workers and advocating the union's interests. It later occurred to me that many of the people I had met had organizing or progressive activism in their blood even if they had never personally participated in a group like Interfaith before: one young organizer recalled sitting in church basements as a child while her mother attended meetings of the Sanctuary movement; other members of the group had participated in the civil rights movement, worked as housing organizers, or more recently, were involved in immigrant rights activism. Still others worked for social justice nonprofits or foundations that fund social action.

Having migrated between multiple social-change efforts throughout their lives, these seasoned veterans often referred to themselves simply as longtime organizers. To be clear, these experienced organizers did not comprise the entire group, which mostly included newcomers to social action. Still, this general understanding of organizing as a way of life pervaded the group's culture. As organizers, their goal was to constantly engage new people in the work of social change and empower them with sufficient confidence, skills, and awareness of their own self-interest so that they could become effective organizers themselves.

By publicly presenting themselves as organizers and displaying the breadth of their relationships—via large crowds at public actions, or diverse groups in small meetings with decision makers—Interfaith members signaled the inclusivity of their community and their orientation toward building enduring relationships with anyone who shared their interest in problem solving for the common good. These qualities were intended to bolster the legitimacy of their public claims. But these practices were also meaningful to many of them as people of faith, and they served as a way for them to express their values through their political action.

Indeed, the topic of the next quarterly leadership meeting was the "art of listening." During this meeting, Rev. Fischer emphasized the sacred value of listening. He also underscored the fact that this was a skill that leaders needed to develop in order to cultivate a "listening community": "I call it an art. It's also a sacred art, a holy art, listening to the sounds inside the heart of the other person. That is the challenge. How [do] we do that? We have to practice, practice, practice, but with a conviction that it never is over. . . . I'm so honored and convicted by this process of listening, one person at a time. And I've noticed that it is extremely powerful." This type of talk might strike some as touchy-feely, a prelude to "Kumbaya" in rounds. But there was no singing that day; this was all about practical skill development. We split into pairs to practice one-to-one conversations. When we came together again, we tried to analyze what had been different about these intentional conversations. People noted the importance of eye contact and of leaning toward the other person. One woman pointed out that we had asked questions. The leader of the exercise asked her to elaborate on what kind of questions they had been: "Were they yes-or-no questions?" "No," she replied, and then considered for a moment. "They were probing, open-ended, 'why' questions."

The political skills they refined in these sessions—listening, storytelling, asking constructive questions—were viewed as meaningful in themselves. But they were also invaluable tools through which Interfaith's leaders gathered knowledge about the issues affecting their communities and then communicated this knowledge to decision makers. In their view, these skills were the building blocks of active and informed citizenship.

Back at the earlier quarterly leadership meeting, after Jon finished his lesson in problem solving, Nora, the group's executive director, had come to the front of the room. A white woman with reddish hair and a round face that directly conveyed her emotional state, Nora always seemed to be in five places at once. When she was not crisscrossing the city in her car, she was tapping out emails on her Blackberry and making countless phone calls to group members who lacked email access, to keep them in the loop. Even when she was exhausted, laughter tumbled out of her in short unaffected bursts. She surprised me the first time I discovered she was also a bold and rousing public speaker. After observing the executive directors of several similar coalitions from around the country, it struck me that this might be a job requirement.

That night she asked the group: "How do we follow the prophets? How can we be prophetic voices in a world that is different, fearful, and blaming?" She had spent the morning at an event to discuss a Muslim community center that was slated to be built near "ground zero" in New York City and had provoked heated protest around the country (indeed, several area Tea Party groups, including the Patriots, were among those protesting the "ground zero mosque"). She reflected that when she had watched the protesters and supporters clash, "I didn't feel like a prophet. I said nothing. It just felt like conflict." Sighing, she asked, "How do we have a conversation?"

She suggested that the role of a group like theirs was to say, "We are prophets, and we have a different way of looking at this—not as partisan politics and not through fear, but through relationships." They forged these relationships, she said, by listening to one another across their differences, and by sharing the stories they heard from their neighbors and friends. "We must answer the call in Exodus," she went on to say, "to respond to public grief."

She described moments from the past several months in which they had done this: a public action with a representative from the Treasury Department, where Interfaith's leaders had reported hearing from people who were afraid of losing their homes; a health-care listening session at her own Catholic church the previous weekend, where they heard people saying, "We're afraid," and learned that one woman was spending thousands of dollars a month on prescriptions just to stay alive. "This is what we hear when we listen!" she shouted, her face flushed. "When we tell these stories, when we bear witness to public grief, there is public catharsis. . . . Public grief is primary. It is how we move forward and work together to solve problems."

For Interfaith members, solving problems required expanding the boundaries of their sacred listening community to include community partners and decision makers alike. This was an ambitious goal, but they believed it began with a set of small acts—namely, standing up, sharing their stories, and listening to one another across their differences. And everyone must do their part; as Nora told them, "All of us are prophets! All of us are called!"

Of course, they were far from achieving this vision, a reality that Nora plainly conveyed to the group. Slowing down, her voice lowered, she recounted, "When I was outside earlier, standing on the sidewalk, I was afraid. Our country is going downhill. We can blame each other. But that can be so ugly. Or we can pray that we can find a way to live together and work together to make the country and the city better for all of us."

ACTIVE CITIZENSHIP IN HISTORICAL AND POLITICAL CONTEXT

In the wake of economic upheaval and political dissatisfaction, individuals—including many who had not previously been involved in political life—flocked to groups like Interfaith and the Patriots. Despite their many differences, participants in these two groups chose to pursue a strikingly similar path to addressing society's problems. By joining citizens' organizations in which ordinary people worked together to develop the knowledge and skills necessary to participate in debates about the decisions that shaped their lives, members of Interfaith and of the Patriots chose to engage in active citizenship.

By zooming out from the polarized political context in which these groups are typically viewed, and situating them in a broader historical and political perspective—as we did in chapter 1—we can see that this was one of many paths that these individuals could have taken. It is thus noteworthy that they selected the same one. Moreover, once we recognize this, and we return to the contemporary political context, we see that in pursuing active citizenship participants in the two groups also set themselves apart from most of their fellow Americans.

Michael Schudson's informative history of changes in the meaning of good citizenship in the United States is summarized in chapter 1, so I will review it only briefly here. Central to this story is the emergence of a more active and informed model of citizenship during the late nineteenth and early twentieth centuries. This new ideal emerged in a wave of reformist fervor and led citizens to take a much more active role in political life than they ever had before. Between 1890 and 1920, these reformers fought to reduce the power of political parties, expand the mechanisms for direct decision-making by citizens, and encourage the development of an independent press that could serve as a check on party-controlled channels of political information. Together, Schudson argues, these changes "provided the institutional groundwork for an ideal of an informed, rather than blindly partisan, citizen."[5]

This dramatically changed the role that ordinary citizens were expected to play in the daily life of their democracy. In contrast to previous models of good citizenship—like the *blind partisan* who unquestioningly fell in line with one of the mass-based parties that had emerged in the early 1800s, or the *deferential citizen* who for most of early American history deferred to the judgment of recognized social elites—the new informed citizen was expected to become knowledgeable about issues, develop informed opinions and positions, and support or reject political candidates on this basis; they were also expected to advocate the policy changes they sought, an activity that would have been viewed as dangerous and inappropriate only a century earlier.

Students of contemporary civic and political engagement will see much that is familiar about the model of active, informed citizenship that emerged during this period. The idea that informed citizens should play an active role in decision making and in holding government accountable looms large in our vision of good citizenship today—so much so that these reforms have become taken for granted as necessary conditions for a well-functioning democracy. This is evidenced by the fact that the qualities associated with active citizenship have become enshrined in our shared ways of talking about what it means to be civic-minded, democratic, and morally good.[6]

Just because this ideal is now widely embraced, however, does not mean it is the only one available. It did not replace the previous ideals of citizenship entirely. Rather, Americans today hold a wide range of understandings of citizens' ideal role, which tap into each of the previous historical ideals Schudson identifies. And new ideals are emerging all the time. The fact that participants in both Interfaith and the Patriots pursued a similar model is noteworthy in light of this variety.

Indeed, despite the fact that citizens flocked to groups like Interfaith and the Patriots, participants in these kinds of groups still represent only a small minority of Americans. Most Americans do not (or cannot) dedicate the substantial amount of time and energy required to engage in active citizenship. Whether this is because they lack the resources, the time, or the motivation varies considerably, but most Americans are not actively engaged in the civic or political life of their communities or of the country.[7] Knowingly or not, many citizens today are enacting a modern twist on the *deferential citizen* model, which suggests that citizens should sit back and trust government officials, experts, and other elites to do what is best for their families and communities.

If they begin to worry that those elites are not truly representing their interests, they are told they have the opportunity to vote for new elected officials during the next election.[8] This is the logic at the heart of representative democracy, and the mechanism of accountability that both politicians and political scientists typically emphasize.[9] Whether one believes that representatives will make decisions based on what they anticipate voters will reward at the next election, based on what they promised during the last election, or based on their superior judgment, elections are viewed as central to the citizen-government relationship, at least in theory.[10]

In practice, however, elected officials make only a fraction of the decisions that actually affect their constituents—as the size and complexity of government grows, nonelected bureaucrats make more of these decisions. Moreover, elections themselves have been so distorted by the influx of money, among other issues, that their efficacy as a mechanism of accountability has been diminished.[11] The current campaign finance system in particular has made candidates and parties alike more dependent upon moneyed interests and wealthy elites than voters. As a result, as the social ethicist Jeffrey Stout notes, "when used in isolation from the exercise of other political rights, voting often provides too little accountability, too late. The electoral process, when not invigorated by a culture of accountability, often becomes a vehicle for domination, rather than a corrective for it."[12] Still, many citizens continue to embrace a *partisan* model of citizenship. They strongly identify with a political party and vote the "party line" when they enter the ballot box, arguing that in an era of political complexity and partisan polarization, Americans must rely on political parties to represent their interests.

For Americans who choose to break from deferential and partisan models of citizenship, and who wish to become more actively involved in their communities, there is a variety of ways for them to do this. But most of these are still not truly consistent with an active citizenship model, in the sense that I mean when I refer to Interfaith and the Patriots. Indeed, much of this energy is limited to more *passive* activities—like signing on to advocacy organizations' mailing lists, signaling support for issues on social media, or writing checks to political candidates—or activities that do not address problems with the political *system* itself, like engaging in charity work.[13]

In contrast, we have seen that when participants in Interfaith and the Patriots described what they were doing together, they did so in part by distinguishing their activities from each of these other kinds of activities. In drawing these distinctions, participants in these groups tapped into widely shared ideas about what qualities are considered good (and bad) for democracy. Although, as Schudson argues, these qualities have evolved over time, those associated with active and informed citizenship are now deeply woven into our shared ways of talking about what it means to be a good citizen. The cultural sociologist Jeffrey Alexander refers to these shared ways of talking as our "civil discourse."[14] This discourse is rooted in sets of widely accepted moral oppositions, including the notion that being active is good, while being passive is bad. Other qualities associated with civic, or "democratic," action include being knowledgeable (rather than uninformed), autonomous (rather than dependent), and critical (rather than deferential).[15] By drawing on this civil discourse, groups like Interfaith and the Patriots not only infuse their actions with moral and political weight but also elevate their actions above those they consider uncivil or undemocratic (or insufficiently civil or democratic).

When members of Interfaith and the Patriots referred to "waking up" or "standing up," when they said that staying home and yelling at the television set was no longer an option, or when they were taught that it was better to pursue "problem-solving" than to engage in "denial" or "blame," they were distancing themselves the furthest from those citizens who remain complacent in the face of the major problems facing society. In some cases, they did this by comparing their current activity to their past complacency, as when Linda expressed her remorse for having been too "busy living the American dream" and not "paying attention" to the problems that were growing around her. Yet she also explicitly positioned her current self against the "50 percent of Americans" who say they are too busy to engage, preferring instead to look the other way and hope the government will take care of things. "It's a choice," she insisted.

Moreover, they also underscored the fact that the *ways* they chose to be active mattered. Especially for members of Interfaith, this meant distancing themselves from the form of civic engagement that was most prominent in their faith communities: charitable giving and volunteer work. As Robert put it, his choice to start a social justice committee at his church was an intentional move away from the existing focus on charity, which he framed as easier, less risky, and ultimately less effective than a commitment to creating systemic changes. Community organizing, he explained, was a means of taking "a more *active* role."

Finally, although participants in the Patriots tended to support Republicans, and participants in Interfaith tended to support Democrats, members of the two groups still worked to distinguish their activities from those associated with excessive or blind partisanship. Many denied partisan labels, calling themselves Independents and insisting on their groups' nonpartisan identities. Recall Nora's distinction between engaging in partisan politics, which was rooted in division and fear, and being prophetic, which was rooted in relationships. Similarly, although the Patriots' use of electoral tactics brought them into relatively close alignment with partisan politics, they also worked to maintain critical distance from both parties. They routinely commented that they were fed up with politics as usual, and they blamed both the Republican and the Democratic parties for failing to represent the American people. As Linda put it, "It's no longer a right-left thing." And as Gilbert communicated at the train station, they were not Republicans or Democrats; they were just "concerned citizens."

In addition to drawing on this broadly shared civil discourse, both groups also drew in similar ways on "civil religious" language and symbols, to borrow the term popularized by the sociologist of religion Robert Bellah.[16] To be sure, not all models of active and informed citizenship are framed in civil religious or religious terms. But as discussed in chapter 1, members of Interfaith and of the Patriots asserted that their religious traditions offered values, lessons, and notions of "the good" that could help solve the country's most pressing problems. Complicating accounts of secularization that predicted a decline in religion's private appeal and public relevance, members of these groups worried that excluding religious values from public debates about issues of common concern could risk threatening democracy itself. For both groups, then, active citizenship involved inserting, not only their voices and knowledge, but also their values, into public life.

Still, both groups approached this task with an awareness of the need to carefully navigate a religiously diverse and secular public sphere. Recall from chapter 1 that Interfaith and the Patriots operated in a context marked by declining religious authority over political life, rising religious diversity, and rising religious disengagement. Members of the two groups had also watched as conservative religious groups endeavored, over the past several decades, to stridently assert the primacy of Christian values in political debates, and had provoked backlash from religious minorities and liberal secularists, who subsequently pressed for a stricter separation between church and state. As a result, neither group pursued the path taken by the religious Right. Both groups were mindful of framing their efforts in terms that would resonate with wide swaths of the population regardless of their religious affiliation or lack thereof. Rather than speaking on behalf of any particular religious community, members of the two groups instead spoke in a broadly shared civil religious language that imbued active citizenship and American democracy itself with sacred significance.

As Robert Bellah first observed in a classic 1967 essay, civil religious language and symbols weave pivotal periods of American history—like the Revolution, slavery, and the Civil War—into a narrative that infuses the nation and the struggles of its people with sacred meaning.[17] This narrative resonates with Americans across the political divide, in part because of its symbolic flexibility. Indeed, as the sociologist Philip Gorski notes, Americans draw on competing versions of this general narrative: one rooted in the *prophetic religion* of the Hebrew Bible, which frames Americans as a chosen people charged with upholding a national covenant with God; the other, a *religious nationalist* variant, rooted in Biblical accounts of military conflict and apocalypse, which frames America as a Christian nation whose original perfection is perennially threatened by evil forces. Yet the civil religious narrative also references the classical *civic republican* tradition of political thought, which influenced the development of America's republican form of government, and which emphasizes citizens' moral and political responsibilities to the political community. Despite taking various forms, this general narrative is widely used as a means of reminding Americans of their sacred role in this fragile political experiment.[18]

When Interfaith and the Patriots articulated the necessity of active citizenship, both groups presented their efforts as a way of playing their role in this transcendent narrative. Interfaith members, for example, framed their action as a means of fulfilling their responsibility as "prophetic voices" in their communities—by calling the nation to account when it fails to live up to God's standards. Meanwhile, many of the Patriots framed their transformation into active citizens as a process of "waking up," akin to religious conversion processes in which converts experience the feeling that "I was once blind, but now I see," to quote the New Testament verse

(John 9:25) that is enshrined in the well-known Christian hymn "Amazing Grace."

Linda likened this process to the one described in the science fiction film *The Matrix,* but others, like Josephine, explicitly highlighted the religious nature of this experience. Among the truths revealed through this conversion was the central role God plays in American democracy. Recall Josephine's pamphlet, which identified "*Faith* In the Lord God Our Creator" as one of three "seeds of liberty." For many of the Patriots, being an active citizen was not unlike being a missionary—defending American freedom required that they remind their neighbors and fellow citizens of God's (and religion's) foundational role in the American democratic project. They had to help others "wake up." Participants in the two groups thus framed active citizenship as a calling and as a means of fulfilling their end of America's sacred compact with God. As Nora told members of Interfaith: "All of us are prophets! All of us are called!"

In sum, despite their differences, Interfaith's and the Patriots' efforts paralleled one another in surprising ways. In the wake of economic crisis and a rapidly changing world, participants in the two groups determined that they needed to join together with their fellow citizens to solve the problems facing their communities and the country. Their solution was a more active model of citizenship, through which they aimed to become informed enough to participate in complex debates about policy issues that affected them. In choosing active citizenship, they distanced themselves, implicitly and explicitly, from deferential, partisan, and more passive and individualistic models of citizenship. Moreover, by insisting that their religious values informed these efforts, they also distanced themselves from a secularist model of citizenship that insists religion has no place in democratic public life.

In the process of defending and enacting this model, members of the two groups tapped into widely shared civil discourses and civil religious symbols and themes. In so doing, they embedded their efforts in an ongoing public narrative in which active citizens play a substantial role in enacting democracy under God's watchful gaze. But the groups drew on significantly different versions of this narrative in the course of their work, with profound consequences for how they put their ideal of active citizenship in practice.

3 Narratives of Active Citizenship

Struggling with the fallout of economic crisis and the anxieties of a rapidly changing world, participants in the Patriots and Interfaith decided to act. They hoped that by joining forces with their neighbors they could solve some of the problems that their communities, and the country as a whole, were facing. They had woken up; they were standing up; they were speaking up. They were refashioning themselves as active citizens.

But becoming active citizens did not simply involve arming themselves with facts and figures about how the political process or individual policies worked. At a more basic level, members of the two groups also realized that if they wished to chart a course toward a better future, they needed to learn the lessons of the past. As they set out to fulfill their roles as active citizens, participants in both groups took inspiration from other men and women whose hard work and bravery had helped steer the country during previous "times of trial."[1]

Members of the Patriots and Interfaith held these men and women up as exemplars, sometimes explicitly and sometimes through symbolic practices that subtly referenced their place in history. In so doing, members of the two groups came to view themselves as carriers of their legacy, and cultivated an understanding of their own work as one small part of a broader historical project. Yet participants in each group referenced different historical exemplars and different pivotal events, and wove them together through plotlines that led them to different conclusions about how the nation's past connected to its future.

The Patriots offered a story of America from the perspective of those who were once at its center, and sought a return to that position. Interfaith members offered an alternative version of that story, in which men and women at the social and political margins demanded inclusion and recognition as full members of the American people and active participants in the American project. Whereas the Patriots' narrative traced the country's decline from a moment of original perfection, Interfaith's narrative traced the country's long and uneven journey to live up to its founding ideals. Finally, while the Patriots' narrative highlighted pivotal moments in which patriotic heroes stepped in to save the country from destruction or further decline, Interfaith's highlighted men and women whose prophetic words reminded their fellow citizens when they drifted off course on their journey to "a more perfect union."[2]

Both of these narratives referenced actual historical figures and actual events in American history. Yet neither group recounted a definitive history; they each told a *story*.[3] The differences between their stories reveal a gulf between how the two groups understood their place in America's past, present, and future. Yet it is also striking that members of both groups conveyed a profound faith in the American democratic project itself and a conviction that ordinary citizens have played a crucial role in propelling this project forward.

"WE THE PEOPLE," PATRIOTIC HEROES

In the large back room of a popular local restaurant, I stood with thirty members of the Patriots as we faced the flag to recite the Pledge of Allegiance. Several people had just shared their outrage that President Obama had omitted the words "endowed by their Creator" when he quoted the Declaration of Independence the previous week. Now we placed our hands over our hearts, and our voices merged as we recited from memory words I had not used for years before I started spending time with this group. When we got to the phrase "one nation under God," people shouted—a small act of resistance against what they saw as the steady erosion of core American values.

Once she called the meeting to order, Linda directed us to a handout. She had broken the preamble to the Constitution into seven segments, with commentary on each piece, followed by discussion questions. She asked if anyone could recite it by heart, like she had had to do when she was in school. Everyone laughed as Pete, who was in his late sixties, raced through the long-memorized words, his eyes pinched closed to show he was not reading them from the paper. When he finished, he took a dramatic breath and smiled, saying, "I guess I still remember it!" Linda then turned to John, a long-haired mechanic in his late twenties who sometimes wore a black "Who is John Galt?" T-shirt,[4] and asked him to read the first passage aloud. He began, "We the people of the United States . . ."

Identifying as "we the people" empowered the Patriots to reclaim their voices as active citizens. Along with other Tea Partiers around the country, they rallied around this identity as a constant reminder (to themselves and their public audiences) that ordinary men and women like them were legitimate participants in public debates about the decisions that shaped their lives. As noted in chapter 2, they chose to stand up, speak out, and organize their neighbors so they could work together to project their values into public debates and hold their elected officials accountable.

When the Patriots identified themselves as "we the people," recited the Pledge of Allegiance, and quoted the Constitution from memory, they were tapping into a deep store of recognizable political and religious symbols and assembling them into a narrative of ordinary patriots standing up to defend American greatness against decline and destruction. They drew on this narrative to remind themselves of why they were compelled to stand up in the first place and what they sought to do together. While I saw this time and again during my fieldwork, a group meeting from early in my time with the Patriots provided a particularly vivid image of the role this narrative played in the life of the group.

Upon entering the restaurant where the group's meetings were held, I ran into Gilbert and Jamie sitting at a table near the front door eating heaping plates of pasta they had ordered before the meeting started. The front room of the restaurant was cozy, with around ten booths and ten tables and a bar crowded into the back. Gilbert waved me over, saying, "Hiya!" He introduced me to an older couple sitting with them and asked Jamie if he remembered meeting me when I helped them pass out newspapers at the train station. "Of course. Hi there," Jamie said, looking up only briefly before digging into his plate of spaghetti with red sauce and shrimp.

Gilbert urged me to pull up a chair, and he excitedly told me there were only forty-two days left until the 2010 midterm elections. They were ready for the fight of their lives, he said. He started to tell me about the FreedomWorks training session that he and Jamie had recently attended, when Linda approached. "Come on guys, it's late. You know how I feel about being late. It's rude. Bring your food in with you," she instructed, and they followed. "Oh, hi, hon," she said, greeting me warmly with a quick kiss on the cheek as she hurried us through a door into a large event space in the back of the restaurant.

In the spacious back room, six round banquet tables were clustered in one corner, presumably to create a more intimate feel for the relatively small group of around thirty that had gathered that evening. One table was covered with stacks of printed handouts: the group's newspaper, the *Informed Citizen;* information about the group; and other assorted pamphlets and printouts that Linda brought to every meeting and rally. Each person had picked up a stack of handouts on their way in and now sat with beers, sodas, and the dinners they had ordered, waiting for the meeting to begin. At Linda's table, I noticed three people who were significantly younger than the rest of the crowd—a man in his late twenties, and two girls who looked like teenage and twenty-something versions of Linda. I realized these were her kids. She had spoken of them frequently, especially her hope that her work with the Patriots would inspire them to become more knowledgeable about politics.

After grabbing my own stack of handouts, I hurried toward the empty seat next to John, the young libertarian with the "Who is John Galt?" T-shirt whom I had met at a rally a few weeks earlier. After we recited the Pledge of Allegiance, Linda pulled a small book from her stack of materials and began reading aloud. Over the sound of forks clinking and people whispering drink orders to the waitress, she read about ordinary citizens during an earlier era of the country's history joining civic organizations, writing letters and pamphlets, holding meetings, and staging rallies. When she was done, she looked around for dramatic effect and explained that what we were doing today was just like what those men and women had done. People looked around their tables and nodded at one another knowingly.

It was not uncommon for the Patriots to connect their activism to earlier episodes in American history. Linda did so explicitly here, but they also signaled this continuity with the past each time they quoted the Founding Fathers, referenced their duty to protect the Constitution, or referred to their movement as the Tea Party. Indeed, by identifying with the Boston Tea Party, the Patriots aligned themselves with American colonists whose acts of protest two and a half centuries earlier changed the course of the country's history.

"We are following the tradition of the original American community organizers, the Sons of Liberty," wrote former House majority leader Dick Armey and FreedomWorks president Matt Kibbe in the organization's "Grassroots Activism Toolkit," which Gilbert and Jamie likely received during their FreedomWorks training session in Washington, D.C. This tool kit was also an appendix in the authors' 2010 book, *Give Us Liberty: A Tea Party Manifesto*, for which the Patriots had hosted a book-signing party and which Linda encouraged members to purchase and read.

"These grassroots Americans helped lead a campaign to build public support for the American Revolution," Armey and Kibbe went on to say, "and were the brains behind the original Boston Tea Party in December 1773. As they understood so well, it does not take a majority to prevail, but rather an irate, tireless minority keen to set brush fires of freedom in the minds of men." Even after Tea Partiers around the country stopped wearing costumes in the style of Revolutionary-era clothing, reflections like Linda's and like Armey and Kibbe's continued to encourage the Patriots to draw parallels between their efforts and those of these earlier groups in American history.

But these were not their only historical role models; and indeed, although the Patriots spoke of the Sons of Liberty with reverence, they did not engage in or condone violent or destructive acts of protest. Preferring rebellion from within the confines of the law, they also looked to the Founding Fathers, and particularly the authors of the Declaration of Independence and the Constitution, for guidance about how good citizens ought to behave.[5] In stories about the drafting of the founding documents, they saw patriotic citizens fighting for democratic ideals that seemed out of reach at the time, as well as headstrong men unafraid to stand up for what they believed in, even if this led to conflict in the short run.

Linda often quoted these men in the *Must Know News,* as in a June 2011 issue, when she included the following two "Quotes of the Day":

> Dissent is the greatest form of patriotism.
>   Thomas Jefferson

> It is the first responsibility of every citizen to question authority.
>   Benjamin Franklin

By reminding group members that towering figures in American history— like Jefferson and Franklin—viewed dissent and the questioning of authority as "the greatest form of patriotism" and "the first responsibility of every citizen," Linda emboldened group members to engage in their own acts of dissent and questioning. Other members of the group followed suit.

At one group meeting, Phil, one of the Patriots' core leaders, split the fifty people gathered into teams. Among the team names he suggested were "Team Thomas Jefferson" and "Team Thomas Paine." Later, he explained one of the projects that the group would be working on: "The solution [to our current political problems] is easy. Simply follow the Constitution! We have to use the tools of the Constitution: education and the ballot box. We have to get off our chairs and become active in the constitutional process to get the country back." Here, Phil encouraged group members to carry forward the tradition the Founding Fathers had set in motion by approaching the Constitution as a set of practical tools for political action. This was framed as a simple and straightforward task, as if the Constitution were an instruction manual left for the Patriots by the men who drafted it. References like these justified their ongoing political vigilance; and by holding their activism up as the continuation of work begun by the Founding Fathers, they also shielded themselves from accusations that their rabble-rousing was inappropriate, undemocratic, or unpatriotic. After all, few would accuse the Founding Fathers of such qualities.

These men not only supplied the Patriots with practical models for their own active citizenship but also supplied them with models for how their elected officials should behave. As Linda once explained to me in an interview, the job of elected officials is quite simple:

> Uphold the Constitution. That's their number one job. Uphold the Constitution. Do what the Constitution allows you to do. Nothing more, nothing less. They can't even do that. Document's been around for two hundred years. Watching them read it, you would swear to God they'd never read it once. . . . Limited government, constitutionally run. How are these bad things? They're not. . . . Stick with the Constitution. You can't go wrong. Can't go wrong! . . . I mean, our founders came together, and my God, they never agreed on anything! But they agreed on that Constitution.

Like Phil's statement at the group meeting, Linda's portrays the Constitution as a straightforward set of instructions for modern-day lawmakers. But in this formulation, it is also akin to a contract that future generations are duty-bound to uphold: lawmakers are obliged to consider whether existing laws and new policies are consistent with the intent of the founders. This approach also implied a clear role for groups like the Patriots—to serve as guardians of this contract. As a result, they regularly pressed their elected officials to evaluate policies ranging from Obamacare to local tax policies based on whether they were consistent with the founders' vision for the country.

In this way, their approach to this document bore much in common with the constitutional philosophy of "originalism," popularized by the late Supreme Court justice Antonin Scalia and widely embraced within conservative circles.[6] Through their originalist lens, the meaning of the Constitution was not only timeless but also plainly evident to anyone who could read it and was familiar with the history of its drafting. Just as biblical literalists assert that all believers can readily understand the meaning of scripture, the Patriots viewed it as completely reasonable to assume that ordinary citizens like them would be capable of making judgments about whether policies were faithful to the Constitution (I discuss the religious roots and resonances of the Patriots' approach to the Constitution in more detail in chapter 4).[7]

Still, this was not a responsibility they took lightly. This is why familiarizing themselves with the Constitution and its history was among the first ways that members of the group enacted their newfound roles as active citizens. As a group, the Patriots encouraged this by reminding one another that the Constitution could be read and understood by ordinary people like them. In a handout Linda circulated at one of their group meetings, she included the following "fun fact": "The Constitution has 4,543 words, including the signatures but not the certificate on the interlineations; and takes about half an hour to read. The Declaration of Independence has 1,458 words, with the signatures, but is slower reading, as it takes about ten minutes." Many individuals that I met carried dog-eared pocket Constitutions, which they proudly pulled from breast pockets and pocketbooks whenever the occasion called for it. This practice had become so common by mid-2010 that *The Hill* published a story about the nationwide spike in demand for the pocket-sized booklets over the preceding year.[8]

Most of the group's meetings during their first year of activity also included a discussion about these documents or issues that related to them. Indeed, at the Patriots' group meeting discussed above, after Linda asked Pete to recite the preamble by heart, she turned our attention to the handout she had distributed at the beginning of the meeting. At the top of the page, the preamble was printed in an ornate script. Below, it was split into seven segments, each of which was followed by a few words or sentences of analysis, including:

> 1. We the People of the United States. The government that came before the creation of the Constitution was an agreement between the 13 state governments, not an agreement between the government and the people. The Constitution created a government by, for and of the people. In a kingdom when a young prince grows up, he will rule. But under the Constitution, the rulers are the people. Future government officials can be your classmates, your neighbors, your teachers, farmers, businessmen, others and even you.
> . . .
>
> 5. Promote the general Welfare. Another way to say general welfare is common good. This clause can be viewed as a general idea to ensure that all citizens are safe and have the freedom to pursue their happiness.
>
> 6. Blessings of Liberty. What freedoms do we enjoy—the list is long.
>
> 7. To ourselves and our Posterity, do ordain and establish this Constitution. The Constitution was designed for both 1787 and for the future, for today. This is what the Framers meant by "ourselves and our posterity."

By closely studying the text and its meaning, the Patriots embodied their newfound roles as the guardians of these documents and prepared themselves to carry forward the tradition that the founders had set in motion.

But their approach to the Constitution was not simply the product of historical reverence; most members of the Patriots also treated the Constitution like a sacred text. This was the result of having immersed themselves in a body of historical scholarship that highlighted both God's role in the founding of the country and the sacred nature of the American project itself. Glenn Beck's role in promoting this version of American history—which he often reminded his viewers was not taught in most schools—should not be understated. Indeed, for millions of Americans who turned to the nation's past for solutions to the country's current ills, Beck's television studio became their history classroom. For those who wished to dig deeper, he even offered a one-day course, "The Making of America." Whether he prompted or simply capitalized on Americans' desire to reeducate themselves, Beck transformed his audience into eager students, and himself into their charismatic professor—tweedy jackets and blackboard included.

The books he recommended shot up the best-seller lists, became the subjects of reading groups, and found their way into local Tea Party groups around the country, including the Patriots.[9] Among these books was W. Cleon Skousen's *The 5,000 Year Leap*, which argues, among other things, that the Constitution was rooted in Judeo-Christian values and inspired by the Bible.[10] During the first several months of my fieldwork, the Patriots' daily email advertised at least three book clubs dedicated to discussing *The 5,000 Year Leap*, and group members cited it by name when they gathered in person. Exposure to these ideas led group members to a shared conclusion—if the Founding Fathers were inspired by God, then the Constitution is the sacred path. By extension, denying the sacred nature of America's founding was a profound threat to the fragile system that the founders had built. Together, these concerns revealed a vision of the country's founding as a "sacred, quasi-religious" moment of perfection.[11] Although the two and a half centuries since had steadily eroded this perfection, the Patriots viewed it as their duty to restore the country to its original greatness.

At rallies and group meetings, they reminded one another that threats of ruin were ever present—the result of moral corrosion, political corruption, or economic calamity. Indeed, at the Patriots' group meeting discussed above, Linda had directed our attention to a 1934 *Chicago Tribune* cartoon that was circulating in the Tea Party blogosphere,[12] which she had printed for everyone to discuss. The cartoon, titled "Planned Economy or Planned Destruction?" depicts a horse-drawn wagon carrying "young pinkies from Columbia and Harvard"—presumably members of President Franklin D. Roosevelt's administration—throwing bags of money into the street. On the back of the wagon are the words "Depleting the resources of the soundest government in the world." In the bottom left-hand corner, a bearded bespectacled man writes on a placard: "Plan of Action for U.S.: SPEND! SPEND! SPEND under the guise of recovery—bust the government—blame the capitalists for the failure—junk the Constitution and declare a dictatorship." The words "It worked in Russia!" float above his head. In the distance, a cross-armed Stalin remarks, "How red the sunrise is getting!"

It took only a moment for people to start commenting aloud about how similar it was to their current situation. They saw in this cartoon striking parallels to the federal government's handling of the current economic recession, in which liberal social elites were spending other people's money—their money—"under the guise of recovery." This suggested more than simply an abandonment of constitutional principles ("junk the Constitution"): for those who were primed to interpret the threat of big government and communism through a religious lens, references to the "young pinkies" and to Stalin's pleasure also warned of the ascendance of Soviet-style atheism over America's Judeo-Christian values.[13]

The cartoon was also a reminder that although the players had changed, the nation was still being threatened by foes within and without. This felt especially pressing since many of the Patriots or their family members had served, at one time or another, in the military and so had personal experience battling these external threats. For many people in the group, military service represented the ultimate expression of what it meant to be an American patriot. By extension, to disrespect the Constitution was to disrespect the considerable sacrifices of the men and woman of the armed forces, who have protected these constitutional values again and again against threats ranging from socialism to "radical Islamic terrorism."[14]

As a group, they often set aside time to show their respect for the military—from ceremonially raising and lowering the American flag at rallies to informally thanking veterans for their service. In so doing, they conveyed the high stakes of the political challenges they faced, and they presented their activism as a way for civilians to carry forward the military's patriotic mission to "support and defend the Constitution of the United States against all enemies, foreign and domestic," to quote the oath sworn by every man and woman enlisting in the armed forces. As one member of the Patriots once told me in an interview: "If some kid can strap on body armor and go sit his ass down in some foxhole in some desert on the other side of the planet and dodge bullets, the least we can do at home is stand and engage."

After members of the group took a few moments to study the detailed cartoon, John, the young libertarian, raised his hand and noted that it showed how close we had come previously to destroying the country. Yet, he said hopefully, they somehow managed to come together and pull themselves out. Someone in the back of the room shouted, "The difference though, is that Roosevelt loved America!" Linda cut him off and said sternly, "It's not just about Obama. And it's not about Democrats and Republicans. This is about us not being vigilant and letting our political leaders take too much power."

She reminded them that even if they felt like they won this time around (meaning during the upcoming 2010 midterm elections), they had to stay vigilant or they would just slip back into the way things were. The man backed down. "It's true," he conceded. "You know what they say. We get the government we deserve. People are people. Everyone's a crook at heart. If we stop watching, it will go right back." An older woman agreed. "We've won the battle," she said, "but we have a long war ahead of us."

When the Patriots reflected on their role in the American democratic project, they called forth this entire narrative of faithful stewardship of America's founding principles. As selective as it was sweeping, this particular telling of America's history was nonetheless familiar to most of the Patriots and provided context for their group practices. In the patriotic heroes who inhabited their story of America, they saw reflections of themselves standing up to distant and unresponsive decision makers and defending the country from destruction and decay. Amid the emotional ups and downs of active citizenship, this narrative elevated them above the profanities of contemporary politics and infused their efforts with sacred meaning.

PROPHETIC VOICES, "SHOULDER TO
SHOULDER FOR JUSTICE!"

As Interfaith's general assembly got under way, Gloria began the ritual roll call. A black woman in her sixties, Gloria was one of Interfaith's most active leaders at that time, and it was a sign of the group's respect for her that she was given such a prominent role in the proceedings that day. This was my first time attending the group's general assembly, and I was struck by the turnout for this annual event that brought the entire coalition together to celebrate their successes over the past year and reflect on the challenges that the upcoming year would bring. Gloria addressed the crowd from the stage. With a pronounced Caribbean lilt, she explained that as she read the name of each of Interfaith's member congregations, its representatives were to stand up. When all of the names had been called, she told the audience, "We will all be standing together, shoulder to shoulder for justice!"

One after another, she and another leader called the congregations by name. Among them were Catholic, Lutheran, Episcopalian, and Baptist churches, a synagogue, and an Arab American organization. They represented neighborhoods across the city, new immigrant communities alongside more established ones. While some of the group's most active leaders—including their executive director and then-chairperson—were white, most of the people present were African American, Caribbean, and Hispanic.

From my seat in the balcony, to which I had retired to get some perspective on the action below, I took a moment to assess the gathered crowd. Next to me, a boy of around eight—the child of one of the staff organizers—had been assigned the task of photographing the event. Under a mop of braided hair, he turned his digital camera this way and that, but he could not quite figure out how to capture the entire scene in one frame. Having spent the past several months with this group, I knew just how he felt.

Seated in the balcony on the other side of the room were a handful of sharply dressed black men in dark suits and bowties. On the stage below, some of the presenters wore business attire. Most of the audience was dressed casually, however, and on this cold day many still wore their parkas and hats. The large sanctuary echoed with applause as more and more people rose to their feet. Eventually, when nearly everyone was standing, the woman assisting Gloria with the roll call shouted, "We are one big family, one church, one faith! We fight for the same cause! We want freedom, justice, and peace!"

The roll call was a moment for taking stock. As I explained in chapter 2, the organization had come together as "one big family" only a few years earlier, and they were working hard to make everyone feel included. As soon as everyone was seated, Rev. Fischer announced that they would be translating the meeting into Creole and Spanish, and that they had headphones on hand for people who were hearing impaired. They then repeated this announcement in Spanish, and I saw a ripple through the crowd as people tapped the shoulders of those they knew might not have heard. Making it possible for everyone to hear one another—not to mention listen to one another, and then eventually speak with one voice—was a central challenge for a group marked by such a high level of internal diversity.

Collective action among such diverse constituencies requires compromises—namely, willingness to set aside their myriad differences and focus instead on their commonalities. As noted in chapter 2, one thing they shared was that they had all chosen to stand up, speak out, and organize their neighbors so that they might eventually be able to hold their elected officials accountable. Moreover, for most of Interfaith's leaders it was *faith*—whatever their faith tradition may have been—that motivated their efforts to stand together to pursue justice.

Once organized, they infused their collective efforts with meaning by imagining themselves as prophetic voices—the latest in a long line of ordinary people doing their small part to urge the country toward "a more perfect union." When Gloria called upon Interfaith members to stand "shoulder to shoulder for justice," and when, as described in chapter 2, Robert proudly declared his intention to "threaten the established order" and Nora explicitly called upon the people gathered at the quarterly leadership meeting to be "prophetic voices," these leaders embedded Interfaith in a historical lineage of prophetic social action that has punctuated American history with its calls for profound changes to the social order.

They returned to this narrative time and again to remind themselves of what they sought to do together as a diverse faith community committed to pursuing justice. Part of what it meant to be members of Interfaith, therefore, was to learn about this tradition and how their efforts could carry it forward, as I saw firsthand during a planning session for their "prophetic voice" quarterly leadership meeting.

On that afternoon, I was hanging out in Interfaith's cramped offices on the top floor of a Lutheran church in Westside talking with a handful of leaders about the next phase of their economic justice work. Sitting at a cluttered desk nearby, Nora was putting the finishing touches on the flyer for the upcoming quarterly leadership meeting. Jackson, a part-time organizer who had been coordinating their economic justice work, handed me the latest draft. A white man in his late forties, he wore his typical outfit of boots and an oversize khaki cargo vest, which made him look vaguely like a photographer in a war zone. As a handful of us scanned the draft, he folded his six-foot-four frame into a small plastic chair and scooted it toward the cluster of elementary school desks that served as our makeshift conference table.

The flyer was covered with so many photographs, quotes, and pieces of information that it took me a moment to locate the name and date of the event it was intended to advertise. It invited guests "to join in the Prophetic Voice Tradition" by attending the upcoming quarterly leadership meeting. At the top of the flyer, a row of small photographs depicted five exemplary "prophetic voices": Moses, Martin Luther King Jr., Abraham, Cesar Chavez, and Dorothy Day. Wedged between the images of Cesar Chavez and Dorothy Day was a sixth photograph—it was less iconic than the others but would be familiar to members of this group. Taken at a recent press conference, it depicted several Interfaith leaders standing behind a large banner reading, "Our Voices, Our Future." At the bottom of the flyer, a quote from the rabbi, Jewish theologian, and activist Abraham Joshua Heschel read, "Others have considered history from the point of view of power, judging its course in terms of victory and defeat, of wealth and success. But the prophets look at history from the point of view of justice, judging its course in terms of righteousness and corruption, of compassion and violence. . . . They proclaimed that might is not supreme, that the sword is an abomination, that violence is obscene."

Jackson tapped the flyer and told us that it had been his idea to add names below each of the grainy black-and-white images of the "prophets." "Some people may not know who they are," he explained. Indeed, this seemed possible. Of course, King was a common reference point for members of the group—many of them saw their work as a continuation of battles first waged by the civil rights movement, and a handful of active members of the group had actually participated in the earlier movement. That King was both African American and a Baptist minister only increased his resonance for members of this racially diverse and faith-based group.

The biblical prophet Moses, too, was commonly referenced by group members. This was likely because of his central role in the Exodus story, which has become a focal symbol for movements committed to social change.[15] The story of Abraham—central to all of the Abrahamic faith traditions—was also likely familiar to most people raised in the Jewish, Christian, and Muslim traditions, which included most members of this group. But Dorothy Day, the journalist, activist, and founder of the Catholic Worker movement, and Cesar Chavez, the Mexican American labor organizer and civil rights activist best known as a founder and leader of the United Farm Workers, may not have been as familiar to everyone.

"Like, do you know who Dorothy Day is?" Jackson asked me, clearly sizing me up. I quickly said that I did, but a fortyish black woman named Raquel, seated next to me, said she did not know who she was. Raquel was an active member of both her congregation's local organizing committee and Interfaith's working group on economic justice, having poured herself into this work during a period of lengthy unemployment. Raquel once described her work with Interfaith as a way for her to connect with people in her community and use her "voice" to bring about positive change. But "volunteering" with Interfaith, as she referred to it, also appeared to be an important substitute for paid work during this time. She was a take-charge kind of person, as I learned during my first encounter with her, when she had burst into this same office, her waist-length braids and long skirt trailing behind her, and found Jackson and me struggling to set up the phone for a conference call. She was breathless after hurrying up three flights of narrow stairs to make it on time, but she marched toward us like she was the CEO of this operation and promptly took over.

So I had been surprised when Raquel admitted she was not familiar with Dorothy Day. As Jackson explained the importance of Day's legacy, she seemed genuinely interested. She asked what they meant by the "prophetic tradition." By then Nora had joined us, and she explained, "It's based on the prophets in the Bible who would wander around and say, 'This is not how things should be! Things should be different.'" People speaking their mind: this was something with which Raquel was familiar.

On the day of the "prophetic voice" quarterly leadership meeting, Nora explicitly aligned Interfaith with this long prophetic tradition. "How do we follow the prophets?" she asked the crowd. "How can we be prophetic voices in a world that is different, fearful, and blaming?" She suggested they do this by building relationships, by listening to one another, and by telling their stories—acts that helped them "answer the call in Exodus to respond to public grief."

In addition, she explained, when they bring values and symbols from their faith traditions into their public actions, they can show people that "things are not hopeless. There is a different way!" Religion, in this view, was less a set of rules that constricted individuals' behavior than a set of tools for broadening society's collective moral imagination concerning what kind of world was possible.

Nora's voice then rose as she began to list prophets who had played this role: "Moses, Martin Luther King, Cesar Chavez, Dorothy Day, Raquel, Jon, Rev. Fischer, Gloria, Robert . . ." She rattled off the names of several people sitting in the crowd. "I am mentioning some of you by name," she noted. "There are too many to say them all. But all of us are prophets! All of us are called!" Her voice had risen to a near shout now and echoed through the large room.

Even while the group sought to emulate the bravery and moral clarity of these biblical and historic prophets, so too did they make lessons of the prophets' failures. Rev. Fischer noted during the "prophetic voice" event that he considered his career one of trying over and over again to play the role of the prophet, although, he noted with a smile, he usually failed. Even so, he explained, he always sought to move forward. He called upon everyone to keep speaking out against injustice, no matter how impossible it might seem—it was this perseverance, he told them, that truly defined them as prophets.

At the same time, he acknowledged that it would often be hard to align their call to prophecy with their role as citizens. After all, Interfaith members were not crying out in the wilderness as many of their biblical forebears had; they were embedded within complex political coalition efforts, from the local to the national level. Moreover, they did not wish to create a new kind of society from scratch: like the Patriots, they saw themselves as stewards of the country's founding principles. But they believed that when the country did not live up to its democratic promise, it fell to modern prophets like them to press the nation to fulfill its potential. Rev. Fischer captured the conflicts they faced between pragmatism, patriotism, and prophecy by quoting from a poem by the social critic and writer Wendell Berry:

> All that patriotism requires, and all that it can be,
> is eagerness to maintain intact and incorrupt
> the founding principles of the nation, and to preserve
> undiminished the land and the people. If national conduct
> forsakes these aims, it is one's patriotic duty
> to say so and to oppose. What else have we to live for?

Closing his book after reading this poem aloud, he quipped, "Prophecy and politics . . . I mean, seriously, right?" A few people in the room nodded and laughed quietly. He had identified a central tension that Interfaith and groups like them faced.

When Jackson, Nora, Raquel, and I had discussed the flyer for this meeting in Interfaith's office a month earlier, I had considered this tension. The cluttered layout of the flyer was a testament to the group's efforts to reconcile their calls to be pragmatic, patriotic, and prophetic. They believed their organizing model, when it was most effective, offered a way to do so. In a large italic font in the center of the flyer was an appeal: "We live in a time of violence in our communities, discrimination, and economic worries about our homes and jobs. . . . From the point of view of *justice*, we ask ourselves[:] what can we do to make life better for those we love? Join us as we discuss together how to create powerful local organizing committees to make the change we need." The answer, for them, was found in a particular style of active citizenship—by joining with one's neighbors to "make life better for those we love" and "make the change we

72   CHAPTER 3

need," and by becoming the latest in a long line of prophets who urged their societies to live up to their stated values.

When Interfaith members referred to themselves as "prophetic voices," and when they stood "shoulder to shoulder for justice," they called forth this entire narrative of prophetic social action. Although the men and women who were central to their narrative were not the standard cast of characters found in most American history textbooks, most group members were nonetheless familiar with their efforts. Some of them had been familiar with these figures' roles in history before joining the group; others had been exposed to their stories within the group itself. In either case, the particular way in which Interfaith members recounted America's democratic journey—a journey in which recurring battles over civil rights were as defining as the Revolutionary War, if not more so—provided context for their group's perspective and practices. In the diverse group of prophets who populated their story of America, they saw reflections of themselves speaking their minds and confronting elites. They saw men and women like themselves struggling over the dilemmas of prophetic social action, just as countless others had done before them. Faced with tensions between different dimensions of their work, and challenges generated by their internal diversity, the group used this narrative to help bind participants to one another and to infuse their efforts with sacred meaning.

NARRATIVES OF ACTIVE CITIZENSHIP AND DIVERGENT DEMOCRATIC IMAGINARIES

There are clear differences between these groups' narratives of active citizenship; but before focusing on these differences, it is worth noting that juxtaposing these narratives also reveals some surprising parallels between them. They share a common structure—in general, both groups developed what the political scientist Rogers M. Smith calls a "story of peoplehood."[16] More specifically, both narratives portray ordinary people as the engine of American democratic life, and as embedded in complex relationships with their fellow citizens and with government officials. Finally, God looms large in both narratives—sometimes at the center of the action, and sometimes just offstage, but always present as a source of empowerment or judgment.

Although the groups populated this general narrative structure with different constellations of characters and historical events, and although they situated themselves differently in relation to other actors and in time, each group embedded its efforts in an ongoing story of the American democratic project. Whether group members imagined themselves as patriots or prophets, fulfilling their duty as Americans, in both accounts, involved engaging in active citizenship.

These narratives thus reveal the groups' understandings of what it means to be an active citizen in a diverse democratic country like the United States. These understandings have three dimensions that are intertwined within each narrative: they combine an articulation of their *collective identities* as active citizens, their *ideal models* of how society as a whole should work, and their *visions* of the country's future, all rolled into one. I refer to these intertwined understandings as the groups' democratic imaginaries. This term borrows from the philosopher Charles Taylor's concept of *social imaginaries*, which he describes as "the ways people imagine their social existence, how they fit together with others, how things go on between them and their fellows, the expectations that are normally met, and the deeper normative notions and images that underlie these expectations."[17] As a kind of social imaginary, democratic imaginaries are rarely made entirely explicit, but rather are embedded and embodied in symbols, discourses, and practices, like these narratives of active citizenship.

The groups' narratives thus helped participants develop a collective sense of who they were (and were not), where they had been, and where they wanted to go together.[18] This was enabled by the fact that both narratives were symbolically flexible, multivalent, and open-ended enough that diverse participants in the groups could imagine themselves as participants in these ongoing stories.[19] When we look closely at the democratic imaginaries that these narratives reveal, however, we can see clear differences between them, which reflect a significant gap between the groups' understandings of their place in America's past, present, and future.

Collective Identity as Active Citizens

First, by situating members in space, in time, and in relation to other actors, these narratives offer windows into the groups' collective identities.[20] When the groups told stories about what it meant to be a good citizen, these stories implied who "we" are as well as offered an account of who "we" are not.[21] This group of "others" was not always visible; but when it was, it was typically encoded as the evil, uncivil, or profane foil to "our" good, civil, or sacred character.[22] Moreover, while the figurative "we" could refer to the people who participated in each group, it more often referred to the broader constellation of actors—past and present—that the groups viewed as aligned with their political project, including the historical exemplars to whom they looked for guidance.

Yet the groups' collective identities conveyed more than just a static definition of who "we" (and "they") are. The sociologist Rogers Brubaker distinguishes between two different meanings of collective identity that are clarifying for our purposes. In the first, more common, usage it means "groupness," or "the sense of belonging to a distinctive, bounded, solidary group"—a "we" that can be contrasted to a "they." In the second, it means "self-understanding," or "situated subjectivity," defined as "one's sense of who one is, of one's social location, and of how (given the first two) one is prepared to act"—a "we" that moves through society, space, and time.[23]

Although subjectivity is typically considered an individual trait, citizens groups are key sites in which this kind of *situated subjectivity* can become shared, by providing opportunities for people to corroborate their experiences with others' and develop more refined understandings of what kind of society they are living in, what it means to be a member of that society, and how they are connected to their fellow citizens and their government.[24] In this way, a group can develop what we might term *situated intersubjectivity,* a collective sense of what kind of group it is, how it relates to other groups, and how (given the first two) it is prepared to collectively act. It is this sense of collective identity that forms the basis of such groups' democratic imaginaries.

When the Patriots studied the preamble, adorned their pamphlets and newspapers with American flags, quoted the Founding Fathers, recited the Pledge of Allegiance together, and read aloud from the Constitution and

NARRATIVES OF ACTIVE CITIZENSHIP

from histories of citizen activism, they defined themselves as the latest in a long line of patriotic heroes that first established and then protected the country and its foundational values. In their narrative, these patriotic heroes faced off against a wide range of threats, including distant illegitimate rulers, socialists, liberal secularists, and radical Islamists. More subtly, this narrative also placed some of the blame for the country's ills on ordinary Americans—indeed, it called them to account for their complacency.[25]

Meanwhile, when Interfaith members assigned their meetings the theme of "prophetic voice," told stories of biblical prophets and historical figures who played a role in advancing principles of justice, fairness, and human dignity, and spoke openly about wanting to change the social order, they defined themselves as the latest in a long line of prophetic voices that have called upon their government and fellow citizens to live up to their shared values and the country's founding principles— principles that, in their view, have never been fully realized. They named fewer specific enemies than the Patriots did, preferring instead to blame systems and those broad swaths of the population that resisted systemic change and engaged in partisan politics and the politics of division.

Whether they imagined themselves as patriotic heroes or prophetic voices, members of the two groups saw themselves as continuing a long tradition in which active citizens changed the course of history during moments in which their country was drifting off course. Yet there were profound differences in the qualities that Interfaith and the Patriots associated with these prophets and patriots, respectively, and in the exemplary models that each held up. Indeed, it is noteworthy that there was little overlap in the exemplars that each group looked to for guidance. As one early reader of this book put it, if you posed the question "Who built America?" to both groups, they would supply very different answers.

For example, many of the Patriots' exemplars—including Revolutionary War–era activists like the Sons of Liberty and, later, the Founding Fathers—were white Protestant men. This is not particularly surprising given the Patriots' emphasis on early American history. Although there have been efforts in recent decades to highlight the role of women, people of color, and members of minority faiths in early American history, the standard historical narratives most Americans are exposed to still place white Protestant men at the center of this story.[26]

But these were not the Patriots' only models—recall that members of the modern-day military, too, occupied a central place in the Patriots' narrative. In terms of race, class, and religion, members of the U.S. military are far more diverse than the Founding Fathers, a point that underscores the significance of military service as a pathway to active citizenship. Moreover, the military is now open to women. Although rarely stated explicitly, Linda's past service in the U.S. Navy—a part of her biography known to many group members—subtly reinforced the fact that women have also played an active role in protecting the nation.

Still, it is undeniable that the Patriots' narrative primarily featured individuals who occupied positions of relative privilege in their time. This pattern comes into clearer focus when their narrative is placed next to Interfaith's version of this story. As we have seen, Interfaith looked to a variety of biblical and historical "prophets" who called attention to their societies' moral failings and urged them toward better futures. Looking just at the Americans among these prophetic figures, they include the African American leader of the civil rights movement (Martin Luther King Jr.), a Catholic woman who founded a radical pacifist movement (Dorothy Day), a Mexican American labor organizer and civil rights activist (Cesar Chavez), and a Jewish theologian and civil rights activist (Abraham Joshua Heschel). In terms of their racial, ethnic, and religious (and to a lesser extent, gender) diversity, these exemplars look quite different from the historical figures who populate the Patriots' narrative. The question is why this is the case.

On one level, it seems plausible that each group sought out role models, consciously or not, that roughly reflected the sociodemographic characteristics of the groups themselves: whereas the Patriots (a predominantly white, middle-class, and Christian group) traced their lineage to figures who occupied positions of relative advantage and social prestige in their time, Interfaith's racially, economically, and religiously diverse membership traced its lineage to figures situated at the social and political margins. But if we look closer, we see that there is not a perfect correspondence between the demographics of the groups and their historical exemplars. Indeed, the Patriots were more diverse, in terms of their gender, class, and religious composition, than the historical exemplars they looked to for inspiration. Linda's strong leadership in particular ran counter to assumptions that groups like theirs view history-making as the sole domain of men.[27] Meanwhile, although Interfaith looked to a more diverse range of historical exemplars, we should not overlook the fact that many of the most active members of the group were white, middle-class, and Christian. If group members had simply gravitated toward historical exemplars that looked like them, there would have been far more references to white, middle-class, Christian prophets.

These incongruities suggest a need to examine how broader cultural forces, and not simply sociodemographic matching, shaped the groups' choices. After all, the groups were neither selecting fully formed versions of these narratives like books from a shelf, nor conjuring these narratives from scratch. They were assembling them from a vast archive of historical and cultural materials that circulate in American political culture.[28] In the course of their interactions and discussions about how active citizenship worked, group members attached their everyday experiences to those historical examples that were most relevant and accessible to them. Members of the two groups were likely familiar with an overlapping set of historical models for their action that most Americans would have encountered in their high school history courses or in popular culture. Technically, these characters would have been equally available to participants in both groups. Yet as we have seen, the groups tended to gravitate toward different subsets of characters. To understand why, we must consider how two processes—experiential filtering and gatekeeping—made some narrative elements more or less familiar and accessible to each group.

First, the exemplars they chose were also the ones that were most prominent within the various *other* social worlds in which they were embedded. As members of Interfaith and the Patriots passed through their religious communities, the military, the conservative and progressive media worlds, and other social movements, to name just a few of these, they were exposed to different clusters of foundational texts, such as the Constitution or the Old Testament; casts of characters, such as the Founding Fathers or Martin Luther King Jr.; and accounts of history, from apocalyptic narratives of moral collapse to hopeful narratives of moral progress.[29]

For example, individuals who had been involved in the broader progressive activist scene would likely have encountered stories and lessons from earlier movements like the civil rights movement, as well as these movements' efforts to present their successes and failures in light of the prophetic religious narrative of the Hebrew Bible. The cluster of texts, characters, and historical narratives associated with these movements would have been *more* familiar to members of Interfaith, many of whom had passed through this scene, than to members of the Patriots, who had not (for the most part).[30] Similarly, the Patriots drew on narrative elements that circulated within the conservative political subculture in which they were embedded, including a religious nationalist narrative that was increasing in prominence. One observer at the time noted Glenn Beck's considerable influence on this subculture: "His genius has been in his recognition that viewers . . . want a coherent vision, a competing canon that the regulated airwaves and academy have denied them. So he, Glenn Beck, is building that canon, book by book from the forgotten shelf."[31] While certainly not every member of the Patriots was familiar with this entire canon, elements of it were visible in group members' efforts to make sense of the nation's history and their place in it. The Patriots were also significantly *more* familiar with this canon than members of Interfaith were.

Meanwhile, actors within each scene also acted as gatekeepers of certain texts, characters, and narratives when members of other social worlds were perceived as misappropriating them. For example, when Glenn Beck staged a 2010 rally in front of the Lincoln Memorial on the anniversary of Martin Luther King Jr.'s historic "I Have a Dream" speech, he tried to align his event with King's efforts. "We are on the right side of history," he said. "We are on the side of individual freedoms and liberties, and damn it, we will reclaim the civil rights moment *[sic]*."[32] But Beck's effort to attach his political project to King's was viewed as inappropriate by progressive groups who viewed themselves as the true carriers of King's legacy. Accusing Beck of "hijack[ing] a movement that changed America," the Reverend Al Sharpton organized a counterrally, "Reclaim the Dream."[33] This clash raises interesting questions about whether historical figures like King *belong* to some political actors more than others. The same question could be asked about the Founding Fathers. Fully answering this question is beyond the scope of this book, but for now it suffices to note that these various cultural forces subtly channeled the groups toward embracing different exemplars of active citizenship.

Ideals and Future Visions of Society

Meanwhile, the groups' narratives also expressed their ideal visions of how society should work and of various possible futures. This is important because a vision of how civic life ought to be structured in the future can inform individuals' understandings of how they can make a difference today.[34] Of course, as we have seen, groups not only are oriented toward the future but also embed themselves in different understandings of the past. These are inextricably connected, as different understandings of the past—whether via memory, stories, or official histories—shape understandings of how change occurs and what the range of future possibilities is. This is why debates perpetually rage over who is allowed to write histories, who gets credit for major social changes, and whose memories of events become official.[35]

In the Patriots' narrative, American perfection is a thing of the past: in the years since the country's founding, threats both within and without have weakened its democratic spirit; yet the nation's precipitous decline has been halted during each of these crises through the actions of patriotic men and women like them. As this narrative reveals, although the Patriots idealized the past and feared for the future, they did not see decline as *inevitable*. In this way, their account was less fatalistic than the apocalyptic narratives of moral and political decline that are associated with contemporary religious nationalism.[36] Rather, the Patriots called upon Americans to take action now and remain more vigilant in the future. When they spoke ominously about the country's imminent destruction, their purpose was not to spread despair but to refocus attention on the urgency and historical import of their actions. Their vision was infused with optimism about the possibilities of restoration—paradise had been lost, but it could still be regained.

In contrast, Interfaith's narrative was rooted in members' recognition of the country's original sins and of its uneven journey toward "a more perfect union." The group understood their work as one small part of a long-term moral and political project that is bending the arc of the country's history, however slowly, toward justice, to paraphrase the words popularized by Martin Luther King Jr. While the heroic actions of certain individuals could be celebrated along the way, the group acknowledged that few changes would be immediate or complete. Indeed, biblical and historical prophets alike were portrayed as fighting against all odds and making only occasional and partial gains. At this closer vantage, Interfaith's vision of history actually resembles a spiral more than an arc—group leaders reminded one another that progress is possible and has slowly been achieved on some issues, but that it is advanced only through a circuitous process involving setbacks, backsliding, and wandering.[37] Recognizing this pattern, which parallels the journey to the Promised Land recounted in the book of Exodus, motivated them to keep moving forward even when they did not have visible evidence of their impact or recognition for their efforts.

Interfaith's and the Patriots' visions of the past also shaped their interpretations of new situations and their hopes for the future. Indeed, understanding how the past, present, and future were linked through each of their narratives helps illuminate a subtle difference in what participants in the groups meant when they commented that the country was not how it used to be, as noted in chapter 1. When the Patriots said this, they referenced an idyllic past, when the country was organized in a way that enabled men and women like them to thrive, assuming they did what was expected of them. Group members did not consistently reference a specific moment in the past that reflected this ideal, but their vision was not limited to the era of the country's founding. Indeed, the journalist E. J. Dionne Jr. observes that contemporary conservatism blends nostalgia for "the government and the economy of the 1890s, the cultural norms of the 1950s, and, in more recent times, the ethnic makeup of the country in the 1940s."[38]

While it is unlikely that every member of the Patriots shared this precise brand of nostalgia, nostalgia in general is a common response to the perceived or anticipated decline in one's economic, political, or social status—a situation that many members of the Patriots faced in the years leading up to their decision to become more active.[39] When people feel as if the life they once enjoyed is threatened, it makes sense they would yearn for a return to the social and political conditions under which they felt they could live up to their potential. As we have seen, the Patriots were sensitive to accusations that this desire necessarily meant they were elitists, nativists, or racists. They thus insisted that the future they sought would not only serve social groups that had thrived during past eras but also benefit everyone who chose to play an active role in the political process.

In contrast, when members of Interfaith noted that the country was not how it used to be, they were not referencing the same idyllic past as the Patriots. Racial and religious minorities, like many of Interfaith's members, do not tend to view early American history (and even much of the twentieth century) as a better time for their communities than the present day, however flawed the country may still be in their view. Still, there had been times in the relatively recent past—such as during President Obama's first presidential campaign—when they had felt more hopeful about the future and more confident that the country was headed in the right direction. Their disappointment during the time I spent with them stemmed from the feeling that the nation was backsliding after a period of hopeful progress. Their prophetic narrative reminded them that such setbacks were an inevitable part of their journey, and that there was more work to do.

In sum, Interfaith and the Patriots assembled two different narratives of active citizenship. Although both of these narratives were based on real historical events and figures, neither group's account of American democracy is historically complete. Indeed, one would be hard pressed to declare any such narrative to be the one true story of America—most societies are marked by multiple and competing narratives of their origins, development, and destiny.[40] But the historical accuracy of these narratives is less important for our purposes than the fact that they were *meaningful* in the context of these groups. While they imagined the journey differently, the groups' narratives reminded them that the ongoing vigilance of prophets and patriots, respectively, was required if the country was going to survive. By embedding participants in shared interpretive worlds, these narratives played an important role in the daily lives of the groups. And this had practical implications—by orienting members toward shared ways of imagining their role in the American democratic project, these narratives shaped the ways that each group put their shared ideal of active citizenship into practice.

4 Putting Faith into Action

As active citizens, members of Interfaith and the Patriots rejected the premise that politics is the realm of elites and experts and asserted their responsibility to become more informed citizens capable of holding government accountable. At the same time, they also rejected the premise that faith has no place in public life and asserted that religion offers values, lessons, and notions of "the good" that can help solve the country's most pressing problems. Both groups sought to project not only their voices and knowledge but also their values into public debates about how to get the country back on track.

This was a complex task. Recall that these groups were organizing against a backdrop in which the relevance of religious values for most public debates had declined. This is not because religious commitment had disappeared. Rather, as modern societies became differentiated into specialized spheres of activity—from science and medicine to law and government—religion became one source of authority among many.[1] While many Americans welcomed these changes or viewed them as inevitable, some religious communities resisted; they described feeling threatened and marginalized in the newly secularized society. Members of

Interfaith and the Patriots cannot be parsed easily into either of these camps—views on this issue varied within the two groups.

Yet across both groups, members expressed concern that American society would lose its footing if it fully lost sight of the moral values that most people of faith share. And members of the two groups generally agreed that any solution to the country's problems must involve bringing these values back into public discussions about how to pursue the public good. In this way, both groups fundamentally rejected the liberal secularist notion that there is no place for religion, or God, in the public life of a diverse democratic society.

Still, members of the two groups were also aware that many of their fellow Americans and public officials viewed religious values as irrelevant to most policy discussions, or viewed discussions about religious values as inappropriate impositions on those who did not share one's beliefs. Concerns like these are especially prominent in the United States, which not only was founded on the principle of religious freedom but also has grown increasingly religiously diverse in recent decades. As detailed in chapter 1, although nearly three-quarters of Americans still affiliate with Christianity or Judaism, the growing presence of Islam, Hinduism, Buddhism, and new variants of global Christianity has reshaped the context in which Americans experience and navigate religious diversity. Meanwhile, nearly one-quarter of Americans no longer identify with *any* religious tradition—a figure that has grown substantially in recent years.[2]

We might expect these trends—of rising religious diversity and religious disaffiliation—to make it more difficult for groups to speak in religious terms that would resonate with diverse public audiences. But a close look at Interfaith's and the Patriots' efforts to put their faith into action reveals that this is not impossible. Indeed, each group developed a distinctive way of bringing their religious values and teachings to bear on public debates about issues ranging from health-care reform to immigration to the very nature of citizens' rights and responsibilities, while also being attentive to the need to respect their fellow citizens' religious differences.

As will become evident, however, the groups' pluralistic approaches to putting their faith into action were rooted in different concerns and took different forms. While Interfaith's approach emphasized *religious inclusion*, the Patriots focused on preserving individual *religious liberty*. Inclusion and liberty are certainly not mutually exclusive, and members of the two groups referenced both values, but each group privileged one over the other. Meanwhile, the groups also differed in terms of the *limits* of their pluralism, or where they drew the line between those religious traditions that should be respected and those that could not be tolerated in good faith.[3] These differences not only reflected different underlying understandings of how citizens in a democracy ought to relate to one another but also shaped the practical ways in which each group put their faith into action.

PUTTING FAITH INTO ACTION IN A RELIGIOUSLY DIVERSE SOCIETY

Interfaith: Religious Inclusion

When I first met Father O'Donnell, he had been the pastor of his Catholic parish for thirteen years. A white man in his midsixties, with reddish cheeks and silver hair, he once described this urban parish, which serves thirty-two nationalities in three languages, as "international, interracial, inter-just-about-everything." But this was apparently not enough diversity, since they were also members of Interfaith. Sitting in Father O'Donnell's office one day, I asked whether it was important to him that Interfaith was a multifaith group. "The best thing that this parish does," he replied, is that, "twice a year, we have a blood drive [in partnership with a local synagogue]. And when you hold up a bag of blood, you can't tell whether it's Christian blood or Jewish blood. You can't tell whether it's black blood or white blood, rich blood or poor blood. It's blood that's saving a life."

"And the same thing happens when we all gather together," he noted. "The meetings that we have when we have Muslims, Catholics, Protestants, Jews—everybody together—that's not the issue. You go back to your synagogue and you believe anything you want. I'll go back to my church and believe anything I want. We have that freedom in this country. What are we there for? Human dignity. And that rises above all of the creedal things."

As an example of how this works in practice, he mentioned Farah, the twenty-something Muslim woman who had recently become a fixture at his Catholic church. She joined Interfaith as a staff organizer after completing a training program in interfaith organizing run by a Jewish organization. Being comfortable working with people from very different backgrounds proved essential to Farah's new job—she was charged with meeting one-on-one with members of Father O'Donnell's diverse congregation and facilitating regular meetings of the church's local organizing committee. "Farah is a Muslim woman educated by Jews to work with Catholics. Go figure," he chuckled, clearly delighted by the unlikely idea of this woman's newfound role in his church.

Watching the two of them approach me for an arranged meeting the following day, it was clear they had settled into an easy working relationship. We had come to a local university so they could talk to a class of graduate journalism students about their work together as part of Interfaith, as an example of the role faith could play in public life. Before class started, they discussed who should speak first. There was no rank-pulling; but even if there had been, it was not clear which of them would have pulled rank. "You tell me what to do" was Father O'Donnell's constant refrain around Farah.

They agreed he would speak first. After he spoke for around twenty minutes about the importance of religion in the lives of the diverse immigrant communities that comprise his congregation, Farah lamented, "It's always hard to follow Father O'Donnell." She knew this firsthand; she sat in the back of the large ornate sanctuary of his church each Sunday morning, knowing that as soon as mass was over her job would begin. While she waited, she often wondered what people thought as they entered the century-old church and saw "some girl in a hijab." She and Father O'Donnell smiled at one another as she revealed this thought process to the classroom full of journalists.

Now it was Farah's turn to explain how Interfaith endeavored to empower ordinary people to solve problems facing their communities (although, as she noted, she does not consider them "ordinary"). As she introduced the values that guided their work together, Father O'Donnell pushed himself to a standing position and paced to the white dry-erase board so he could take notes while she spoke. As she listed their shared values, he wrote, "1. Justice. 2. Human dignity. 3. Hope. 4. Respect. 5. Concern for the vulnerable. 6. Care for the youth."

Watching their presentation, it occurred to me that without context, the scene would likely confuse an onlooker. The petite Muslim woman seated at the front of the classroom held everyone's attention, though she looked younger than most of the students. She was dressed in a stylish black-and-white patterned silk dress over slim black pants and taupe flats, her small, round face framed by the draped black silk of her headscarf. She spoke from typed notes with scribbles along the margins, her large eyes scanning the room for comprehension after each point. Twice her size and nearly thrice her age, the white priest in suspenders and a starched, white collar played the role of her teaching assistant, jotting notes while she spoke. He cut in occasionally, asking her if he could add one point or another. They traded compliments and smiles. They were an unlikely duo but had forged a partnership that was clearly rooted in mutual respect.

Like the friendship between them, neither individual conformed to expectations. Father O'Donnell had an old-fashioned manner (he once responded to an email confirming a meeting with me with the single word "Be-you-dee-full"). But he also had a radical spirit that was rarely associated with the Catholic Church anymore. "I don't care what church you go to or what God you worship," he told the class, "as long as you don't worship me, because I know I'm not God."

He reiterated this point some time later, adding, "I want to see how you put it into action. Because the credibility of what you believe is in the action that you take. It's not in how many knees on your jeans you wear out praying. It's: 'Did you feed the hungry? Did you clothe the naked? Did you . . .' That whole list." After an early education in antiwar activism in Paris during the 1960s, he had pursued peace and justice throughout his career. His one regret: never having been arrested. One day he will be, when he has fewer responsibilities, he once promised me, "just as a statement of my own commitment."

Farah's pious dress, like Father O'Donnell's starched, white collar, may have given the impression of traditionalist rigidity; but as she told the journalism class, she had struggled with her faith and was currently a bit of a "mosque hopper." "My faith journey—my spiritual journey—is something that ebbs and flows all the time," she explained. "My hijab reminds me . . . of who I am. But it is something that is constantly fluctuating in my own life."

As she shared this experience, you could see the students letting down their guard, seeing her as someone a bit more like them. This was perhaps the kind of instinct for connecting with people that Father O'Donnell was thinking about when he told the class that members of his congregation had come to trust Farah even though they sometimes did not seem to trust one another: "This is an easy person to relate to," he said.

At the end of the day, Farah explained, their work with Interfaith was about a "shared vision for a more just country that we all call home." This was why they called their work *faith*-based organizing. "It's not *religion*-based organizing," Father O'Donnell explained. "There is a difference. . . . We both have faith. We base our activism in faith, not in the religion. I'm not a Muslim. She's not a Catholic. Okay." He threw his hands up, as if this were the most obvious thing in the world.

For Interfaith, this kind of cooperation was at the heart of their work to improve communities throughout the city. Organizing in and across diverse urban neighborhoods required cooperation between various communities that came together in the interest of solving shared problems. Faith communities were well-organized spaces in which groups already gathered regularly, trusted one another and spoke a common language. Why not start there? As Farah told the class of journalists, "It just makes sense to organize people [in congregations], if they're just sitting in the pews."

This is not to say that organizing through congregations was purely instrumental. For Interfaith, building a more just society started in one's own neighborhood, by creating diverse and inclusive communities of mutual obligation and care. To this end, they intentionally worked to bring participants together from a wide range of congregations. Learning to work together across different faith traditions was both a means of building greater power in the community and an end in itself.

Interfaith had worked hard to attract a religiously diverse membership. The majority of the Interfaith coalition was drawn from the Catholic (44 percent), mainline Protestant (30 percent), and Black Protestant (15 percent) traditions. Jews (7 percent) and Muslims (4 percent) were represented in smaller overall numbers within the coalition, but they were actually overrepresented compared to their numbers in the U.S. population as a whole.[4] Moreover, their influence was felt—a handful of active

Jewish and Muslim leaders occupied positions of leadership within the group, and their clergy were regularly asked to appear at public events.

Interfaith's strategy of organizing through a diverse range of congregations reflected a desire to be as inclusive as possible of the many faith traditions represented in their communities, but their congregation-based model also limited the religious diversity of their membership in subtle ways. For example, because participants in Interfaith's work were recruited almost exclusively through their member congregations, it was difficult for individuals to become meaningfully involved in the group if they were not affiliated with one of these congregations. A case in point: I was once seated at the same table as two young women from the neighborhood who had showed up at an Interfaith training session after seeing an announcement of the event. They had participated with enthusiasm, but did not belong to any of Interfaith's member congregations, and I never saw them again. In fact, I knew of only two regular participants in the group's work who had not joined through their religious congregation.[5]

This is not to say that people were unwelcoming, but to point out that there was no organizational infrastructure through which to include unaffiliated individuals. Indeed, this was a practical barrier that I personally confronted throughout my fieldwork. Despite the fact that Interfaith's leaders and active members welcomed and encouraged my research, information about smaller group gatherings was often communicated informally within congregations, rather than through group emails or mass listservs. After missing a handful of these meetings, I learned to be more proactive about staying in the loop. But I also took note that this relatively high barrier to entry stood in contrast to the Patriots' approach—they embraced online and email communication, advertised their meetings and public events widely, and viewed all newcomers as necessary to the growth of their movement.

Interfaith's congregation-based model also subtly limited their ability to recruit members from some minority faiths. Indeed, despite their over-representation of Jews and Muslims, the group had no Buddhist or Hindu participants.[6] And although Interfaith worked hard to cultivate a relationship with a local Arab American organization, Farah struggled to bring more Muslims into the coalition's work. In conversations with me, she attributed this to the fact that it was difficult to use a congregation-based model to organize adherents of certain religious traditions—such as Buddhism, Hinduism, and certain forms of Islam—which either do not emphasize congregational life or do not view places of worship as spaces for political action in the same way that many Christians and Jews do.[7]

Finally, although Interfaith never explicitly excluded evangelicals from their work, no evangelical Protestant congregations were members of their coalition; and indeed, relatively few evangelical congregations are involved in this kind of organizing nationally.[8] This is despite the fact that large (and growing) numbers of evangelicals embrace the idea of working on behalf of social justice.[9] Still, it is difficult for evangelical congregations to officially sign on to faith-based community-organizing efforts, particularly when these involve interfaith work—a pattern likely due to a combination of political and cultural differences and discomfort with interfaith cooperation.[10]

Despite these limitations on their efforts, however, members of Interfaith worked hard to embrace an ethos of religious *inclusion*. Not only did they recruit a religiously diverse membership base (which also happened to be racially, ethnically, and socioeconomically diverse), but as we will see, they also developed a variety of group practices intended to make everyone feel included in a shared project. This can be contrasted to the way in which the Patriots understood their call to put their faith into action, which reflected an emphasis on religious *liberty*.

Patriots: Religious Liberty

Cam was a financial planner by day, folk musician and blogger by night, and an active member of the Patriots. The first time I saw Cam he was standing on top of a flatbed truck that had been set up as a makeshift stage. He was warming up the crowd of around 150 Tea Partiers who had gathered after work to "spread the word of Fiscal Responsibility and Limited Government" and share "the 'ahh haa' moment that inspired them to get active," according to Linda's report on the event the following morning. He wore faded blue jeans, sandals, a slightly rumpled fedora, and a white T-shirt that appeared from afar to be emblazoned with a large American flag. Closer up, it became apparent that the flag was actually starred-and-striped block letters spelling out the words "Liberty and

Freedom." Red, white, and blue bunting lined the edge of the stage beneath his feet. With a guitar slung across his chest and a harmonica perched in front of his mouth, he looked every inch the "conservative Bob Dylan" he was later dubbed in a review of his new album, a folky meditation on the political awakening that had led him to that stage.

The next time I saw Cam was a few weeks later, on a bus bound for Washington, D.C. Along with around fifty other members of the Patriots, we were traveling to the nation's capital for Glenn Beck's highly anticipated Restoring Honor Rally. At the end of the rally, while we waited for others to return to the bus, Cam sat down in the seat behind me and sipped a cold drink. He seemed tired but also eager to talk. "I meant to ask you," he said after catching my eye when I stood up to stretch. "Has seeing all of this changed your opinions about anything?" I told him the truth—that I was learning a lot and was not yet sure how to make sense of it all—and then I asked him what he thought of the rally.

He repeated a refrain I heard from nearly everyone who returned to the bus that afternoon: that he had not been able to see or hear much, but that it had been important for him to be there. I asked him why he thought so, and he told me that he had had a realization at work several months earlier. It had occurred to him that what was missing in our society was honor. His experience as a financial planner had taught him that "people can't trust each other when they make an agreement." He connected this to the fact that "they don't trust their government." When Beck announced the theme of this event—"restoring honor"—Cam said, "I had been like, 'Aha!'"

Beck's solution to the problem Cam encountered at work was straightforward—we need to bring God back into our lives. Cam thought Beck was exactly right about this. He does not belong to a church but considers himself a spiritual person and is focused on "a daily practice of godliness." Yet it had not been until recently—prompted, in his telling, by his regular viewing of Beck's television show—that he started thinking more about the role of God in his life.

While we waited for a few stragglers to return to the bus after the rally, Cam told me about an experience that had brought these ideas home in a very personal way. His bandmates had been over for practice one Sunday afternoon, and everyone had stayed for dinner afterward. They were just sitting down at the table when his drummer asked if he could say grace. As Cam later recounted to me in more detail during an interview:

> So we're sitting at the table . . . with the kids. There were probably about ten of us. And [my friend], before we started to eat, puts out his hands to say grace. And we all take hands. In prayer. [I thought,] "Jesus, this is cool! I haven't done this since I was a kid." And it just was a weird . . . it . . . it just kind of struck me, how . . . what has happened to us? It kind of felt that . . . slowly, what we've done is we've shoved God in a closet.

As he explained it, "We've kind of gone full spectrum." Although the country was founded on the idea that everyone could freely practice whatever faith they chose, "now we've got all these separation-of-church-and-state issues, which has totally been perverted from the founders' intent." He elaborated: "The founders just wanted us to not have a government-sponsored religion, like the Church of England, where you pay your taxes . . . they take your taxes. But the founders never meant for us not to be able to pray in school. Or, or . . . you know? And everywhere you look, they're extricating our most sacred symbols from the public square." On the bus after the rally, after telling me about his experience praying before dinner, he concluded, "We need to bring that kind of thing back into our lives."

The Restoring Honor Rally had been devoted to exactly this cause. It was part political rally, part religious awakening, and Beck had spoken that day about the need for Americans to "turn back to God." Although he took the tone of a preacher, he spoke in broad theological strokes that would be accessible to a religiously diverse audience. Media accounts equated the rally to a modern-day tent revival, but few recognized the varieties of spirituality that were gathered under Beck's big tent.

Beck himself is a Mormon, having converted to the faith after recovering from an alcohol and drug addiction and engaging in a spiritual journey that led him to the Church of Jesus Christ of Latter-day Saints. Although he commonly writes and speaks about his Mormon faith, he also speaks in a more general spiritual language that appeals equally to evangelical Christians, unchurched spiritual seekers, and a wide range of others. For example, I spent much of the Restoring Honor Rally with a recent convert to Seventh-Day Adventism and a former Catholic who briefly explored, then abandoned, Buddhism, both of whom were former addicts.

Although these men could not have been more different, Beck's message of personal and national redemption appealed to them both.

This broad appeal may have been part of why he was embraced by the Tea Party. Indeed, although it is often assumed that political conservatives are also religious conservatives (and more specifically, evangelical Christians), the Patriots included members with varied religious identities and relationships to organized religion. Although not representative of the entire group, an informal survey of group members who traveled to the Restoring Honor Rally offers a window into the religious diversity of the group. Of the forty-two people who reported their religious identification to me, 31 percent identified as Roman Catholic, 21 percent as Evangelical Protestant, 14 percent as mainline Protestant,[11] 10 percent as either atheist or members of no religion, and 7 percent as Jewish. Five percent opted not to respond, and 12 percent identified as "something else." Among the latter were individuals who identified as pagan, as Christian/Buddhist, and as a "very lapsed Catholic."

It is possible that the group of people who traveled to this rally represented a subset of the larger group that was disproportionately likely to be religious, since they were clearly comfortable with Beck's brand of public religiosity. But 10 percent of that group still reported *not* being religious, and one-third was not Christian. In this way, the Patriots who traveled to the rally generally resembled the group as a whole, which included some conservative Christians, but also many small business owners, veterans, and libertarian-leaning independents who were drawn to the group for reasons beyond their concerns about the nation's soul, and who varied widely in their reported relationships to faith and organized religion.

Of course, it is also possible that the religious profile of the Patriots differed from that of other Tea Party groups around the country. The Patriots' location in the Northeast, proximate to a large and diverse metropolitan area, may have contributed to their religious diversity and the relatively low number of evangelicals. Yet national surveys of Tea Party participants confirm that the diversity of religious affiliation and practice found within the Patriots was not atypical within the movement as a whole. Indeed, the national movement had significantly higher levels of religious diversity than the religious Right (our prototypical example of a conservative religious movement) in terms of both religious tradition and practice.

According to one survey, roughly half of national Tea Party participants reported also being part of the religious Right. Even so, Tea Partiers were, on average, significantly less likely than white evangelical Protestants to attend church at least once a week or believe that the Bible is the literal word of God, suggesting that the white evangelicals within the movement were counterbalanced by individuals reporting much lower levels of religious engagement and orthodoxy. Moreover, nearly one-fifth of the movement was composed of non-Christian religious minorities and religiously unaffiliated individuals, groups that would be unlikely to be found within the religious Right.[12]

Not only did the Tea Party have greater religious diversity than did previous models of conservative religious activism, but also the place of religion within the life of the movement was more ambiguous. For example, the Patriots' original website stated prominently that they lived by the "Nine Principles and Twelve Values" of Glenn Beck's 9/12 Project, the first two of which were "America is Good" and "I believe in God and He is the Center of my Life." Yet group members, including Linda, explicitly distanced the group from the religious Right. In this way, they echoed a theme that national Tea Party leaders had been insisting upon since the movement's beginning. As Jenny Beth Martin, founder of the Tea Party Patriots, told a reporter, "It's not about religion. . . . Our movement started and has been more focused on fiscal responsibility and we really haven't focused on religious issues or social issues. Each member within the movement has their own religious beliefs. Generally those don't come into play at Tea Party events."[13]

For the Patriots, avoiding the social issues that had occupied the religious Right was partially strategic—they worried that wedge issues like abortion had only divided self-identified conservatives into camps. In contrast, they worked to bring those groups back together around broader unifying themes: strict adherence to the Constitution and a restored commitment to the Judeo-Christian values on which the country was founded. Beck's Restoring Honor Rally brought both of these themes together in a simple argument—namely, that the former was not feasible without the latter.

"This is a day that we can start the heart of America again," Beck told the crowd gathered on the National Mall that day. "And it has nothing to do with politics. It has everything to do with God. Everything [to do with] turning our face back to the values and principles that made us great." Tapping into a language that fused individualized spirituality with civil religious themes, Beck asserted that America's greatness could be restored only if each American recommitted to living out his or her faith values.[14]

But honoring God's place in this system did not necessarily require that everyone become religiously devout or march in religious lockstep. Indeed, many of the Patriots honored their God-given rights by expressing their freedom to disagree about religion. It was not uncommon for the Patriots to spar over issues that are typically barred from dinner parties—religion and politics were at the top of this list. Although many reported feeling like part of the "silent majority" before getting involved in the Tea Party, most of the Patriots I knew had grown comfortable debating these issues with their families, friends, and fellow Patriots. They often told me about these disagreements with a degree of pride. After all, the freedom to disagree was central to their understanding of what it meant to be an American.

Cam spoke (and blogged) frequently about the disagreements that had erupted within his marriage since he had become more politically and religiously active. As he explained in an interview, he navigated these differences in a manner that was consistent with his individualistic understanding of religious liberty: namely, by approaching them not as irreconcilable differences but as learning opportunities, especially for their kids:

> My becoming engaged and becoming a little bit more active has created a little bit of friction in the house. But [it's] interesting, because the kids—and we have two; one fourteen and one twelve—have the benefit of growing up in an environment where they get both sides of the fence. So I think . . . [*laughs*] as much as it makes my wife crazy [*laughs*], that's a good thing for them. Let them decide. So I made a commitment two years ago. I said if some kid can strap on body armor and go sit his ass down in some foxhole in some desert on the other side of the planet and dodge bullets, the least we can do at home is stand and engage. And question. And do it with a certain respect and a certain level of fairness. That's what this country's about.

As his comment "That's what this country's about" suggests, the way Cam practiced pluralism at home reflected his more general understanding that being American required this kind of contentious engagement with others. He later elaborated on this point: "Regardless of what your faith is or what you believe in, or what have you[,] . . . my understanding or my . . . appreciation of this country is that . . . that's basically why the Pilgrims came here; [it] was to escape religious persecution and [the] Church of England and all that. To be able to practice their faith . . . in the way they saw fit for themselves and their families."

Cam's approach to religion differed substantially from that of the Pilgrims. He once wrote on his blog that his readers should consider adding to their New Year's resolutions a promise to "make time for meditation and prayer (to the Sun God if that's your higher power)." The notion that members of this group would view prayer to the Judeo-Christian God and to the Sun God as equally viable paths to a virtuous life will likely come as a surprise to those who associate political conservatism in the United States exclusively with evangelical Protestantism. But it should by now be clear that the Patriots, and the Tea Party more generally, broke this mold; efforts to understand them through the same frame as the religious Right will miss the complex ways in which this movement approached the relationship between faith and politics. Cam's "to each their own" spirituality, while not fully shared by everyone in the group, embodied the Patriots' shared emphasis on individual liberty.

But there were also limits to Cam's (and the Patriots') pluralism. I discovered the first limit when Cam talked to me about "social justice"—a term that, again thanks to Beck, has become widely associated among conservatives with *socialism.* Cam told me that his wife was active in a Reform Jewish temple where the rabbi played guitar and led musical services that Cam enjoyed from time to time. The congregation was, in Cam's words, a "wonderful group of people." But he worried when his wife brought home brochures that highlighted the issue of social justice. These were, in Cam's telling, "the two words that send a chill down my spine."

Cam made a similar comment on the bus ride home from the Restoring Honor Rally. When I asked why he was so concerned about social justice, he responded with a question of his own. "You know liberation theology, like what Obama talks about, and what they teach in Rev. Wright's church?" Before I could answer, he explained, "They talk about 'collective salvation.'" [15] I began to notice that other members of the Patriots with whom I spoke also made this distinction between individual and collective salvation. After some research, I found that their formulation bore a close resemblance to Beck's extended discussions about this issue: he described individual salvation as "an individual relationship between a person and God through Jesus' sacrifice on the cross." Beck then explained, "When Jesus died on the cross he died for everyone that ever lived, but individually. It was one act for the entire collection—it was for each person individually."[16]

Echoing this logic, Cam explained that collective salvation was just an excuse for socialism. Although he carefully made exceptions for his wife, for the members of her liberal synagogue, and for me (who, he explained, "honestly believe . . . that being liberal is being compassionate, being liberal is helping people that can't help themselves"), he declared elite proponents of social justice to be "pure evil." His concern about the synagogue's social justice agenda was not rooted in differences between Judaism and his Christian and Buddhist-inflected spirituality, or between liberalism and conservatism. It was rooted, at least in part, in these more abstract understandings of the proper relationship between individuals and God.

The second limit involved Islam. Many members of the Patriots were concerned that Muslims wished to fundamentally transform American culture—a common anxiety about new immigrant groups. This was a topic that came up frequently during my fieldwork. At one rally, a conversation I was part of turned to whether it was possible for Muslims to truly "become American." The unanimous answer was "no," but the various reasons offered reveal the complexity of discussions about this topic.

One man explained that he could never trust Muslims: "They want you dead!" he said, looking directly at me, "They want you dead!"

"You think *all* Muslims want me dead?" I asked.

"Every one of them," he responded. "Their book, their Bible, the Qur'an, says that they should lie to us. You're an infidel. Because you're not a Muslim! You're an infidel! They're gonna lie to you."

A woman added, "They don't *want* to be Americans."

An older man worried about their capacity for patriotism: "Muslims can never become good Americans. They have one allegiance. Only one. And that's to Allah. So they can never have allegiance to the flag, or the government, or anything else."

"Well, people used to say similar things about Catholics, too, right?" I asked him. "Do you think it's similar?"[17]

"Through the different generations, the Italians, the Irish, the Germans, they all came into this country" he explained. "They came in, they were glad to come here. They assimilated. They learned English. They learned the American ways. They became Americans. Americans! What is happening with the Muslims—they're not assimilating. We have to change our culture for them."

This was a common sentiment within the group. Evidence of this was found not only in visible landmarks like the "ground zero mosque" in New York City but also in more quotidian presences, like their children's textbooks. At one Patriots meeting, a woman reported on her child's history book: "There were only two pages on Christianity. The rest of it was on Islam!" On another occasion, an elderly man told me, "You wouldn't believe some of the stuff they are trying to sneak into textbooks these days. All this pro-Islamist stuff!" He then handed me a card for an organization called ACT! For America, which raises awareness of the "increasing pro-Islamist and anti-American and anti-Israeli bias in high school and college courses and textbooks."[18]

But these cultural concerns were only part of the reason that Islam tended to be excluded from the Patriots' vision of American pluralism. Anxieties about the global spread of Islamic law, which had been mounting since the terrorist attacks of September 11, 2001, had gained passionate new adherents in Tea Partiers who viewed it as a fundamental threat to the Constitution. During the peak of the Patriots' activities, national political commentators like Beck and Pamela Geller detailed this threat through various conservative media channels, public appearances, and books, like Geller's 2011 *Stop the Islamization of America*, which became an influential part of the Tea Party canon. In the *Must Know News*, Linda linked regularly to Geller's writings and promoted local events featuring Geller as a speaker, including an October 2010 rally hosted by several area Tea Party groups. At that rally, one speaker described Geller as "an American hero because she will talk about Islam, even if that means she has a fatwa on her head!" The crowd cheered enthusiastically when he reminded them that she would be speaking later that evening.

For the Patriots, there were common threads linking Muslims and religious groups promoting social justice—both sought to transform American society; and by undermining the individualized nature of God-given rights

and the singularity of the Constitution, both threatened the very foundations on which Americans' religious liberty rested. As a result, although
the Patriots' emphasis on protecting and preserving religious liberty led
them to take a more pluralist approach to religious diversity than is often
associated with conservative movements, these groups were placed outside the boundaries of their pluralist vision. They could not be tolerated—
for the good of the country.

PRACTICING RELIGIOUS INCLUSION AND RELIGIOUS LIBERTY

As we have seen, Interfaith was concerned with religious inclusion, and
particularly with a desire to take the beliefs, values, and perspectives of
religious minorities into account in discussions about the public good.
This infused their efforts to develop collective religious practices that
could (at least in theory) bind them together as an interfaith community
that could credibly speak with one voice. Meanwhile, the Patriots were
concerned with preserving and protecting each individual's religious liberty, including individuals' freedom to practice whatever faith they chose
(or no faith), within certain limits. This led them to generally view religious practice as an individual pursuit. But this did not prevent them from
developing certain collective practices that communicated a civil religious
vision of God's role in the American democratic project.

Interfaith: Collective Religious Practices

Because Interfaith members identified collectively as people of faith, they
regularly incorporated religiously salient practices into their work. This
was a way of signaling their group's faith-based identity to outsiders
(which was a mark of distinction for them, especially when they worked in
coalition with secular groups); it was also a means of infusing their political action with sacred meaning and of interpreting their varied religious
teachings and values through a shared political lens. The group thus
developed a variety of religious practices in which their religiously diverse

membership could participate, whether individuals were Protestant, Catholic, Jewish, or Muslim.

The most visible of these collective practices involved public prayer. This may seem surprising, if one conceptualizes prayer as a private mode of communication that links individuals to God, or as a ritualized practice specific to each individual faith tradition.[19] Yet every Interfaith meeting—internal or public, large or small—opened with some kind of prayer or reflection. This was not without complications, but group members (and especially the clergy) developed ways of publicly praying together that highlighted their shared identity as people of faith while also attempting to be as inclusive and respectful as possible of multiple religious traditions.

Over the years, Father O'Donnell had developed a particular style of doing this, which was on display one night when his congregation's local organizing committee hosted a public accountability action. They had invited two local city council members and three officials from the city's housing department to their church so they could explain their concerns about a delinquent landlord who refused to make legally required repairs to a building on their block. I discuss this action further in chapter 5, but here my focus is on how Father O'Donnell opened the meeting.

Once the guests were seated at a head table and the audience was seated in rows of folding chairs that had been set up in the church auditorium, Father O'Donnell rose to provide a brief faith reflection. He began by noting that a diverse crowd had gathered that evening—a nod not only to Interfaith's internal diversity but also to the fact that this meeting, although held in a church, was open to the public. He noted that while we were all different, we were there together to fight for justice. He then called upon those gathered to pray "to the God of your understanding" and asked everyone to "allow yourself to be called by that God to do the good work that will make us all better neighbors." Continuing, he noted,

It is good and it is pleasant when people come together in unity. But sometimes that unity needs to be ironed out. Sometimes there are wrinkles. Sometimes there's stuff that we have to do to make sure that we're not in the way. And if we see somebody who's in the way, make sure that they're not hurting themselves. Okay? We have a responsibility to one another, and as much as I have a responsibility to you, you have a responsibility to me.

Ultimately, we are who we are. And I am glad that you're here, being who you are, as you represent your own interests, but also the interests of the people of the building across the street.

This opening prayer blended elements of two types of prayer practices that were common within Interfaith.[20] First, it was an interfaith prayer. His call for people to pray "to the God of your understanding" drew people of various faith traditions into the act of prayer while allowing them to pray in the manner that was most meaningful to them. Similarly, a priest once opened a large public meeting by directing the audience to pray in their own faith languages, together: "If you are Jewish, stand for Adonai. If you are Muslim, stand for Allah. If you are Christian like me, stand for Jesus." At larger events, they also sometimes signaled their interfaith inclusivity by asking multiple clergy from different traditions to pray, each in his or her own tradition and style, and sometimes even in different languages, most often Spanish, but also Creole, Chinese, Russian, or Arabic. It was common at those events to see several audience members with headphones, receiving simultaneous translation.

Father O'Donnell's prayer also contained elements of what I came to call a prefigurative prayer. Like interfaith prayer, prefigurative prayer was common within Interfaith. This kind of prayer referenced the group's shared values and goals, as well as how the group's work together modeled the kind of society they sought to bring about through their actions. In this case, Father O'Donnell called attention to the fact that community members and public officials had come together not only out of their own economic and political interests but also out of shared responsibility to one another as neighbors. Moreover, when he remarked, "It is good and it is pleasant when people come together in unity," he was paraphrasing Psalm 133, which communicated to those primed to hear it that in addition to being bound as neighbors, they were also members of the "blessed community" that groups like Interfaith sought to build.[21]

Sometimes prefigurative prayers did not reference any specific religious tradition or quote scripture. Although Father O'Donnell did so here, clergy also drew on recent news articles, social criticism, or even poetry as their inspiration. For example, during a training session to address the challenges of racial injustice in their work and in society at large, Rev.

Fischer, the Lutheran pastor we met in chapter 2, drew on the writing of W. E. B. Du Bois:

> For me, I needed to always turn to some sources of wisdom during this time. . . . And I went back to read W. E. B. Du Bois, some of his language, his words, because he said at the very turn of the last century very similar things that we are thinking and feeling and understanding today. So I'm gonna read just some snippets of his, what's called "Credo," written in 1918. Snippets of "Credo." "I believe in God," he says, "who made of one blood all nations that on Earth do dwell. I believe that all men," he said, "black and brown and white are brothers, varying through time in opportunity, in form, in gift, in feature, but differing in no essential particular, and alike in soul, and the possibility of infinite development."

He continued reading for several minutes. When he was done, he said, "We are people seeking to make the world better and to align ourselves with many other voices, which is the beauty of what's happening around our country. People are speaking again, and not recognizing each other's differences. That is power. . . . In my language, when we're done with meditation, we always say, 'So be it. Amen.'" By using public prayer as an opportunity to specify their vision of what a diverse and healthy democracy should look like, clergy orient group members, despite their many other differences, toward a shared democratic imaginary.

Looking beyond the *content* of their prayers, the *form* their prayer practices took also encouraged diverse members of the group to recognize their shared goals and identity as people of faith. Typically, in internal settings, like group training sessions, clergy would use their opening reflections to encourage coalition members to physically interact with each other—to hold hands in a circle, shake hands with their neighbors, or collectively learn a new ritual. Practices like these encouraged transgressions of personal space and drew group members together into shared embodied experiences, breaking down the norms of inhibition and polite restraint that often prevented strangers from interacting, even within groups like these.[22]

Finally, the group sought to build trust and mutual recognition by creating opportunities for everyone to learn more about the others' religious traditions, and particularly about minority religious traditions. While not a regular occurrence, members of minority faiths were occasionally asked to lead prayers in their own traditions. One example of this came during a prayer retreat when a Muslim leader led about thirty of us in his daily prayer ritual, explaining what each step signified as the group of all non-Muslims, including several clergy members, followed along.

Another example took place in the smaller and less reflective setting of a health-care working group meeting. A Jewish woman named Helen, who was actively engaged in Interfaith's work, expressed discomfort (she explained she was "not mad, just mentioning") that the group had scheduled a meeting on a Friday night, the beginning of the Jewish Sabbath. The organizer suggested she start the meeting by saying the hamotzi, the Jewish blessing over bread that is traditionally said before the Friday night meal. Although raised Jewish, Helen had only recently become observant and was self-conscious about being a spokesperson for Judaism. But she agreed. Before the meeting began, she spent a few minutes explaining the meaning of this blessing for Jews, then closed her eyes and quickly recited the prayer in Hebrew before slicing a fresh loaf of bread for everyone to share. As this example shows, these practices could sometimes feel awkward for the people involved; but even in such moments, they communicated the groups' commitment to religious inclusion.

There were also more informal occasions for participants to learn more about one another's faith traditions. This happened through small talk before and after meetings, through new friendships that emerged within the group, and through the less visible daily challenges of respectfully navigating different faith communities' needs and preferences. Scheduling around everyone's holy days, selecting menus that respected dietary preferences: these were the mundane habits on which shared culture was built.[23] But this was not always easy, as I saw during a meeting of the economic justice working group during my first summer with Interfaith.

As our small meeting had drawn to a close, five of us pulled out Blackberries, iPhones, and paper calendars to schedule our next meeting. After a pause I looked around, confused to find the others shaking their heads as they flipped pages or swiped screens. "August and September are tough because you run up against either Ramadan or the Jewish High Holidays," Nora explained. While people rattled off possible dates, she held up a finger and said she was looking for an email from one of their Jewish leaders telling her when all of the relevant Jewish holidays were that year.

Jackson, the day-to-day organizer working with the group, whom we met in chapter 3, suggested the second or third Thursday in September. Nora had found the email and now began to list the dates that interfered with the Jewish holidays. My head spun. With none of the Jewish leaders in the room, a few people briefly debated whether it would be kosher, so to speak, to schedule a meeting during the week between Rosh Hashanah and Yom Kippur.

Nora relayed a conversation she had had with a rabbi active in Interfaith's work, who explained that scheduling an event during that week would be like scheduling something two days before Christmas. To my right, Raquel and an older man, both Catholics, nodded in understanding. Jackson was staring at his phone. "What about that Wednesday?" he asked. His voice had an edge. Nora repeated that it was still during the High Holidays. He said, "I'll be honest, I've been to meetings three days before Christmas."

There was some shifting in seats. Nora paused before speaking. "Sure, we of course have the option of scheduling the meeting and just telling [the Jewish leader] we don't expect her to be there." This was, in fact, what the health-care working group had done the night Helen led the group in the Sabbath prayer. Raquel then suggested late August instead. Jackson worried aloud, "This is too soon, no? And isn't that during Ramadan?" He put his phone down. Nora explained that it was Ramadan now, and that it was okay to schedule meetings during Ramadan: "They go to meetings. They just don't eat," she explained, referring to their Muslim leaders.

Raquel suggested late August again. Jackson countered with early September. We decided on September 1. Exhausted, we headed down the back stairs of the old church and parted ways. But before we scattered, Jackson reached over and handed me a blue button with "Interfaith" written in white block letters. Witnessing how they had navigated this painstaking task felt like my official initiation into the group.

Finally, at the most informal level, the group forged a sense of community through what we might call interfaith small talk. During those brief moments before group meetings began, during coffee breaks, and in car rides to and from events, they asked one another relatively "safe" questions about their traditions, rules, rituals, and holidays.[24] They signaled their openness to learning about one another's traditions by telling self-deprecating jokes about their own traditions and trading stories that showcased their commitment to diversity or vilified others who were religiously closed-minded. Through these informal exchanges, they found common ground in their shared acknowledgement of the importance that religion played in their lives and in their shared commitment to fostering interreligious relationships.

These interactions also had the potential to lead to deeper personal relationships between participants. Farah and Father O'Donnell's strong working relationship was only one manifestation of the group's work to help a diverse set of people feel like part of a single interfaith community. Many other examples existed within the group. A Jewish woman and a Lutheran pastor often compared notes about their faith traditions during the health-care working group's coffee breaks. During a period when a Muslim leader was absent from group activities for an extended period of time, a Jewish woman and a Catholic woman spoke of him frequently, updating one another on what they had learned about a difficult situation in his personal life. The week that the elderly father of a Catholic leader in the group passed away, I attended services at a progressive synagogue that was central to Interfaith's work. Several members of the congregation stood during the service to talk about how important their friendships with him had been—friendships that had been forged through their work with Interfaith.

"We learn because we're willing to learn," Father O'Donnell once explained to me in an interview. "But also because we have people who are willing to teach us." Asking lots of questions, and being willing to answer—this was how strangers became neighbors. "If there were people who say, 'No, I'm sorry, we don't talk about that . . . ,'" he remarked, "well, then I remain a stranger. If you talk about it with me, I'm not a stranger anymore." Sometimes these conversations were awkward, or even unintentionally hurtful. But Interfaith members endeavored to make the group a safe place to have them.

At the end of the day, Interfaith worked to build their group culture in the same way they worked to build their public power—through relationships. "There's a respect that we each have for one another's tradition," Father O'Donnell said. "And the respect, I would say, is based in not so much the theological respect but the sociological respect. You're here, I'm here, she's here—and we're all here together for the same purpose. And that purpose is not to discuss how many angels dance on the head of a pin. That purpose is to say, 'How do we get justice for the people?'"

Through these formal and informal practices, Interfaith members sought to build a group culture that was rooted in their shared values, which were drawn from their respective faith traditions. This, they believed, gave them credibility to speak collectively on behalf of their diverse communities and publicly communicated the relevance of these values to the issues their communities were facing. By grounding their political demands in these broadly held values, they hoped to tug at the moral conscience of public officials and remind the public of the moral imperative to act.

Patriots: Individual Religious Practices

The Patriots' practices differed significantly from those of Interfaith's members. One visible difference was that the Patriots did not tend to pray together when they gathered. This may have been because, unlike the members of Interfaith, they did not identify as a faith-based group, and there were no clergy or other religious leaders involved in the group. To the extent that members referenced any elite perspectives on questions about the role of religion in their work, they tended to cite Beck. This had implications for how the group approached religion.

Although Beck encouraged them to think in new ways about the political significance of prayer, he also conceptualized prayer as an individualized practice that involved one's personal relationship with God. While it is impossible to say with certainty how much influence Beck's message had on each individual's practices, the way in which Cam and other members of the Patriots reported engaging in prayer was consistent with his approach.

Beck's approach was front and center at the Restoring Honor Rally. Recall his words to the crowd gathered on the National Mall that summer day: "This is a day that we can start the heart of America again. And it has nothing to do with politics. It has everything to do with God. Everything [to do with] turning our face back to the values and principles that made us great." In other words, if America could still be saved, it would be ordinary Americans like Cam who would save it. They did not require money or power; all they needed was a little faith. Through small daily practices, like prayer, the nation could welcome God back into their lives, one person at a time. "I ask not only if you would pray on your knees," Beck told the crowd, "but pray on your knees with the door open for your children to see." Cam took this request to heart, and months later he revealed on his blog that after attending the rally he had "re-established a practice I had long ago abandoned . . . praying on my knees."

On the bus after the rally, when Cam first told me about his experience praying before dinner and his growing concern that Americans had "shoved God in a closet," I asked him what any of that had to do with politics for him. "It doesn't," he said. "It's more of an individual thing." At the time, this answer surprised me, especially since he had just spent several hours on a bus so that he could attend what was, at least from some vantages, a political event. This answer was even more surprising in light of his later recounting to me that these experiences had led to a number of specifically political involvements: he started writing more about his political views, first on Facebook and then on his own blog ("to my wife's horror"); he started attending (and then headlining) local Tea Party events; and he got involved in the campaign of a local Tea Partier who was running for Congress. Yet, as I came to understand, these were, for Cam, not simply political acts; they were acts of devotion—to God and to country. It was individual acts such as these, aggregated millions of times over, that Cam (and Beck and many other Patriots) believed would bring salvation to the nation.

Beck's instructions to pray "with the door open for your children to see" reveals much about his vision of how society could be reshaped through individual practices like the ones discussed here. It was a process that started with individuals and rippled outward. By praying with the door open, one welcomed God back into one's home and provided a model for one's children. By praying before meals with friends, one brought one's religious values into one's broader social relationships. And by being present to pray alongside hundreds of thousands of Americans on the National Mall, each individual citizen did his or her part to "start the heart of America again."

This path to national salvation resonated closely with Cam's approach to faith, grounded as it was in individual practice and a "to each their own" spirituality, rather than in elite authority or congregational life. But I assumed it would offer little to those in the group who disavowed religious affiliations and belief. I was thus surprised to find that Beck's message *also* resonated for many of these individuals. In a written response explaining why she was attending the Restoring Honor Rally, one woman said, "Although I do not believe in 'God,' I was brought up as a Catholic[;] and historically I know that Jesus lived. I feel that I have retained my Christian moral code. I believe this is very important to the success of our country. Therefore, I believe all children should at least be exposed to religion. The Ten Commandments are a good moral code for anyone." Even though they did not personally believe in God, this woman and many others I spoke to supported the idea that religious values—like those enshrined in the Ten Commandments—were necessary "to the success of our country" because they were important sources of individual moral virtue.

But this was not the only reason why many of the Patriots felt it was important to be mindful of God's place in the American democratic project. In their view, religion was not merely a source of virtue: God was also the source of individuals' rights. And although members of the group insisted that each individual's relationship with God was a personal one, they also agreed it was their collective obligation to remind the American people that by "shov[ing] God in a closet," citizens risked forgetting the source of their freedom. It was in this way that God subtly seeped into the Patriots' collective practices.

Patriots: Collective Civil Religious Practices

As a group bound by their shared commitment to preserving individual liberty, members of the Patriots, who had widely varying relationships to faith and organized religion, found common ground in their agreement that Americans needed to recognize God's role in the American democratic experiment or else their liberty was at stake. This point was reinforced and reiterated through various group practices: they recited the Pledge of Allegiance, sang "God Bless America," immersed themselves in early American history, and collectively studied the Constitution. These practices framed the country's founding as a "sacred, quasi-religious" moment, highlighted the influence of Judeo-Christian values on the nation's founders, and underscored God's role as the source and guarantor of citizens' rights.[25] And although superficially these practices may not seem religious, a closer look reveals their religious roots and resonances.

Let us begin by discussing the Pledge of Allegiance, which the Patriots recited at the beginning of every meeting and rally. Most people do not think of this as a religious ritual, and indeed, the pledge's presence in public schools around the country is predicated on its secular nature. But its religious significance became clear to me during one of their group meetings when I found myself out of sync with the group during this familiar ritual. As recounted at the beginning of chapter 3, this meeting had begun like any other, with everyone standing to face the flag and recite the pledge. But that night, when we reached the phrase "one nation under God," several people raised their voices. Startled, I had looked around for some sign of what had happened, but everyone had continued unfazed. Only afterward did I realize what prompted this dramatic gesture. I recalled a discussion among several group members before the meeting had started, about the fact that President Obama had omitted the phrase "endowed by their Creator" when quoting the Declaration of Independence a week earlier. Linda had addressed Obama's omission in that morning's issue of the *Must Know News:* "As we heard for ourselves the President left out a meaningful part of the Declaration of Independence," she wrote, citing as evidence an article in the conservative magazine, the *Weekly Standard,* titled "Does President Obama Think Our Rights Come from Our Creator?"

For the Patriots, the words "endowed by their Creator"—like the phrase "one nation under God" in the Pledge of Allegiance—confirmed their transcendent vision of America's founding and justified continued recognition of God's place in the nation. The Patriots' forceful recitation of the words "one nation under God" during the pledge was a small act of resistance against what they viewed as hostile secular forces intent on obscuring God's role in the American democratic project.

Of course, the words "under God" were not inserted into the Pledge of Allegiance until 1954, in part as a means of highlighting America's religious character in contrast to atheist communism in the midst of the Cold War. According to the historian Kevin Kruse, this change was also precipitated by longer-term concerns about the expansion of the federal government in the wake of the New Deal.[26] Today, these concerns are echoed in claims that America's religious heritage is under attack by radical Islamic terrorists around the world and by liberal secularist and big government ("socialist") forces at home.[27] Obama's reported omission of the phrase "endowed by their Creator" from the Declaration of Independence was interpreted as the latest blow in this intensifying attack.

Following reports that Obama had omitted this phrase on a few additional occasions, Cam addressed the situation on his blog. Calling "endowed by their Creator" the "four most essential words" of the "Inalienable Rights" passage of the Declaration of Independence, he wrote that this phrase "is the very fuel of Liberty and the essence of our American Exceptionalism." In Cam's view, removing this phrase was troubling not only because it is part of the original text but also because the phrase is the key textual support for their claims that citizens' rights are granted by God and, therefore, not by government.

Although this message was subtly communicated each time the Patriots recited the pledge, they more explicitly highlighted God's role in the American democratic project by singing "God Bless America." Originally performed on the radio in November 1938, this patriotic anthem has been sung during the decades since as a reminder of American freedom in the midst of world war, as a statement of support for the military, and as a protest song by groups on the political left and right.[28] As with the pledge, however, it has most recently been embraced by conservative religious groups concerned that America's religious heritage is under attack.

At one fall 2010 rally, the Patriots and other Tea Partiers from around the state sang this song not once but twice. As was customary at such events, the organizer of the rally kicked things off by leading the crowd in the Pledge of Allegiance and "God Bless America." About an hour later, when one of the featured speakers closed his remarks with the words "God bless America," this prompted several people in the crowd to start singing the song again. "God bless America, land that I love . . ." they began, haltingly, as if unsure whether their impromptu singing would catch on. But soon the rest of the crowd joined in, and they sang the full song for the second time that evening, closing with a high-spirited "God bless America, my home sweet home!"

While some Patriots members entered the group with the conviction that God played a key role in America's founding and history, many reported being introduced to this idea by Glenn Beck around the time they became involved with the Patriots. In the early days of the Tea Party movement, Beck's television studio became a history classroom for millions of Americans who sought, in the nation's past, solutions to the country's current ills.[29] The books Beck recommended shot up the best-seller lists and became the subjects of reading groups around the country. Among these books was *The 5,000 Year Leap*, by the Mormon author W. Cleon Skousen, who argues that the Constitution was rooted in Judeo-Christian values and inspired by the Bible. During the first several months of my fieldwork, the Patriots' daily email advertised at least three book clubs dedicated to discussing *The 5,000 Year Leap*, and group members cited it by name when they gathered in person. Exposure to these ideas led group members to a shared conclusion—if Skousen and Beck were right, and the Founding Fathers were inspired by God, then the founding documents were the sacred path: Americans needed only to trust that they were right and follow them.

As discussed in chapter 3, the Patriots often underscored this point when they were together. As Phil reminded the group during one meeting: "The solution [to our current political problems] is easy. Simply follow the Constitution." Similarly, Linda once explained to me in an interview how this same logic applied to elected officials. In her telling, their job was simple: "Uphold the Constitution. Do what the Constitution allows you to do. Nothing more, nothing less." As these comments suggest, the Constitution was viewed not simply as an important legal document but as the *only* text needed for the American democratic project to flourish—the *sola scriptura* for the national community.[30]

Moreover, the Patriots viewed themselves as guardians of this sacred text. While it may seem unusual that ordinary Americans without any formal legal training would claim this role, they did not see this as inappropriate or implausible. This is because they asserted that the meaning of the Constitution was both timeless and plainly evident to anyone who could read it and was familiar with the history of its drafting. This approach, which echoes that of Constitutional originalists, also bears a striking resemblance to the one that many evangelical Christians take to the Bible—not only do constitutional originalists and biblical literalists treat their respective texts as sacred, but both groups' approaches are also rooted in a deep distrust of elites' interpretations of these texts, which are viewed as reflections of political bias and self-interest.[31] Moreover, both deny that elites' specialized knowledge is even necessary, asserting instead that the meaning of the Constitution, like the meaning of the Bible, is accessible to all.

In this spirit, the Patriots studied the Constitution with the zeal of evangelicals studying scripture. As noted in chapter 3, they carried dogeared pocket Constitutions, read passages aloud during group meetings, broke down the meanings of the text, and quoted it chapter and verse whenever the occasion arose. They also practiced how to respond to common critiques of the original Constitution. The fact that they did so using a style of argumentation that resembled Christian apologetics only underscores the sacred significance of this text for members of this community.

For example, at one group meeting, Linda turned the group's attention to a handout that included a series of questions, which she explained were intended to help them debunk some common myths about the Constitution. Among the questions were: "How many times does the word 'slavery' appear in the original Constitution?" "None." But Linda spent the most time that night debunking the idea that the founders extended rights only to white men—a common critique of the Tea Party's nostalgia for early American history. The handout asked, "According to the original Constitution of 1789, who was permitted to vote in federal elections? Everyone! No one was forbidden by the Constitution." Rather, she pointed out that this power was delegated to states by article I, section 2.

Each of these questions was designed to defend against accusations that the Constitution in its original form promoted institutions or values now viewed as abhorrent to most Americans—such as slavery, white supremacy, and male domination—and thus needed to be interpreted in light of more modern values. The need for more robust interpretation was threatening, not only because it suggested the original text was flawed, but also because it shifted the locus of constitutional authority from ordinary people to experts. This had both political and religious significance. Studying the Constitution thus equipped group members to confidently assert their authority—not only as "we the people" but also as a kind of "priesthood of all constitutional believers."[32]

In their commitment to defending the original text of the Constitution, the Patriots also reinforced their vision of the country's founding as a moment of perfection that they must attempt to restore. Through this lens, the country's founding era was sacred, the Constitution's authors were divinely inspired, and over the past two and a half centuries the country has gradually fallen from grace. Although the Patriots spoke ominously about this decline, their vision was also infused with optimism about the possibilities of restoration. In this way, their decline narrative differed subtly from the most fatalistic apocalyptic accounts of imminent destruction that have been associated with some religious nationalists. Rather, their narrative of national perfection, decline, and potential restoration echoed more hopeful Christian narratives of sin and redemption. As discussed in chapter 3, the Patriots viewed themselves as the latest in a long line of patriotic Americans dedicated to halting this decline and restoring the country to its former greatness (the name of Beck's 2010 rally—*Restoring* Honor, which was followed by a 2011 *Restoring* Courage tour, and a 2012 *Restoring* Love rally—clearly communicated this vision). As a result, putting their faith into action was an act of both civic duty and national redemption.

It was thus fascinating to observe that members of the group did not need to personally believe in God in order to participate in these group practices. Harry, a self-proclaimed atheist, represented an extreme case in point. I met Harry at an election-returns-watching party held at the home of a couple who were active in the group. We were alone in the TV room watching local news coverage of the election when he turned and told me, in a hushed confessional tone, that some of Glenn Beck's "religious stuff" made him uncomfortable. This troubled him, he said, because he thought that pretty much everything else Beck said was right, and he watched the show regularly.

He had provoked an argument earlier that evening by suggesting to some of the other guests that the founding documents were "secular documents." I had overheard the end of this conversation. The wife of a local elected official had countered, "You can't take God out! What would be the basis for our rights? It's only because our rights are God-given that the government isn't able to take them away. It's the source of our freedoms and liberties." Everyone around the table had signaled their agreement, and her comment seemed to close the case for the moment. But Harry insisted they had misunderstood his point.

As he explained to me, he believed he had found a way of reconciling his atheism with the notion that Americans' rights are God-given. The way he saw it, the founders were religious, and their belief in God inspired them to write the founding documents and create the American democratic system. Although he did not personally believe in the God they believed in, this did not change the fact that he viewed the Constitution, the Bill of Rights, and the Declaration of Independence as brilliant and sought to protect them. The founders drafted the documents "under God," he explained, but "they drafted them *for everybody*—under God, under Allah, under Buddha, whatever."

Although their personal faith commitments differed, most of the Patriots that I encountered referenced this common vision of God's role in the American democratic project. Whether real or symbolic, God was the source of their individual rights and, by extension, individual freedoms; to forget God's place in this system would be to risk losing those rights and freedoms. As a result, they engaged in collective practices that served as reminders of God's role and the dire consequences of forgetting it.

For a group who denied having a religious purpose and distanced themselves from other conservative religious movements, it may seem unusual that the Patriots would engage in practices like these. It is thus necessary to put these practices into context. Although symbolically powerful, rituals like reciting the pledge and singing "God Bless America" were relatively brief interludes between more explicitly political discussions and activities. And studying American history and reading the Constitution were likely understood by most group members as political, rather than religious, practices, although the form these practices took had clear religious (and specifically Protestant) roots and resonances. In light of the religious diversity of the group, it is also likely that these practices meant different things to different participants. While they may have had religious salience for some, they may simply have had vague civil religious significance for others, akin to noting that a dollar bill is imprinted with the words "In God We Trust."

Still, the centrality of these collective practices within the Patriots' group life—and their absence from Interfaith's—highlights the distinctiveness of the Patriots' style of putting their faith into action. Overall, through their individual and collective practices, group members underscored each individual's freedom to worship (or not) as they pleased, but also recognized a collective obligation to bear witness to the role that God plays in undergirding that very freedom. This was a difficult balancing act, but it was one that most people in the group—even nonreligious members—managed to embrace.

FAITH IN AMERICAN DEMOCRACY

Divergent Styles of Putting Faith into Action

As we have seen, Interfaith and the Patriots both rejected the liberal secularist premise that religion is irrelevant to or inappropriate in the public life of a diverse democracy. Both groups demonstrated through their actions that certain religious values could be widely shared among people who differ in their personal religious commitments. And perhaps more importantly, they both made the case that it is essential to keep these values in mind if we want the country to better serve ordinary citizens.

Yet members of these groups emphasized different religious values, developed different ways of engaging with religious others, and engaged in different kinds of religious practices. Put simply, they developed quite different *styles* of putting their faith into action—one oriented toward religious inclusion and the other toward religious liberty. When we view the two groups side by side, we can see that these differences reflect each group's distinct way of imagining how citizens should relate to one another and to God.

Interfaith, for example, sought to build a coalition that reflected the religious diversity of the nation as a whole, with particular attention to including minority religious voices. Although there were limits to the diversity it was able to achieve, its members nonetheless built interfaith relationships and worked together to identify the values that they all shared across their differences. In so doing, Interfaith showed by example what a diverse and inclusive moral community could look like, and prefigured a society in which diverse communities could pursue a shared vision of the common good, even while respecting differences in individual beliefs and values.

Meanwhile, the Patriots cultivated an understanding of God's relationship to citizens in highly individualized terms, rooted in the premise of individual religious liberty. This entailed respecting each individual's right to his or her own religious views, including the choice to reject religious belief—but only up to a point. It was their very commitment to religious liberty that required they speak out against those forms of religious commitment that they viewed as potential threats to that liberty.

The individual and collective practices that Patriots members developed allowed them to express this complex set of orientations toward religious others. They did not develop collective prayer practices like Interfaith did, but instead enacted their religious liberty by praying as individuals and debating their religious differences. Still, although the Patriots were more religiously diverse than many might assume, they ultimately cultivated collective practices that underscored a shared understanding of God's central role in the American democratic project—as the guarantor of their individual rights and freedoms.

They distinguished their understanding of God's role, which was rooted in an individual relationship between God and each citizen, from one that framed this relationship in collective terms. This explains their discomfort with social justice, which they associated with collective salvation and, by extension, socialism. In contrast, the idea of social justice was at the heart of Interfaith members' vision of what their faith—and their citizenship—required. These disagreements were not rooted in partisan or sectarian religious differences. Rather, they reflected differences in the groups' democratic imaginaries and, specifically, in their understandings of the proper relationship between citizens, the nation, and God.

Despite these differences, however, it is important to keep in mind that for participants in *both* Interfaith and the Patriots, engaging in active citizenship required they put their faith into action. To this end, both groups developed novel practices that politicized their religious values and sacralized their active citizenship. By putting their faith into action, both groups prefigured the kind of society they sought to bring about through their collective action.

Rethinking the Role of Faith in Public Life

More generally, this comparison also enlarges and complicates our understanding of the role of faith in American public life, in three ways. First, as discussed in chapter 1, public religion has, for the past several decades, primarily been viewed as the domain of conservatives. During the 1970s, the religious Right successfully placed conservative Christian morality at the center of the Republican Party's national agenda. Meanwhile, concerns about the antidemocratic role that religion could play in the public life of a diverse democracy led Democrats to generally avoid public religious talk. Although liberal and progressive religious groups were working below the radar all along, their voices were eclipsed by these conservative religious voices. The result was a conservative monopoly on public morality during the last quarter of the twentieth century. In recent years, progressive religious groups like Interfaith have disrupted this monopoly.[33] Meanwhile, contemporary conservative groups have also developed innovative, if ambiguous, ways of fusing religion and politics that depart from previous conservative efforts. Yet observers of political life have not sufficiently reordered their picture of the American political landscape to take these developments into account. This comparison pushes us toward a fuller understanding of the relationship between faith and democracy across the political divide.

This fuller understanding requires us to broaden our notion of not only the kinds of religious groups that engage in public life but also the issues in which they are choosing to intervene. During the period in which the religious Right was ascendant, religion was primarily mobilized in public debates about *sexual* politics—most notably abortion, gender roles, and same-sex marriage. But during the past decade, political actors have increasingly mobilized religion as a framework through which to evaluate and defend different visions of economic inequality and opportunity, of political processes, and of what it means to be an American citizen. This is not to say that sexual politics are absent from contemporary debates, but rather that religious and moral arguments for freedom and justice, respectively, are now far more visible than before.[34] Both the Patriots and Interfaith are carriers of these new kinds of arguments.

Finally, by observing the ways in which both groups frame these arguments, we also gain insight into broader changes in the American religious landscape itself. As discussed in chapter 1, American society has been secularized—religious belief is now understood as optional, and the authority of religion over most domains of social life has declined. There have also been profound changes in the religious composition of American society—namely, a combination of rising religious diversity and rising religious nonaffiliation. In light of these changes, one might expect that religion would become more divisive and less relevant to public life. But observations of the Patriots and Interfaith suggest that the opposite is true. It seems that these changes are encouraging groups to reimagine religion's place in the life of a diverse democratic society and develop innovative new styles of putting faith into action.

Through the varied practices described in this chapter, Interfaith and the Patriots worked to interpret the American democratic project, and by extension their active citizenship, as sacred. For both groups, engaging in active citizenship was thus not simply an opportunity to put their faith into action: the religious practices they developed also lent meaning to their efforts to put their faith in democracy into action.

5 Holding Government Accountable

Shortly after President Obama took office in 2009, he took steps to make good on a promise he had made during his campaign: he would "strive to lead the most open, ethical, and accountable government in history." On the first day of his administration, he set into motion several initiatives, each of which was "geared toward increasing public participation in government, and making government more accountable to the American people."[1] This twenty-first-century government, as he called it, would be "Of the People, By the People."[2]

In making government accountability central to his administration, Obama said he was responding to concerns he was hearing around the country. Citizens across the political divide increasingly worried aloud that the relationship between the government and the governed had become indirect and tenuous, and that the locus of decision making had grown distant from the people whose lives were affected by decisions. They watched as local programs were shaped by federal guidelines and regulations rather than local input; as policies were informed by statistics interpreted by experts and without reference to on-the-ground experiences; as political elites became mired in partisan battles that did not speak to the concerns of ordinary citizens; and as government appeared to answer more to corporations than to ordinary people like them.

At any time in the country's history, these trends would have been viewed as problematic. But they had taken on a new urgency in the wake of the economic crisis. Amid anxieties about the state of the American economy, ordinary people also expressed concern that they were not being included in decisions about how to chart a course back to the world they had been promised. And in those instances when they disagreed with the course that was selected, they lacked the tools to effectively demand change. They especially sensed a breakdown in one of the key relationships that undergirds a healthy representative democracy—the one between citizens and their elected representatives.

In this context, groups like Interfaith and the Patriots were key settings in which citizens collectively reimagined how this relationship should work. At the heart of both groups' visions was the idea of accountability—that in order for government to be considered legitimate, it must be accountable to the governed. But accountability would not happen automatically or naturally—without ongoing pressure from citizens, it was unlikely that authorities would hold themselves to account. Members of the two groups thus viewed it as citizens' duty to actively *hold government accountable.*

In their efforts to put this vision into practice, Interfaith and the Patriots faced a number of similar challenges. This should not have been surprising. After all, despite significant racial and socioeconomic differences between the groups, neither was composed of *elites*—far from it. As ordinary citizens endeavoring to influence the political process, members of the two groups had to overcome the following four challenges, and did so in generally similar ways.

First, most ordinary citizens find that their power as an individual is insufficient to demand accountability from government and other elites. As a result, the very act of participating in a group like Interfaith or the Patriots reflects an analysis, however informal or unconscious, that citizens must work together in order to leverage whatever power they do have. Groups may ultimately choose to build different kinds of organizations and exercise different forms of collective power—for example, by pressuring authorities as a bloc of individual voters, as a mass of disruptive protesters, or as a moral community. These choices will vary not only across groups but also within groups across settings.[3] Despite this potential for variation, however, it is important to recognize that the memberships of both Interfaith and the Patriots felt they had to work alongside their fellow citizens to make their voices heard.

Second, before beginning their work together, they had to develop a shared understanding of accountability itself—and more specifically of what the relationship between government and the governed should look like in practice. We can think of this as an accountability frame, a kind of "collective action frame," to use the term coined by the sociologist William A. Gamson.[4] While groups may conjure subtly different visions of what a relationship built on accountability should look like, an accountability frame that encourages collective action typically defines unaccountable authorities as immoral and illegitimate, and defines citizens as morally worthy agents with the power to improve their situation through their collective action. In this way, they empower groups to confront government. The memberships of both Interfaith and the Patriots referenced this kind of accountability frame in the course of their work.

Third, like most nonexperts, participants in Interfaith and the Patriots were often stymied by the sheer complexity of public policy issues. In light of this complexity, it makes sense that specialized experts increasingly dominate these debates.[5] While some argue that these professionals' knowledge and experience allow them to craft policies that best serve the public good, others ask whether a society can be truly democratic if citizens lack sufficient knowledge to understand policy decisions.[6] Indeed, the ideal of "informed citizenship"—introduced in chapters 1 and 2—is premised on the notion that it is citizens' responsibility to be informed participants in these decisions, lest society become corrupt or elite-driven.[7] Citizens groups have often been called "schools of democracy" because they are spaces in which ordinary people are encouraged to develop this capability, by cultivating the knowledge, skills, and confidence necessary to participate in the complex political life of their communities.[8] Although less visible than other aspects of grassroots political action, education is often central to the internal lives of these groups.[9] Members of both Interfaith and the Patriots felt they needed to become more informed if they wished to influence policies or the political process itself, and they dedicated significant amounts of time to this endeavor.

Finally, in order for groups to actually exert political influence, decision makers need to view their knowledge as legitimate and valuable and to take it into account when crafting policies. But there are typically multiple actors vying for this kind of influence, armed with competing demands and knowledge claims. Meanwhile, many public officials are uninterested in yielding to pressure from any of these outside groups—even if their own constituents are among them. In light of these challenges, groups like Interfaith and the Patriots have developed a range of tactics designed to pressure public officials into recognizing the legitimacy of their voices and knowledge. Sitting as these groups do in a boundary niche between social movements and civic organizations, they have access to a wide range of tactics—from protests and demonstrations, to lobbying and legal action, to collective and individual forms of political engagement.[10] Both Interfaith and the Patriots drew on tactics designed to achieve this common end.

In sum, participants in Interfaith and the Patriots faced similar challenges in their efforts to hold government accountable, and at a general level they responded to them in similar ways: by organizing for collective action, developing an accountability frame, becoming informed about policies and the political process, and selecting tactics designed to pressure public officials into taking their voices seriously. An in-depth look at Interfaith's and the Patriots' accountability efforts reveals surprising parallels between them that are typically obscured. At the same time, however, juxtaposing these portraits of accountability in action reveals patterned differences in *how* they organized, conceptualized accountability, became informed, and pressured officials. At this closer vantage, we can see that they developed different styles of holding government accountable, and moreover, that each group's style reflected its respective way of imagining the proper relationship between citizens, government, and God.

INTERFAITH

Organizing for Collective Action: Power through Solidarity

It was already dark when I arrived at Father O'Donnell's Westside parish for a public accountability action that the congregation's local organizing committee had been planning for the past few months. Their goal was to convince city officials to demand that a delinquent landlord make legally required repairs to a building on their block. Although local in scope, the task ahead of them was complex: they desired to hold the landlord accountable for his failure to meet his legal obligations to his tenants and to the community in which he was a property holder; but lacking sufficient power to do so as tenants and neighbors, they also sought to persuade their public officials to fulfill their responsibilities as regulators in the public's interest.

As I approached, I saw one of Interfaith's staff organizers shivering outside a side entrance hanging flyers. She looked exhausted but smiled warmly and pointed inside. "They're downstairs," she said. "I think they're running behind." This was unusual, I thought. I made my way down to a large basement, which looked like a cafeteria with rows of folding chairs set up facing a long table. The front of the table was adorned with a long blue banner with "Interfaith" printed in large gold letters. Name tents were set up to identify each of the invited guests: two city council members; three mid- to high-level officials in the city's housing department; and the owner and managing agent of the property in question.

Although the meeting was scheduled to begin any minute, no one was sitting at the table. I wondered if none of the invited guests had shown up. Some members of the audience were seated, others milled. I realized the organizers were stalling. I checked in with Nora, Interfaith's executive director, whose young son was entertaining a small group of onlookers with yo-yo tricks. He was one of the few children present, even though it was early evening on a weeknight. Then I looked around for Helen, the active Jewish leader I had gotten to know through Interfaith's health-care working group. Although her synagogue was not formally involved in this action, she made an effort to attend as many of the other congregations' events as possible and had emailed me that afternoon to make sure I was coming, too.

Helen lived in Hillside, a gentrifying neighborhood halfway between Westside and Riverside. Although her synagogue was more racially diverse than most, its membership was nonetheless predominantly white, as well as highly educated and upper-middle class. But as a congregation they were committed to social justice—and not just as an extracurricular activity in which some congregants participated; after attending a handful of worship services and other events there, I saw that the pursuit of social justice was woven into every aspect of their community's life, from worship services to social gatherings. So, too, was their interest in cultivating diversity. Participating in Interfaith was a natural extension of these efforts, and their charismatic female rabbi was a high-profile supporter of Interfaith's work. During this period, Helen was one of the most active members of the synagogue's social justice committee, and she was ubiquitous at Interfaith events around the city.

She had told me she wanted to be at the action that night to support the work this congregation was doing, partly in an effort to build stronger ties between Interfaith's member congregations; partly out of her and her husband's long-standing interest in housing justice and tenants' rights; and partly because the owner of the property was Jewish. She felt it was important to show that Interfaith's Jewish (and, although it went unstated, white) members stood in solidarity with this Catholic congregation, whose membership was mostly composed of low- and middle-income people of color.

To this end, she had emailed me that afternoon, along with several members of her social justice committee, to remind us to attend. Although I was not a member of their congregation, she included me as if I were, having confirmed early in our time together that I was nominally Jewish but without a congregation I called my own. She arrived soon after me, instantly recognizable under a shock of blondish gray hair. She looked discombobulated, as if she had rushed. She impatiently pushed her hair back from her face and adjusted her colorful scarf as she scanned the room. Finding that we had not begun, she appeared to relax momentarily, before setting off in search of an explanation.

Though few people were seated in the rows of folding chairs, the room was crowded, and it echoed with the chatter of conversation. I recognized several members of this congregation from previous actions, as well as a handful of other people who, like Helen, were active participants in Interfaith's broader efforts and who attended events like these even when their congregations were not involved. Off to the side, I spotted Father O'Donnell conferring with a few other members of Interfaith's staff and the members of the congregation's local organizing committee who were responsible for organizing the action.

At the edge of this group, I saw Doris, a petite black woman with cropped grayish hair, who had been appointed the leader of this effort. She was a longtime resident of the building in question, and she had recently become involved in Interfaith primarily because it offered her a channel through which to address her concerns about her building. While her status as a rent-paying resident and a taxpaying citizen could presumably have served as her primary grounds for demanding that the building be repaired, she acknowledged by joining her congregation's local organizing committee that her individual power was insufficient. That night, she would speak instead as part of a collective and faith-based effort, which she hoped would be more effective.

Finally, there were also unfamiliar faces, whom I assumed were residents of the building or neighboring buildings. I knew Doris and the other committee members had reached out to her neighbors in an effort to build solidarity among the building's residents, as well as to residents of neighboring buildings in order to build a case that a large number of people in their community were subjected to substandard living conditions because of negligent landlords. Now, with these assorted supporters gathered as witnesses, Doris and her fellow committee members would try to convince the public officials that this was a matter of public—not just individual—concern.

Accountability Frame: Public Officials as (Potential) Partners

Eventually, the housing department officials took their seats at the front table. The seats reserved for the city council members and the building owner and manager were conspicuously vacant, but Father O'Donnell rose to open the meeting. As we saw in chapter 4, he had developed a distinctive style of addressing diverse audiences in such settings. Although the religious significance of his opening prayer has already been discussed, here I highlight its role in the group's accountability efforts.

Standing at the front of the auditorium in his typical garb, a black button-down shirt, suspenders, and a starched white collar, he began by calling attention to the diverse crowd that had gathered that evening—a nod not only to Interfaith's internal diversity but also to the fact that this meeting, although held in a church auditorium, was open to the public. He remarked that although everyone was different, they were there together to fight for justice.

After calling upon those gathered to pray "to the God of your under-standing," he asked everyone to "allow yourself to be called by that God to do the good work that will make us all *better neighbors.*" He continued:

> It is good and it is pleasant when people come together in unity.[11] But some-times that unity needs to be ironed out. Sometimes there are wrinkles. Sometimes there's stuff that we have to do to make sure that we're not in the way. And if we see somebody who's in the way, make sure that they're not hurting themselves. Okay? We have a responsibility to one another, and as much as I have a responsibility to you, you have a responsibility to me. Ultimately, we are who we are. And I am glad that you're here, being who you are, as you represent your own interests, but also the interests of the people of the building across the street.

As clergy in the group often do, Father O'Donnell used this opening prayer as an opportunity to establish the tone and communicate the group's expectations for the meeting. By noting that the community members and public officials had come together out of shared responsibility to one another *as neighbors*, as well as out of their own economic and political *interests*, he realistically recognized the terms under which they were all bound together.

Although Father O'Donnell addressed the public officials as members of their community, that night they were also their invited guests and would be the "targets" of their demands. The next part of the reflection, directed at these officials, reveals much about how Interfaith approached their complex relationships with these men and women: "I want to wel-come the people who have come, the public officials, the people from vari-ous agencies; and I anticipate the arrival of a couple of the people whose names are up there on the signs. Some of them have a reputation for being late [*quiet laughter*], and so we don't take it very seriously. But you know, that's what happens when you're in public life. But for those of us who are here, we are here, and it's time for us to begin."

Father O'Donnell was respectful of the invited guests, but he also took the opportunity to point out that the city council members were late, an act that was typically understood as a sign of disrespect to their constituents. Indeed, the group frequently spoke of their efforts to "respect time," a subtle means of achieving the moral high ground in interactions with chronically late public officials. Starting and ending meetings on time also meant that more people could attend, especially community members with less flexible work schedules. As a result, Interfaith made an effort (although not always successfully) to start and end events on time and asked public officials to show them the same respect.

Yet Father O'Donnell was not overly harsh in his criticism of the absent city council members' tardiness; rather, he signaled that Interfaith had established long-standing relationships with them, through which they had come to understand the council members' lateness as a sign of the pressures of public life. This comment is exemplary of the way in which Interfaith members approached their relationships with elected officials: through compassion, seeking to understand why they make decisions and act in certain ways rather than starting from a stance of opposition or distrust.

This approach makes sense in light of Interfaith's perspective that these officials are potential partners in making their community a better place. This is not to say that they will not confront or pressure them. But as Nora explained during one of their coalition-wide training sessions: "When we have public actions, we want to hold our leaders accountable; but first we need to know what they're thinking, why they're doing things. We need to ask what their interests are. We want the world as it should be, but first we need to know what it is." As she explained, even Moses had to listen to Pharaoh during their negotiations for the release of the Israelite slaves. When it came down to it, Pharaoh had a genuine economic reason for wanting to keep the slaves—they had built his city, and in the language of community organizing, it was in his self-interest for them to stay.

Yet, even while Interfaith emphasized the need to understand officials' self-interest, the organization also consistently reiterated the message that they all share a common interest in the good of the community. As another active clergy member, Rev. Fischer, once put it when testifying before the city council: "As a faith community, we collaborate with you in public life when we share the desire for broad-based stability. That line of separation between the faith community and public life has always been a line of conviviality when justice and mercy is our shared objective. I thank you for your work and your insight to listen to a local voice which, like you, seeks the welfare of our beloved city, for in its welfare is our own welfare." Through comments like these, Interfaith publicly signaled that its members were (at least potentially) aligned with government officials in a project to promote shared values and advance the welfare of their city as a whole. Accountability actions—however small or large scale, local or broad reaching—were opportunities for Interfaith to transform these hypothetical partnerships into practical ones, by demanding that public officials commit to working with them in specific ways to enact these shared values.

Becoming Informed: The Art of Listening and Storytelling

After the opening prayer, Father O'Donnell did not play a public role in the action. He turned the microphone over to the lay leaders in his congregation, who began as they begin all public accountability actions, by giving a brief "credential" that explained who Interfaith and the PICO National Network were and established why they should be considered credible spokespeople for their community. The group's standard credential delineated the number of congregations—and by extension the number of individuals, religious traditions, and neighborhoods—that Interfaith represented. They repeated a similar set of statistics for PICO's national network as a whole, making clear that although they might appear to be a small band of ordinary people in one church in one neighborhood, their efforts were linked to a national movement of people like them, whose collective power could be marshaled to their cause. They ended the credential more modestly, by articulating their expectations for this event: "We're just hoping that by congregating here tonight, some of the officials that are here will listen to our concerns, and as a result, we'll have some sort of solving of some of the problems that our community faces."

Doris, the resident of the building in question who was also a member of the local organizing committee, was then charged with presenting the findings of their research about the scope of the building's problems. Her authority to speak on behalf of this group had been "earned," as the social ethicist Jeffrey Stout would say, by developing one-to-one relationships with her neighbors and fellow congregants.[12] While the size of the crowd at actions like this one served as an outward sign of the depth of these relationships, it was not sufficient for members of Interfaith to claim to speak for a large number of people; they also sought to demonstrate that they were knowledgeable about the issues their community faced.

To this end, the organization had developed a set of practices that helped them gather and deploy this knowledge. After identifying a problem in their community, members of the local organizing committee typically commenced a lengthy research process that began with conducting intentional one-to-one conversations with people in their congregation and the broader community who were affected by the problem in question. In this case, Doris reported to me in an interview that she and other members of her local organizing committee had gone door to door in her building, surveying each tenant about the issues they faced, the ways they had filed complaints, and the responses they had received from the landlord and the city. They then spoke to residents in a handful of other buildings in the neighborhood to determine if the issues were more widespread.

Once they defined the scope of an issue, they identified the various channels for effecting their desired change and endeavored to conduct "research actions" with all of the relevant decision makers and stakeholders. This typically began with some research online or in consultation with partners, like nonprofit organizations, who had expertise in the issue. In this case, they met on a few occasions with one of the representatives of the housing department, who was at the public accountability action that night, and members of his staff, in order to learn more about how they could address the problems in the building. They also sought out a meeting with the owner of the building, and had met with him privately in order to better understand the situation from his perspective and discuss the best way to move forward. But private meetings like these were primarily used for information gathering, not deal making—they asked people to make commitments to them in public. As a result, the final step of the process involved putting together a research report that could be presented during a public accountability action.

This process was considerably more difficult for some issues than others, and for some local organizing committees than for others. Within some of Interfaith's member congregations, all of the active leaders had access to personal computers and the Internet; in others, few did. As a result, they typically pooled whatever resources they had and worked together and with Interfaith's staff organizers to do this work collectively. They formed research committees whenever they took on a new issue, and they assigned roles to each member based on the individuals' particular skills and resources. In the process, they not only bolstered their collective knowledge about the issue but also developed skills that empowered each of them as individual citizens and as collaborators.

At the heart of these research practices was a commitment to listening, which, as we saw in chapter 2, Rev. Fischer referred to as "a sacred art, a holy art." Learning to listen, he often stated, was a prerequisite to speaking prophetically. In this way, they emphasized the importance of listening to one another's experiences and seeking out others' stories. When done effectively, these listening practices not only strengthened their network of relationships but also supplied them with knowledge about how issues were affecting people's lives. By extension, this knowledge undergirded the credibility of their claims that the solutions they proposed served the common good of their community.

Before proposing any specific solutions, however, they publicly relayed the information they had gathered from their communities. They typically did so, first, by presenting the summary findings of their research, and then, more dramatically, by asking a handful of community members to recount personal stories, or testimonies, about their experiences with the issue. They did not necessarily seek to debunk official accounts of the problem; nor did they insist their experiences trumped others'. They simply demanded that their communities' experiences be taken into account alongside those of other impacted communities. Their stories and research were framed as additional data points, offered in the spirit of expanding the official understanding of the issue.

When it was time for Doris to present the research that the local organizing committee had gathered for this action, she stood at the front of the room. The microphone and projection screen had been set up to the left of the table where their invited guests sat, and she stood at an angle so she could speak simultaneously to these guests and the audience. A petite woman, she was dwarfed by the large projection screen behind her and had to pull the microphone downward. The tardy city council members had finally arrived and now turned toward her as she started to speak. Although she occasionally met their gaze, she mainly looked out at the broader audience. She spoke slowly while a woman nearby advanced the PowerPoint presentation.

Though Doris appeared nervous at first and had some trouble coordinating her remarks with the slides, she provided a clear picture of the bleak conditions that she and her fellow tenants had been dealing with: "For the past two and a half years, the tenants of 914 Mitchell Street have been working together to resolve the problems in the building. These problems have included lack of heat and hot water, leaks in ceilings, bathrooms and toilets, rotting [of] doors and windows, an infestation of rodents, roaches and bedbugs. In our building, there were seventy-six violations in the last two months, not including violations for no heat and hot water." She then explained that they had surveyed fifteen out of the twenty apartments in the building and found similar problems, underscoring once again their authority to speak on behalf of the building's residents. Her voice grew more confident, then indignant, as she listed the actions that residents had already taken to address the issue: filing forms with the city, calling a citizen hotline managed by the city, and meeting with several representatives from the city's housing agencies. Still, the landlord had been unresponsive to their demands.

She closed her report with a plea: "We all deserve to live in a safe and comfortable environment. . . . Let's make our building the best building on the block. Let's pray that we can begin to work toward that goal." The crowd applauded.

Pressure Tactics: Covenants and Public Commitments

Now turning to the table where the officials sat, Doris said pointedly, "Tonight we're asking for a *covenant* to maintain this building as the beginning of a campaign to ask for good maintenance for all the buildings in this community." As she said this, I could not help but take note of her use of the term *covenant*. I had heard this term repeatedly during my time with Interfaith, and with Doris's reference I flashed back to another accountability action I had recently attended, which also had involved a symbolic covenant between public officials, various other stakeholders, and members of the community.

This earlier action had taken place in one of the poorest neighborhoods in the country, in a city a few hours from where Interfaith was based. I traveled there with several of Interfaith's core leaders to take part in a national campaign called Bring Health Reform Home. The action was framed as an opportunity for community members and stakeholders in that city's struggling health-care system to enter into what they dubbed a Covenant for a Healthier Community. A brief description of this action offers deeper insight into how these groups used the concept of a covenant to press public officials to work with them to solve shared problems.

The small church was filled to overflowing with racially and religiously diverse representatives from local PICO affiliates around the country. At the front of the sanctuary, the dais strained under three rows of chairs reserved for the "targets" of that night's public accountability action. The names of these targets—a "Who's Who" list of local healthcare power brokers—were now all familiar to me, as this action was the culmination of two long days of training sessions, presentations, and meetings with many of the men and woman now seated on stage.

Members of the predominantly black congregation welcomed people to their church, and showed them to the few remaining seats. They had hung large banners in each of the four corners of the room that said, "Covenant for a Healthier Community." Looking down, I saw the text of this covenant was also printed in our programs, which I had seen the group's executive director editing only a few hours earlier on his laptop.

Moments later, we began. Members of the congregation's local organizing committee presented their credentials as an organization, shared a detailed research report, and then invited community members to share stories about their experiences with the local health system. The pastor of the church then turned to the stakeholders sitting on the dais. He asked them if they would be available to meet during the following month to talk about moving forward with the specific plans that the local organizing committee had just proposed to improve the health of their community. This can be a tense moment for the targets of these actions, as they are typically only allowed to answer "yes" or "no" to these "pinning questions." The goal is to force the officials and other stakeholders to make a public commitment to work with the local organizing committee to solve the problem in question. But before they could individually answer, the pastor said to them: "What we're going to do is actually make a covenant. A covenant is a binding agreement, where two people, two parties decide that we've come to a place of common understanding, and that we're gonna join hands and work together and walk together and suffer and struggle together, and not to leave one another out, and just to walk two together. And scripture even says, 'Can two walk together lest they be agreed?'"

Next to me, a man murmured, "Amos 3:3, Mmm hmm." The pastor then proceeded to read the terms of this covenant in a call and response style:

> We pledge to work together for a healthier city.
> We pledge to collaborate, even when it gets hard. . . .
> We pledge to be accountable for measurable improvements over time.
> We pledge to work toward a system where patients can find timely access to high-quality health-care services.
> We pledge to not call 911 or go to the emergency room when there are better options for care.
> We pledge to eat well, get plenty of sleep, and exercise. *[People in the audience laughed and groaned.]* . . .
> We pledge to address the poverty, unsafe living conditions, and environmental contamination that lead to poor health outcomes. . . .
> We pledge to seek a different way to pay for health care that rewards good outcomes and creates a healthier community.

After each line, the entire audience, including the officials and stakeholders, responded, "We pledge."

The reference during both of these actions to a *covenant* was not an accident. This term references the notion, rooted in Puritan covenant theology and more broadly in the Old Testament, that God has entered into a special relationship with a community. Among the requirements of this kind of relationship is that members of the community must privilege the common good over their individual self-interest. Indeed, the covenantal community is conceived as "members of the same body," according to Massachusetts Puritan John Winthrop in his famous sermon "A Model of

Christian Charity." As such, it is the community as a whole—rather than the individuals who comprise it—that will be judged for its failure to "do justly, to love mercy, to walk humbly with our God." As Winthrop made clear, "Seeking great things for ourselves and our posterity" constituted "the breach of such a covenant."

By referencing this concept, Interfaith's members and their partners evoked a vivid sensation of drawing those present into a relationship of mutual obligation to work for the good of the community as a whole, under God's watchful gaze. References to covenants subtly infused these accountability actions with sacred significance and import. Unlike empty political promises, a covenant was not something to be taken lightly, or broken. In theory, framing this relationship in moral terms made it more difficult for partners to change their minds or fail to follow through.

Of course, it was also the *public* nature of these actions that created pressure on officials and other stakeholders to conform to Interfaith's demands. One of Interfaith's staff organizers, Farah, who was introduced in chapter 4, once explained this to a class of journalism students:

> One very important part of our organizing . . . is that we do our business in public, through these large meetings with elected officials, with stakeholders. And I think . . . these public meetings that we have are not only a place to hold the people that we put in power accountable; but what's really important is that they are actually creating these spaces for faith communities to be heard, to actually listen, and to work together with different stakeholders for a better neighborhood and for a stronger community.

In a coalition-wide training session, Nora expounded on this message. She asked the group if they understood the difference between private relationships and public relationships. No one responded. A private relationship, she explained, is when "I go in a small room and I meet with somebody, and I'm like, 'Yeah, you do this for me, I do that for you.'" A public relationship is when "I make a commitment in front of a lot of people." She emphasized that they wanted to build public relationships. Doing their "business in public," in Farah's words, not only enhanced their power to hold officials to their word but also was a means of building (and modeling) the kinds of public relationships with officials that Interfaith members believed were required in a healthy representative democracy.

Publicly "pinning" their targets was thus the dramatic high point of any accountability action. But this did not always work as smoothly as it did at the Bring Health Reform Home action, where the organizers had orchestrated a public covenant that laid the groundwork for future collaboration with a number of prominent stakeholders. The action at Father O'Donnell's Westside parish was less effective in demanding that the public officials enter into a covenant with the community to address the substandard housing conditions in their neighborhood.

When given an opportunity to respond to Doris's research report, the invited guests each expressed their solidarity with the building's residents and pledged to do whatever was in their power to address the issues Doris outlined during her presentation. The two popular and charismatic city council members in attendance expressed particular outrage at what the residents were going through, but had few specific solutions to offer. Meanwhile, the local organizing committee members running the meeting were not disciplined about cutting off the statements of officials who went on at length. Learning to exert control over the meeting agenda, particularly when that meant interrupting a local political leader, is daunting to the newly initiated. Like most of Interfaith's leaders, the members of this local organizing committee were still learning; mistakes were inevitable.

Soon, the officials and audience got restless. But there was still more to do. Another resident of the building had been given the role of posing the "pinning question" to each of the officials after they spoke. The idea was that the official had to provide a clear "yes" or "no" answer while a public audience served as witnesses. But the woman kept forgetting the officials' names and titles and stumbled over several of the questions, even though they were printed on placards at the front of the room. These events were delicate performances of citizens' power, and with each mistake the balance of power shifted back to the officials. One senior housing official could barely contain her impatience—she turned to the housing inspector sitting beside her and rolled her eyes slowly, as if pained to be put through this. Meanwhile, the true targets of their demands—the property owner and the manager—had never shown up. Although their empty seats served as powerful symbols of their unwillingness to fulfill their obligations to this community, their absence also denied Interfaith's leaders the catharsis that would have come from publicly demanding accountability from them.

It was nearly eight o'clock by the time the public question-and-answer session began. Several audience members clamored for the microphone, but suddenly one of Interfaith's staff organizers signaled to Doris that it was getting late. Ending the event on time was consistent with their efforts to "respect time." But cutting off the question-and-answer period after their neighbors had patiently sat through the long program risked undermining the fragile solidarity they were working to build. Still, they ended the action abruptly, and the crowd soon dissipated.

Typically, the mood was jubilant at the end of an accountability action, with the crowd cheering and the organizers congratulating one another. After all, these actions were the culmination of months of work on an issue. But this action had been smaller and its results less clear than they had hoped for. They would have to wait and see if the officials would press the absent landlord to make the necessary repairs to the building and, ultimately, whether their approach to holding these actors accountable would be effective in this case.

Yet Interfaith's accountability strategy did not rest wholly on the success of any individual action. While the organization certainly cared about the outcome, each action was only one piece of a much larger project. For the individuals involved, these actions were opportunities to deepen their knowledge about issues, practice new democratic skills, and become comfortable standing up to public officials. For the public officials involved, these actions sent a clear message that communities were organizing to demand change and would no longer sit back while their voices were ignored. As a result, whether or not it was successful in the short run, this action contributed to the group's larger goal of developing active citizens capable of strengthening accountability within their community.

PATRIOTS

Organizing for Collective Action: Acting as Individuals, Together

Halfway through one monthly meeting, Jamie, whom we met in chapter 2, walked around the room and handed out pieces of paper with three phone numbers printed on them.[13] It was early afternoon on a winter Saturday in 2011, and about twenty of us were sitting around tables in the side room of a local Italian restaurant. Jamie's gait as he paced the room was stiff and upright, but occasionally, as if by some momentary effort, it was infused with lightness. The same could be said of his general demeanor.

Jamie had just led a discussion about President Obama's proposed Jobs Bill, and we now paused and listened while he explained what would come next. "We talked about the Jobs Bill," he said. "You may want the Jobs Bill passed. You may not want the Jobs Bill passed. Phone out, because the next ten minutes, we're all going to call [our congressman's] office, and we're all going to tell him what we think about the Jobs Bill and whether or not we want him to vote for it."

The group did not arrive at a collective position on the bill before starting the calls. Jamie underscored the fact that people were free to have their own opinions, just as Linda typically did when she explained that the Patriots did not endorse candidates. Whether the choice involved which candidate to support or which bills to protest, the group discussed the issues together and circulated news and information through Linda's daily email and their social networking sites. For the most part (although not always), they tended to reach similar conclusions. But they still insisted it was the responsibility of each individual to do his or her own research, come to an informed decision, and then seek to persuade others to join them in that decision.

They maintained this individual autonomy because they ultimately saw themselves as free agents, working through Tea Party groups but not bound by them. As Gilbert, the small business owner, liked to say, "The thing about the Tea Parties is that there's no central leadership. It's like herding cats." Frankly, he acknowledged, it was hard to get such individualistic and strong-minded people to work together: "And that's okay."

Before they began calling the congressman, someone asked, "Can we tell him what we think of him, too?" Everyone laughed. "Yes, if you want," Jamie deadpanned, and then flashed a sly smile before shifting back into his businesslike mode. "And after you get through one number, call the next. We're going to see if we can't tie up all of his machines and fill up his mailboxes." More important than their position on the bill, this was a show of force—a reminder that they were watching.

People spent the next fifteen minutes on their cell phones dutifully calling the numbers on the slip of paper. It was a Saturday afternoon, so they all left messages. Any individual constituent could have performed this type of action—this is one of the main channels elected officials offer to constituents who wish to register complaints or offer input. Yet this group of men and women chose to do it while they were all together, and to leave all of their individual messages during a short period of time. Because they had discussed this issue together right before they called, their messages likely shared common language and arguments. It would be clear to the congressman's staff that this collection of individuals was working as a group.

But this was also a skill-development and confidence boosting exercise. I knew that the more practiced activists among them regularly made calls like these on their own time. I once sat with Gilbert in his office as he explained that he often toggled between calls with customers and calls to the governor's office. He then showed me he was serious by actually calling the governor's office while I sat there, and fielding customers' calls on the other lines while he was on hold. But the novices among them were not as experienced in calling their elected officials. Doing this as a group provided them with the extra confidence they needed to assert themselves in this unfamiliar way. This was typical of the type of accountability action that the group took together. They learned from and supported one another as they practiced using their individual power as voters and constituents. With enough practice, they became more comfortable confronting their elected officials in public settings as well.

Accountability Frame: God-Given Rights, Tar and Feathers

Confronting public officials was framed not only as an important civic skill but also as a bold patriotic act. By bringing politicians who had grown distant and elitist down a peg, the Patriots did their small part to close the yawning gap in power between the government and the people. This was colorfully demonstrated at a rally that brought together several Tea Party groups in the area. Several hundred people had gathered after work in front of a large arena in the center of a midsized city. The crowd was not unruly, but local police officers stood sentry between the rally and the streets beyond, their cars positioned as blockades around the perimeter of the designated rally area.

It was a crisp evening in the fall of 2010, and the theme of the event was "Remember in November," a slogan coined by the national organization FreedomWorks and used as a rallying cry by Tea Party groups around the country. It was a catchy reminder to elected officials that the voters were in charge, and they would come after them during the upcoming midterm elections if they did not heed their demands.

One of the hosts of the rally approached the microphone to warm up the crowd. He led them in the Pledge of Allegiance and then "God Bless America." After announcing the speakers who would follow him, he shouted into the crowd: "How many of you hate the health-care reform?" The crowd roared, and he continued, his voice rising: "Yes! Yes! You are the majority! They passed it against your will!" The cheering continued.

He then turned the microphone over to Phil. A financial planner by day, Phil was also the Patriots' resident philosopher and historian, as comfortable quoting Frédéric Bastiat and Friedrich Hayek as he was lecturing on the dangers of socialism or explaining how to obtain a license to carry a firearm in the state.[14] He was also a popular emcee at area Tea Party rallies. With a carefully manicured gray goatee and tinted glasses, he did not look the part of a rabble-rouser. But his usual steady demeanor belied an intensity that brewed just below the surface—an intensity he was able to unleash when he was on stage.

When I had greeted him before the rally, he had nervously waved me off, saying he had to rehearse his speech. But as he took the microphone and looked out into the crowd there was no trace of those backstage jitters. He proclaimed ominously that America was under attack. His voice rose with every word that he spoke about the country's descent into socialism. He called the crowd to repeat with him, "Wake up, Washington. We're done!" They repeated after him once, then twice, then again, gaining confidence with each round: 'Wake UP, Washington. We're DONE!"

He then shouted, "The government is out of its mind if it thinks it can take our rights away, because our rights don't come from the government. They come from our Creator! They come from God! And if you're offended by my religion, by my speech, or by my guns, then I say to you, GET OVER IT!" His face was crimson as he called upon the crowd to "bear witness to the truth of what is happening in this country!" The crowd erupted in cheers.

The rally's host returned to the stage while he waited for the musician to set up. Riding the wave of energy coming from the crowd, he said he had noticed that there were several political candidates in the crowd. He suggested that if people got a chance to speak with any of them, they should make sure to ask them "hard questions." Everyone cheered. "And if they don't answer," he added, chuckling, "we've got some tar and feathers in the back!" His reference to this Revolutionary-era ritual, associated especially with resistance to tax collectors, sent the crowd into a combination of laughter and spirited flag waving.

Becoming Informed: Fact-Finding and Truth-Telling

Although the Patriots had developed a clear argument about the rights of ordinary citizens to hold their government accountable, they shared with Interfaith an understanding that their ability to do so in practice was severely limited by a knowledge gap between the government and the people. As a result, the Patriots, like Interfaith members, spent a great deal of time—together and separately—developing the knowledge and skills necessary to understand and intervene in policy debates. As Linda once explained to me: "Knowledge is power. When you know what you're speaking about, and you're comfortable with what you're speaking about, then you have no problem walking up to [your elected official]. Because you're confident. . . . When you're an authority on something, [you can say,] 'No, these are *facts*. You can't fight that *fact*.'"

For the Patriots, the first step in becoming informed involved reading voraciously. Linda helped encourage this habit with her daily email, the *Must Know News*, which as we saw in chapter 2 contained a compendium of news clips, links to reports, and information about issues being debated by their representatives. In addition to reading this, members also engaged in independent research on specific issues that interested them. They did this on their own time, by combing through a vast online world of news websites, blogs, and publicly available documents.

I once sat next to a woman during a meeting who told me she had been researching the Federal Reserve. "It's very corrupt," she said. "And I never knew all of that stuff until I researched it, so it's been very eye-opening for me, being in this for the past four years." I asked how she did research, and she explained that she found a lot of information online. "Just read a lot. That's how you learn!"

In addition to reading, they also tuned in to media across the political spectrum, something they believed most people on the left were unwilling to do. Cam, the folksinger and blogger we met in chapter 4, told me in an interview that one of the biggest lessons he had learned since becoming more politically active was that, often, when "you look a little closer, . . . you find out that there's something else behind the curtain." His solution? "You do your homework." "So how do you do your homework?" I asked him. His reply:

> Read a lot. I read a lot. I go to *The Blaze*.[15] . . . Unlike my wife, I'm just as capable of sit[ting] down and tun[ing] in to Rachel Maddow and Ed Schultz as I am to turn on Fox and watch Hannity or Limbaugh or Beck. And that's one of the things that I see: there's a real interesting thing here. . . . The Left seems, ironically, the one trying to oppress and silence, and . . . get Beck off the air and do this. Whereas the Right, you don't see the same kind of attacks from them. They want to engage. They want the discussion out and in the light, you know? Generally. Now, obviously there's always going to be exceptions to this.

After asking a number of Patriots how they became more informed, I heard very similar accounts—they read widely and were interested in finding the "truth" by comparing multiple different accounts, including those from nontraditional sources like blogs and social media. They worried that their counterparts on the left were unwilling to do the same, however, which led them not only to challenge their motives but also to question the factual accuracy of their arguments.

They also insisted on the importance of consulting primary sources. As Linda once explained to the members of a local taxpayer's watchdog group, the Patriots' newspaper, the *Informed Citizen*, and their daily email, the *Must Know News*, "do not contain opinion. We just give you the truth. What you do with the truth is your business." An audience member pressed her on this: "You say you only print the facts," he said. "Where do you get these facts? I find things on the Internet and they turn out to be lies." She agreed that the Internet could be dangerous and explained that everything she prints has been verified on government websites. "If I read reports that conflict, I will go directly to the bill they are referencing," she explained. "I have read that twenty-five-hundred-page health-care bill more times than I can count." Referencing her daily email, she added, "Every link I use is there, so I'm verifiable."

As with their approach to the Constitution (discussed in chapters 3 and 4), they approached the Affordable Care Act (the health-care bill Linda referenced) and other official documents with a literalist and populist sense of suspicion that has become common among contemporary American conservatives.[16] They tended to distrust elites' interpretations of these documents and to deny that elites' specialized knowledge was even necessary in order to understand the basic issues at stake, asserting instead that the meaning of these texts was plainly evident to anyone who took the time to read them. Truly knowing was, thus, in reach, albeit with considerable effort; acquiring knowledge simply required that ordinary citizens have access to pure, unfiltered sources of information and devote themselves to "doing their homework."

Their approach to becoming more informed must also be viewed in the broader context of growing distrust of the media among citizens across the political spectrum. Whereas public belief in journalists' adherence to "objective" standards of reporting had previously (at least to a greater degree) certified major news outlets as trusted sources of information, decades of talk about bias has brought the media's legitimacy into question among large swaths of the American public.[17] Specifically, accusations of liberal bias produced a conservative backlash, of which Fox News was a part; and accusations of elitist bias produced a populist backlash, represented by the proliferation of citizen journalists across the political spectrum. Groups like the Patriots embody both of these sentiments. Armed with blogs, listservs, and a stockpile of public documents now readily accessible to anyone with an Internet connection, the Patriots joined a broad-based movement of modern muckrakers.

When they gathered as a group, they put their newfound knowledge to work. This happened informally, as when the woman who had been researching the Federal Reserve could not resist sharing with me the information she had discovered, whispering excitedly to me even after the meeting started. But there were also more formal opportunities to showcase this new knowledge during group meetings. Phil, for example, led a collective exercise that I came to call "stump the liberal." A combination of Socratic and sarcastic, Phil would ask group members to respond to arguments hypothetically posed by liberal friends and family members. He began one such exercise with the following prompt: "Ask your liberal friends, because I've been stumping them lately, 'Can anybody tell me what *fair* is?'" The group then spent almost half an hour practicing rebuttals to their liberal friends' potential responses. Exercises like these were opportunities to showcase the research they had been doing on their own since the last meeting, as well as to learn from one another how to draw upon their newfound knowledge in everyday interactions with friends and neighbors and in communications with decision makers.

Pressure Tactics: Vigilance and Public Confrontation

Once members of the Patriots felt they had become authorities on a particular issue, they were encouraged to confront their elected officials and debunk any claims they believed were untrue. For the most part, they used confrontational tactics available to them as individual voters and constituents. They called and wrote letters to their representatives, spoke as individual citizens at public hearings and town hall meetings, and submitted letters to the editors of local newspapers. In each case, their demands reflected their own research, concerns, and interests rather than the negotiated common ground of the whole group.

For example, several members of the Patriots attended a public hearing about their county budget, where they planned to voice their concerns in front of their local elected officials and hundreds of their neighbors. The Patriots had supported a new county executive during his campaign earlier that fall, and his first order of business when he took office was to propose a new budget that sharply reduced taxes and spending. Linda had included updates about the budget process in her morning email for weeks and encouraged everyone to attend one of the scheduled hearings on the issue. As she wrote in one email: "By now you've read [the] budget proposal. You've read the facts—you're in a position to counter what the left is telling you—you have the truth. . . . We need to . . . send a very loud and clear message that . . . taxpayers are done playing games and mean business."

For many of the Patriots, this would be their first time attending a hearing like this, and they did not know what to expect. On the day of the final hearing, Linda suggested that people arrive before six o'clock in order to get seats and, if they wished, sign up to speak in support of the proposed budget. I did not heed her advice. By the time I arrived, a long line had formed in the lobby. The guard informed me that the main room was at overflow capacity, and the police had told them they could not let anyone else in. One hundred sixty-three people had signed up to ask questions. At three minutes each, it would be a long night.

Once I was allowed to enter the large auditorium, I saw Gilbert and Stan, both small business owners, sitting close to the front of the room. Between Gilbert's early mornings spent handing out newspapers at the train station and these evening events, it often seemed as if he were working with the Patriots full time. Gilbert's and Stan's numbers were called as I took my seat. I knew they must have arrived hours earlier in order to speak so early in the evening. But as their own bosses, they had the flexibility to arrive late or leave work early every once in a while. In some ways, being there actually counted *as work* for them. As far as they were concerned, these hearings had a direct bearing on their ability to run their businesses—they believed they were being taxed and regulated to death.

They filed toward the microphone at the front of the room, their backs to the throngs of people waving handwritten signs bearing the names of programs that risked losing funding during this round of budget cuts—a community garden, a battered women's shelter, a day care program, a health clinic. The group of five people who had been called to speak stood only a few feet from the raised stage, where a panel of about twenty local legislators looked alternately bored and overwhelmed. Though the speakers' backs were turned to the general audience, the latter could hear everything. Via microphone, speakers' words reverberated through the large hall and were fed by a closed-circuit system to two adjacent rooms packed with the overflow crowd. Reporters and bloggers recorded notes to be shared with even broader audiences.

Stan had been elected to a local political office during the previous month's election, a "Tea Party candidate" who had actually been active in a Tea Party group (the Patriots) before running for office. Still, that night he waited for his three minutes alongside everyone else who signed up to speak: he was there as an ordinary citizen, not as a politician. When it was finally his turn, he bellowed into the microphone, his voice far larger than his small frame. He expressed his concern that the county was not using his tax dollars wisely, and he made it clear that as a *taxpayer* he was the legislators' boss; they worked for him: "We are telling you, just as we do in our family, just as we do in our business, this is $1.78 billion dollars that you were given to spend by *WE the taxpayers,* by the taxpayers, . . . the people who are footing the bill. We are asking you to spend it wisely. This is what we elected you to do. This is what your responsibility is. Do not expect another penny from us!" He slammed his fist on the podium.

When it was his turn to speak, Gilbert, too, reminded the officials who was boss, although he focused on citizens' power as *voters* rather than as taxpayers: "I think the electorate's spoken," he warned them. "I hope you're listening." He closed his statement with the tagline Tea Partiers around the country had used in the run-up to the 2010 election: "We'll remember in November!" He was booed. But he had delivered his message—that the people were in charge.

After engaging in activities like this, group members often reminded each other that they were engaged in brave acts of truth-telling. Sometimes they were booed when they did so, but this only strengthened their resolve. As Linda wrote in her group email about the hearings: "It takes guts and a strong belief in fiscal responsibility to stand up in front of hundreds of people that oppose every word you say. Bravo gentlemen!" Whether or not they were successful in the short run, the very act of standing up and demanding to be heard advanced their goal of holding government accountable.

ACCOUNTABILITY IN ACTION

Common Goal, Divergent Styles

Both Interfaith and the Patriots organized in order to more effectively hold government and other institutions accountable. They did so in response to similar challenges and concerns: as individuals they had lacked the power to demand the outcomes they sought; as nonexperts they had lacked the knowledge to intervene in debates about complex issues that affected them; and as ordinary people they had lacked the standing to demand decision makers' attention. And the two groups responded in similar ways: by organizing for collective action, developing shared understandings of what accountability meant in practice, becoming informed about issues and the political process, and employing tactics designed to pressure public officials into taking their voices seriously.

They were not always, or even usually, successful; for both groups (and indeed, all groups like them), success was difficult to measure, partial, and rarely achieved immediately. My goal in this chapter was not to evaluate which group's approach to accountability was more effective. Rather I have sought to show that for members of the two groups, the very *act* of holding authorities to account was an important part of their work together, and that they interpreted this as a meaningful way of playing their part in the story of American democracy. Whether group members believed they were playing the role of a prophet or a patriot, working vigilantly to hold authorities accountable was at the heart of both groups' understandings of what it means to be an active citizen.

The public typically sees only the end result of these efforts: the groups' public demands. And in most cases, the groups demanded very *different* things of their governments. While the Patriots (and the Tea Party more broadly) demanded lower taxes and less government intrusion, Interfaith (and other faith-based community-organizing coalitions around the country) supported government action that protected the most vulnerable citizens in their communities. That the demands of a conservative group and a progressive group would differ is not terribly surprising. But a focus solely on the content of their demands fuels the perception that groups like these do not share anything in common. As we have seen, that is not the case.

A closer look at the ways in which Interfaith and the Patriots organized to hold government accountable reveals parallels between these groups' efforts that are often obscured. When their accountability efforts are placed side by side, our attention is drawn to aspects of each group's work that might otherwise go unrecognized. For example, little has been written about the amount of time that Tea Party groups spent doing research and refining their political knowledge and skills. But because groups like Interfaith formally place research at the center of their organizing model,

I became attuned to the importance of these practices and paid closer attention to them in *both* settings.

Moreover, the few researchers who have attended to this aspect of Tea Party groups' efforts have emphasized the frequency with which these groups circulated factually inaccurate information about policies (in contrast, researchers found high levels of knowledge about the political *process*).[18] My focus in this analysis has not been on fact-checking the groups. Rather, I have sought to demonstrate that the process of becoming informed was a central and meaningful component of both groups' efforts.

At the same time, however, these groups became informed in markedly different ways. For example, they viewed different authorities and sources of information as credible and had different ways of doing research. Interfaith members primarily gathered information by documenting their own experiences and collecting the stories of other community members. Meanwhile, the Patriots learned about issues by comparing multiple media accounts and referencing primary sources of information. They also understood the practical meaning and role of this knowledge in different ways. Interfaith typically presented the experiential knowledge they gathered as subjective and partial but nonetheless worthy of consideration—a means of broadening the official understanding of an issue. In contrast, the Patriots sought to dig through political bluster and what they perceived as biased reporting until they found what they viewed as undeniable facts. They then presented their findings as objective truths that were superior to all competing claims.

When groups like these are called "schools of democracy," this typically suggests they are sites in which citizens develop relatively neutral and straightforward "civic competencies."[19] This approach leads scholars to expect that although groups may vary in terms of *how* informed they are, the actual knowledge and skills they develop would be relatively similar. But as we have seen, the knowledge that members of Interfaith and the Patriots developed, as well as their very ways of knowing, differed significantly.

Juxtaposing the groups' efforts side by side brings these kinds of subtle differences between their practices into sharper relief (see table 1). The question is then: What factors are driving these different approaches to accountability? The differences are not easily explained by reference to the groups' political ideologies—indeed, the organizational styles, practices,

Table 1 Divergent styles of holding government accountable

Elements of the Groups' Accountability Efforts	Interfaith's Approach	Patriots' Approach
Organizing for collective action	Power through solidarity	Power as individuals acting together
Developing an accountability frame	Public officials as (potential) partners to community	Rights-bearing citizens as check on government power
Becoming informed	Listening and storytelling	Fact-finding and truth-telling
Selecting pressure tactics	Covenants and public commitments	Vigilance and public confrontation

and tactics that each group developed are not intrinsically conservative or progressive. For example, the Patriots joined groups across the political spectrum—from the far Left to the far Right—by embracing the research practices of citizen journalists. Meanwhile, they chose a relatively decentralized and nonhierarchical organizational form that bore a resemblance to many experiments in "participatory democracy" on the political left.[20] It would make little sense to conclude these choices were expressions of their conservative ideology. But an analysis of the organizational choices that each group made, as well as of differences in these choices across both of the groups, confirms these were not a random collection of choices either. Rather, a clear pattern emerged: the groups developed different styles of holding government accountable that consistently corresponded to their democratic imaginaries.

Accountability Styles and Democratic Imaginaries

In chapter 3, democratic imaginaries were defined as groups' background understandings of how a democratic society should work and of the proper role of ordinary citizens like them within it. The accountability styles that Interfaith and the Patriots developed reflected their respective imaginaries. This can be further specified by looking at how each group's style

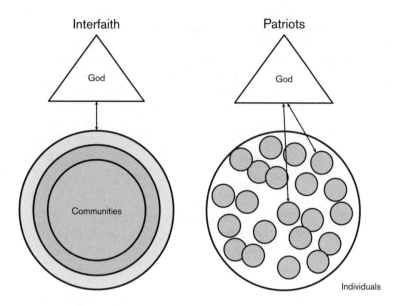

Figure 1. Imagined relationships among citizens.

reflected a different understanding of the proper relationship (1) among citizens, and (2) between citizens and government.

First, we can look at how the groups' styles reflected different understandings of the proper relationship among citizens (see fig. 1). Through their accountability efforts, members of Interfaith framed the citizenry as a set of overlapping and nested moral communities (e.g., their congregations, their neighborhoods, their city, or the nation as a whole) that have certain collective interests and moral obligations. This view draws on the prophetic religious tradition of the Hebrew Bible, whose emphasis on covenants as the basis of political community entered American political thought through the Puritans. According to the sociologist Rhys H. Williams, variants on this general idea have entered social movements through a "covenantal" model of citizenship that frames individual interests as inseparable from the good of the moral community as a whole, which is in turn obliged to pursue God's will.[21]

While the covenantal model has Protestant roots, it has since been taken up by Catholics, Jews, and other religious groups advocating social justice and the common good. Yet this model is not inherently *progressive*—a covenantal vision also undergirds conservative Christian interpretations of natural disasters and national crises as God's punishment for collective "sins" like the legalization of abortion or same-sex marriage.[22]

By referencing the idea of "covenant" and building an organization that mobilized a racially, economically, and religiously diverse set of communities, Interfaith's members connected their efforts to this complex tradition. By developing relationships that were built on listening and storytelling, they demonstrated their commitment to discovering how their varied interests intersected in the common good. Meanwhile, they also understood that in order for their collective claims to be credible, the relationships they forged had to be marked by mutual accountability to one another and to God—a key feature of covenantal relationships. They demonstrated this understanding by creating a leadership structure that empowered members like Doris to speak on the community's behalf, by convening public audiences as a show of solidarity and support for the group's demands, by holding accountability actions inside places of worship, and by opening these actions with prayers that communicated the shared values guiding their work.

Meanwhile, the Patriots framed "the people" as a collection of autonomous individuals endowed with God-given rights to pursue their own self-interest. This view resembles what Williams calls a "contractual" model of citizenship, in that each citizen's role rests, not on the ongoing renewal of collective covenants with God, but on the idea that God granted individual rights to each citizen that cannot be taken away from them.[23] This is not to say that individuals are untethered from moral obligation—rather, each individual must answer individually to God and is personally responsible for determining what kinds of actions are right and good. From this vantage, citizenship and accountability are individual pursuits.

Although in recent decades some groups on the political right have embraced an individualized vision of citizenship, Williams argues this is not an inherently *conservative* way of imagining how democracy ought to work. He shows that movements across the political spectrum have deployed contractual rhetoric, ranging from those emphasizing "the right to the means for achieving inclusion" to those calling for the "right to be left alone."[24]

By explicitly referencing the idea that their individual rights come from God, the Patriots connected their efforts to this complex tradition.

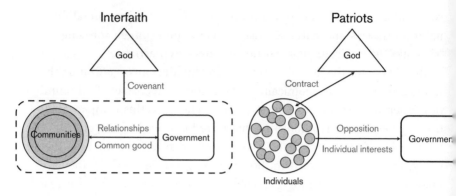

Figure 2. Imagined relationships between citizens and government.

Through this lens, it makes sense that they intentionally resisted creating a rigid organizational structure or empowering any single person to speak on behalf of collective goals. They created an organization that was a loose network of autonomous individuals rather than a collective actor—a fact they highlighted by likening the process of organizing Tea Partiers to "herding cats." They underscored this point by reminding the group that individuals should make their own decisions about issues and political candidates, based on their own evaluations of the facts involved and their individual interests and moral consciences.

Meanwhile, the groups' organizational styles and practices also reflected different understandings of the proper relationship between citizens and government (see fig. 2). In Interfaith's imaginary, public officials were bound in the same covenant community as ordinary citizens. This understanding is consistent with the Puritan notion that the covenant community is bound by what the legal scholar John Witte Jr. calls a "tri-party agreement between God, the civil ruler, and the people."[25] When Interfaith members met one-on-one with public officials or publicly shared their stories with audiences that included both neighbors and public officials, they endeavored to expand the boundaries of their moral community to include all of these partners, so that all would feel bound, in mutual accountability, to pursue the common good of their community. These practices were natural extensions of their vision of the proper relationship among citizens, in which citizens are not atomized individuals but are nested in moral communities. These visions were brought together and reinforced through the practice of publicly asking political authorities to enter into a covenant not with each of them as individuals but with their diverse community as a whole, under God's watchful gaze.

On the other hand, the Patriots' accountability style expressed an understanding that citizens would be free to pursue their individual interests only if they vigilantly opposed government control. Practically, they knew that citizens needed to work together to strengthen their individual capacity to demand accountability from public officials, but ideally this arrangement should be temporary and allow for maximum individual flexibility and creativity. Although less institutionalized than Interfaith's actions, the tactics the Patriots selected routinely reflected this oppositional logic: they engaged in individual accountability actions together; they made demands of their elected officials based on their individual self-interest or moral conscience rather than the negotiated demands of the group; and the actions they were drawn to typically involved publicly reminding public officials that individual citizens are the true authorities in a representative system.

In sum, there was a clear correspondence between each group's style of holding government accountable and their respective ways of imagining how democracy ought to work and the role of active citizens within it. But more difficult questions remain: Did the groups' imaginaries actually shape their practical choices? And if so, what were the specific processes or mechanisms through which these imaginaries channeled the groups toward certain practices and away from other, seemingly plausible, options?

6 Styles of Active Citizenship

Interfaith and the Patriots each developed a style of holding government accountable that reflected a different ideal vision of the proper relationships among citizens and between citizens and government. Similarly, each group's style of putting their faith into action reflected different understandings of how citizens ought to relate to one another and to God. Although it is clear there was a correspondence between the groups' styles of active citizenship and their respective democratic imaginaries, we must now turn to the more precise question of *how* the groups' imaginaries influenced their practices.

Stepping back, it is helpful to recall, first, that Interfaith and the Patriots did not develop their respective styles of active citizenship from scratch. They assembled them from a vast "repertoire" of organizational styles, cultural practices, and tactics that are available to all citizens groups operating within the United States today.[1] When we view group cultures as projects of *selection* rather than *creation*, this prompts us to consider what factors led each group to select the organizational, cultural, and tactical elements that they did.

Certainly, their choices were likely shaped in part by their understanding of what would be most *effective*, but this cannot fully explain the choices they made. As we will see, they did not change course each time their efforts were unsuccessful, and they defended tactical choices that were not especially effective, at least in the short run. As noted in chapters 4 and 5, their practices did not consistently reflect "conservative" or "progressive" ideologies either. Whether they were putting their faith into action or holding government accountable, both groups incorporated some practices that are more typically associated with groups on the opposite side of the ideological spectrum, as well as some that are not associated strongly with either side.[2]

Rather than being driven by judgments of effectiveness or by ideology, the groups' choices, as I came to realize, were more consistently linked to judgments of *appropriateness*. It is a core tenet of sociological thinking that, consciously or not, most individuals tailor their behavior to suit the social context in which they are embedded.[3] For example, we expect most people to behave differently in a work meeting and at after-work drinks with friends, understanding that each setting carries different norms and expectations about what is appropriate and what is not. This logic applies to political life as well, as when activists consider what kind of behavior is appropriate in, say, a public protest versus a private meeting and choose different styles of action accordingly.

While members of Interfaith and the Patriots were attuned to such social conventions, this is not precisely what I mean when I say that the groups' choices were shaped by judgments of appropriateness. In addition to taking their context into account, these groups also considered what kinds of actions were appropriate for "groups like them" in light of how they imagined their roles as active citizens.[4] This is the mechanism through which their democratic imaginaries gained the power to shape their group practices.

This second meaning of *appropriateness* differs in two key ways from the first. Importantly, it highlights the significance of *group identity* in shaping styles of action. Recall from chapter 3 that these groups' democratic imaginaries were rooted in their situated intersubjectivities, their collective sense of who they were as a group, how they related to other actors, and, on that basis, how they were prepared to act together.[5] This dynamic sense of group identity was intertwined in their democratic imaginaries with their ideal models of how democracy should work and their visions of the country's future, and served as a lens through which members evaluated choices about how to engage in collective action.

Moreover, as we will see, this evaluation process was often quite *conscious*, with group members explicitly discussing how "groups like them" should act. At first glance, this finding may seem to contradict a large body of research demonstrating that human behavior is relatively automatic, intuitive, and habituated, motivated by a combination of unconscious cultural schemas and instinct. Yet this research also suggests that there are conditions under which action can be the product of more conscious deliberation in light of one's self-understandings.[6]

Although less common than the former, this latter type of action is most likely to occur, I contend, under the following conditions: first, when action is undertaken collectively rather than individually; second, when perceptions of social and cultural upheaval prompt groups to articulate shared visions of how society ought to work; and third, when a group's internal culture or routine is unsettled, requiring members to reaffirm "who we are" and "how we do things." I elaborate on each of these conditions below. But simply put, where these conditions are present, we should expect to observe groups (at least periodically) making relatively deliberate choices about how to act based on collective considerations of whether behaviors are appropriate for "groups like them."

With regard to the first condition, we know that individual action and collective action work in very different ways. A large body of sociological research building on the work of Pierre Bourdieu, and a growing body of interdisciplinary research on human cognition, point to a similar conclusion about individual action: that individuals' self-understandings profoundly shape their actions, yet individuals are rarely conscious of this influence. Rather, the actions they take based on their self-understandings are typically embodied, habituated, and routine.[7]

There are reasons to believe that the opposite is true of collective action. While people involved in collective efforts like social movements or civic organizations may have different individual motivations for participating, groups must typically establish shared understandings of "who we are," "what we want," and "why we are doing it" in order to justify their choices to act collectively.[8] Developing these shared understandings is not simple; it requires ongoing negotiation and compromise. As a result, we should not be surprised to observe participants in these kinds of groups making some choices about how to act collectively based on deliberations about what kinds of behaviors are appropriate for "groups like them."

But this distinction between individual and collective action is not perfect. Just as there are cases in which individuals engage in deliberative action, so too can groups settle into habituated or automatic action. This is why we must also consider the second and third conditions, concerning the context in which groups engage in collective action. Specifically, insights from cultural sociology suggest that groups are more likely to consciously consider whether their actions are appropriate for a "group like them" when the *broader culture* and/or their *group culture* are relatively unsettled and in a state of flux.

Both of these considerations are rooted in the observation by the sociologist Ann Swidler that people tend to act unconsciously, according to tradition and common sense, when they are in relatively "settled" cultural contexts. In contrast, during "unsettled" moments of social upheaval and transformation, taken-for-granted habits and traditions are disrupted, and people turn to more "explicit, articulated, highly organized meaning systems (both political and religious) [to] establish new styles or strategies of action."[9]

This is a helpful distinction, particularly when studying political groups like Interfaith and the Patriots, which tend to emerge during (or bring about) periods of cultural and political upheaval. Since members of these kinds of groups often perceive the political moment in which they are acting as an unsettled one, they commonly work together to imagine what a better future would look like and how groups like theirs can help to create that future. As discussed in chapter 3, these kinds of future-oriented discussions can inform groups' choices about how to act.

But groups like these almost always operate in unsettled cultural contexts (at least from their perspective), and yet their actions are not always so deliberate. Indeed, a growing body of research on the cultural dynamics of civic groups finds that even groups determined to challenge the social order eventually settle into group routines and habits.[10] As the sociologist Kathleen M. Blee found in her study of emerging grassroots activist groups, groups' understandings of "how we do things" can quickly become taken-for-granted, habituated, and even unspoken, preventing members from revisiting assumptions and decisions that no longer serve the groups' interests.[11]

Yet we should not overstate the extent to which these groups are on autopilot. They are still likely to encounter situations that challenge or unsettle their routine ways of acting: for example, when new members breach unspoken group norms or propose ideas that are inconsistent with the group's style.[12] As the sociologists Nina Eliasoph and Paul Lichterman observe, it is precisely during such unsettled moments in groups' internal lives that we would expect to observe participants reaffirming "who we are" and "how we do things."[13] Group members can then tap into these understandings to justify taking one path forward or another.

In sum, groups that are engaged in collective action, are organizing in a context of perceived cultural and political upheaval, and whose internal cultures are temporarily unsettled are settings in which conscious considerations of appropriateness are likely to shape group practices. As we will see in the case of Interfaith and the Patriots, it was particularly during moments when the groups' routine ways of acting were temporarily disrupted that group members debated about what course of action would be most appropriate for a "group like them." Their judgments of appropriateness were often made explicitly with reference to their ideal models of how democracy ought to work and how active citizens like them ought to behave. Through this process their democratic imaginaries subtly but powerfully shaped their group practices.[14]

As group members reaffirmed their commitment to these shared ideals, this led the groups to interpret organizational, tactical, and cultural choices that aligned with them as the most natural, sensible, and meaningful options—a good "fit" for them—while interpreting alternative choices as implausible, inappropriate, or even undemocratic. This ultimately helped each group adjudicate between competing options and bring outliers and dissenters into alignment with the group's style. The following accounts center on moments like these, revealing the subtle ways in which the groups' idealized understandings of how citizens ought to relate to one another and to government channeled them toward certain behaviors and away from other (seemingly plausible) options.

HOW IMAGINARIES CHANNEL ACTION

Civility versus Confrontation

Let us return to the Westside parish where, as described in chapter 5, Father O'Donnell, Doris, and a handful of other Interfaith leaders pressed city officials to work with them to improve housing conditions in their community. After the action ended and the crowd dispersed, we stacked folding chairs and tables against the walls. This last task completed, Father O'Donnell and the lay leaders who had organized the action met at the front of the auditorium. They motioned for me, Helen (the active Jewish leader who attended in solidarity with this Catholic congregation), and a few other partners who had been sitting in the audience to join them in their huddle. It was time for the ritual postaction evaluation session, where each person shared his or her thoughts about how the action went and how it could have been improved.

These postaction evaluation sessions were central to the leadership development process at the center of Interfaith's work. Although each accountability action represented the culmination of months of work, it was also just one step in the group members' journeys toward becoming more effective and powerful citizens. As they identified areas for improvement and discussed how they could have managed aspects of an action differently, they did so against a set of background assumptions about what an effective and powerful citizen ideally would do in their situation. Staff organizers and clergy played key roles in subtly reinforcing these ideals.

As we went around the circle, the first few people said they thought the action had gone well. But the group's energy was lower than it usually was at the end of a public action; and in light of this, these initial positive evaluations rang hollow. When it was Father O'Donnell's turn, he said he was disappointed and a bit angry. He was upset that the landlord had not shown up, especially after they had met with him privately in order to better understand his perspective. Father O'Donnell noted he had been under the impression they were working together in good faith, and he could not understand why the landlord would now disrespect their relationship. It went unmentioned that reporters from a local news outlet had shown up at the apartment building in question earlier that day to report on the action, or that these public actions were more intimidating for their "targets" than private meetings were, although these factors likely had something to do with his absence that night.

A tall white man in his thirties was standing next to me at the back of the huddle. He was the lawyer they had been working with through a local nonprofit. One of the staff organizers asked him what he thought. "I've done these before," he said, "where tenants confront landlords in the lobby of their building, but this was so different. This was so much more powerful, because you not only had tenants from this building, but you had tenants from other buildings join you to say, essentially: 'You mess with one of us, you mess with all of us.'" He also noted that he thought it was "powerful" that they were still not satisfied. They looked around at one another, nodding, seeming buoyed by this reinforcement that their approach seemed powerful to an outsider.

But Helen seemed dubious of this rosy analysis. Before the huddle, she mentioned to me that she and her husband, who used to work as a tenant organizer, were surprised by how bad conditions had gotten in the building. She said they were curious about why the tenants had not simply gone on a rent strike, and she hoped to learn more during the evaluation session. Now she raised her hand and asked if it would be appropriate for her to say something. She began most questions this way, particularly when she was a guest in another congregation.

She said she generally agreed with the lawyer, but noted that it was actually surprising that the landlord had not come. She spoke carefully now: "He shouldn't have been so scared, because you are all so . . . nice." Everyone laughed, and so did Helen. Then she continued: "But sometimes maybe you're too nice. I am listening to all the things you're saying you've dealt with, and this is just . . . ," she measured her words, ". . . it's just outrageous! It's unacceptable. You should not have to live this way. And you need to keep reminding yourselves of that. Honestly, it's outrageous." Several people stared at her wide-eyed. Others nodded their heads, as if her indignation reinforced their own feelings.

Raquel, whom we met in chapter 3, mentioned that she had spoken to tenants from neighboring buildings who were facing similar problems. "They were pretty angry," she noted with a nervous chuckle. She and a staff organizer glanced at one another as if there were more to this story. Raquel then explained she was disappointed more of them had not come, but added, "But we told them it would be a *peaceful* meeting, so maybe they didn't want to come. We kept telling everyone it would be a *peaceful* meeting."

At that point, Father O'Donnell jumped in and reassured Raquel and the others that they had done the right thing. "Like I keep saying," he said, "it needs to be peaceful. We would rather have a peaceful meeting with a lower turnout than have them come in here yelling and being disrespectful." Around the circle, several people nodded in agreement, and Helen let the subject drop.

Generally speaking, Interfaith leaders were mindful that these public actions could be seen as quite threatening to the "targets" of their demands. This was in some ways the entire point—by demanding commitments in public, they made it much more difficult for their targets to make vague promises or fail to follow through on their commitments after the fact. This kind of public confrontation was a staple of the community organizing tradition going back to Saul Alinsky. As a dramatic display of a coalition's "people power," such actions were intended to disrupt the power relations and social norms that typically marked interactions between citizens and public officials, even if this was uncomfortable.

But the community-organizing field is not unified in its approach. One emerging divide concerns a distinction between *congregation*-based and *faith*-based organizing. Whereas for decades the field viewed congregations primarily as useful organizational building blocks, PICO and its member coalitions (including Interfaith) endeavor to ground their work more deeply in their congregations' shared faith values. This approach was important to Interfaith's leaders and prompted them to reevaluate many long-standing tactics through a moral as well as a pragmatic lens and, when necessary, to modify them.

In this vein, some members of Interfaith expressed concern that the more they leaned toward a style that felt threatening, the more they risked undermining their moral authority and the tenuous bonds that held them all together. Father O'Donnell even took issue with the term *target* and did not use it. As he once explained to me in an interview: "*Target* means you're going to shoot them, and I don't like that."

He was not alone in being sensitive to this issue. Interfaith's health-care working group once hotly debated the best way to handle their relationship with a congressman who had not voted for the Affordable Care Act. Robert, then the chairperson of Interfaith, suggested that they consider partnering with a local union that had lobbied the congressman to vote for the bill. A partnership with this powerful union could have strengthened Interfaith's capacity to hold the congressman accountable for promises he had made to them before this vote. But Robert also warned that this relationship needed to be handled delicately, because the union "wants to bludgeon the congressman." This comment triggered concerns. One woman asked with alarm: "Is that how you see Interfaith's role in this?" Another man responded, "I'm not into political attacks. I joined Interfaith because it was addressing the *moral* dimension of the health-care debate." Robert suggested that part of their role involved working with partners who shared their interests, even if they had different styles of pursuing them. But then he conceded that perhaps this was going too far. "We're not here to bludgeon," he affirmed. "That is against our values." They concluded that working closely with the union was not a path that a group like them should pursue.

Months later, Tanya, an active participant in the health-care working group, raised the possibility of organizing a Catholic parish that was merging with hers. But she explained that when she had approached the pastor to propose working with Interfaith, he "panicked at the idea." She acted out his response, throwing her hands up, her face contorting. People around the table looked intrigued, but confused. Nora explained that decades earlier some of the older clergy members in their neighborhood had bad experiences with organizers from another community-organizing network, which they viewed as too aggressive and confrontational. This community-organizing network was still active in other areas of the city and exerted considerable influence in city politics. Still, Interfaith members had described them to me on various occasions as too "hard-nosed" and "in your face." As one man put it, they did not even "pretend to be faith-based." The group agreed that Tanya should keep talking to this priest about how their work would benefit his congregation, and that she would need to distance Interfaith from this negative impression of community organizing. She agreed to do so, and reported that she had promised him that there wouldn't be "anything aggressive or anything too stressful. It would be low-key."

In each of these cases, the group struggled to determine the best way to hold public officials accountable, yet resisted forms of action that might be viewed as overly aggressive or uncivil. Not only did they worry that this kind of behavior could jeopardize their relationships with public officials and potential allies, but they also worried that it could risk undermining their moral authority. Moreover, it contradicted their idealized understanding of how good citizens ought to behave—as potential partners with stakeholders, seeking the common good rather than facing off in a zero-sum battle over opposing interests. Despite some debate about alternatives, the group ultimately made choices that were consistent with these ideals, even if this meant avoiding activities that might have been more impactful in the short run. They distanced themselves from the other community-organizing network, even though the latter exerted a great deal of power in the city. They chose not to pursue a close partnership with the union, even though that organization was far more powerful. They did not encourage the angry neighbors to attend their accountability action, even though broader community involvement might have led the public officials to address their concerns with more urgency.

Rather than enabling them to achieve political victories in the short run, their democratic ideals oriented them toward creating a different kind of politics. This started with cultivating a different kind of citizen and different kinds of relationships between citizens and public officials. When clergy referred to public officials as "partners" rather than "targets"; when they held public accountability actions in places of worship, where widely recognized norms of decorum discouraged angry outbursts; when leaders were encouraged to share their feelings in postaction evaluation sessions where raw emotions like anger and disappointment could be channeled into more constructive sentiments, these were all subtle means of communicating that their relationships with public officials should be marked by civility.

As we saw in chapter 5, this stands in marked contrast to the Patriots' approach to these relationships. Concerned that public officials were too elitist and distant from the people they served, the Patriots developed practices that reflected the group's desire to bring these officials down a notch. For example, the Patriots publicly reminded officials that as taxpayers and voters *they* were really the boss, and that as a potentially angry mob they could "tar and feather" the officials (metaphorically) if they did not treat their constituents with respect.

In some ways it is surprising that the more progressive group would favor civility while the more conservative group would favor aggressive confrontation. After all, calls for civility are generally viewed as conservative—as one means of controlling the emotions and behaviors of the masses. Meanwhile, public confrontation is typically associated with groups on the left, who have more often than groups on the right resorted to mass disruption and protest. But just as behaving with civility allowed Interfaith members to live out their visions of how citizens ought to interact with government officials, confronting public officials with threats of replacement or embarrassment was consistent with how the Patriots imagined good citizens ought to behave—as vigilant checks on government power.

Self-Interest versus the Common Good

For Interfaith, accountability was not just about how the group related to public officials: it was also about their relationship to their own community. Their moral authority to hold officials and others accountable rested, in their telling, on their interest in serving the common good of their community as a whole. But in practice, determining what was good for the community was complicated, and it involved extended negotiations between individuals with competing interests, priorities, and notions of the good. In the course of this process Interfaith members often helped one another connect their individual self-interest to a broader conception of the common good, which was viewed as aligned with their shared faith values. A disagreement within the group demonstrates how they referenced the moral and democratic ideals that animated their work together in order to manage situations like these.

Tanya was a member of a Catholic church in Riverside and had joined the health-care working group at around the same time I did. She was employed in the public school system as a teacher's assistant and was working toward her master's degree at night, while also raising her kids (and soon, a new grandchild). At around five feet tall, she would pass as petite if it were not for her solid build and square jaw, which communicated a certain toughness before she even opened her mouth. When she spoke, a thick northeastern accent covered any remnants of the Russian language of her youth. Although she was about to become a grandmother, her round face glowed with a youthful feistiness.

During her first few meetings, she seemed unsure of what she was doing there. I had responded to this same feeling by sitting quietly until I became acclimated, but her playful yet tough demeanor did not have a dimmer switch. During her time in the group, Tanya routinely challenged the group's unspoken norms against emotional outbursts and confrontation. In the process, she brought issues to the surface that others avoided, and she made visible some of the challenges Interfaith members faced in translating their abstract ideals into practical action.

She originally became interested in Interfaith, she told me one night after a meeting, because she wanted to address issues facing the undocumented immigrant population in their community. Her husband, who was Mexican, was undocumented when they met. He was lucky, she explained. "He got amnesty, and then we got married and started a family and the 'whole nine.' You know, the American dream!" She explained that she believed that most of the undocumented people in the country had good intentions: "They want the same things and have no choice. And it's not fair that they let Russians in but not Mexicans. How do they decide these things? It's not right! What kind of world . . . ?"

But she had not gotten seriously involved in Interfaith's work until she mentioned to Nora at church one Sunday that she was worried about her unemployed and uninsured nineteen-year-old son. As a public employee, she hoped he could be covered under her policy, but she discovered that he could not. When she looked into various subsidized health insurance options for him, she was surprised and upset to discover that they all took her income into account in addition to his when determining his eligibility. She had, in the group's parlance, identified her *self-interest* in this issue.

Helping people locate and articulate their self-interest is a primary purpose of the one-to-one conversations that Interfaith leaders have with members of their congregations and communities. This is based on the premise that people will not take action unless they have a personal stake in the outcome. This is not to say that each person's self-interest was

defined narrowly in terms of personal material gain; after all, many articulated the belief that lowering inequality and advancing justice in their
community was in their self-interest. Still, as Nora repeated over and over
again at their meetings, pursuing their self-interest was not the same as
being selfish; but it was also different from being selfless, and they needed
to be comfortable with that.

For everyone who joined the group, self-interest was the starting point
from which they were taught to assess issues. As a result, Tanya originally
believed the group would be a resource to help her advance her self-
interest. But after several meetings, she came to understand that Interfaith
worked differently. While the group did wish to find a solution to her
problem, her personal experience was also a resource they would use to
reform the system so that it better served their entire community, including other families like Tanya's.

Over the next several months, Tanya regularly updated the group on the
status of her son's insurance coverage. When the Affordable Care Act
required insurance companies to cover children up to age twenty-six under
their parents' plans, she became the group's resident expert on how this policy change was being implemented. As she told me, "Until I see his name on
an insurance card, I don't believe it." Months after the new law went into
effect, her insurance company had still not allowed him to enroll on her plan.

Meanwhile, Tanya grew increasingly restless as the group vacillated
between different paths forward. Should they focus primarily on "bringing
health reform home" by educating their congregations about changes in
the new health-care law that might affect them, like the new rule about
coverage for children up to twenty-six years old? Or should they voice
their criticisms of the bill—namely, that it did nothing to address the
needs of the large undocumented population in their community? She
cared about both issues, but one felt more urgent. The group went back
and forth, weighing the pros and cons of pursuing these and a handful of
other issues. They would move forward with one, then go back to the
drawing board. This continued for months.

Finally, the group resolved to organize a public accountability action
with a representative from the U.S. Department of Health and Human
Services. The centerpiece of the action would be testimonies from several
members of their communities who would publicly describe the issues

they continued to face following the passage of the new health-care law. Tanya was asked to tell her story. During a prep meeting, Nora asked her what she planned to say. It was typical for speakers to rehearse in advance of a public action. Rev. Fischer suggested that she should share some details of her own situation, but only as an example of the kinds of challenges that a lot of people were facing. She should not expect the representative to provide a solution to her specific situation on the spot.

Tanya nodded. "Right, right, I will just tell them my situation as an example." She started running through the details aloud: her son is nineteen, he is not in school or working, she works for the city, her insurance plan allows open enrollment only during November, and so on. She rehearsed as they had discussed, but then closed with the question "When will my child be covered?" She looked around the table. "I will polish it up a bit, but I don't want to pussyfoot around it. If we don't figure this out, my whole family could end up on Medicaid, and then Riverside [the local safety-net hospital] here we come!" Everyone laughed awkwardly at this pointed comment.

But this had been her attitude all night. Earlier, she had interrupted Nora to discuss her situation and, when told to wait her turn, had said defensively: "I gotta look out for number one, ya know?" Now Helen turned to her and said, "You need to ask this question not just for yourself but for the thousands of others in the state who have the same problem as you." Nora cut in to say, "We found out that this affects tens of thousands of children in this one congressional district . . ." Yet Tanya was undeterred, again launching into the details of her situation. They finally convinced her to move on so they could turn to selecting the other testimonies, which would highlight the ways in which immigrants in their community were struggling to find adequate health care.

When the night of the accountability action arrived, Tanya stood up and faced the official from Health and Human Services. She told her story clearly and with an unquestionable authority that came from months spent becoming informed about the issue. Importantly, she also placed her personal experience in the context of the more general issue facing their community. In the end, she adopted the group's style. Afterward, she beamed as she posed for pictures alongside other members of the working group.

Had I simply observed this public accountability action, it might have seemed that Interfaith's style of action came naturally to its members. But access to the backstage negotiations that preceded the public performance revealed that this style was actually the product of ongoing group discussions in which participants (especially newcomers) were encouraged to align their individual interests with the common good, in a manner consistent with the group's shared values. Although Tanya ultimately conformed to the group's style, reaching this point required delicate interventions by more established group members.

And this situation was not unique; indeed, group members routinely helped one another work through this tension. Even clergy acknowledged that most people's natural tendency was to pursue their self-interest; and as a result, they often used their prayer reflections to orient the group toward the shared values that helped them identify the common good. Recall Father O'Donnell's prayer recounted in chapters 4 and 5, which reminded everyone present that although they had different interests, they were "called by God to do the good work that will make us all better neighbors." These efforts were not always successful, but the fact that group members referenced these ideal models of good citizenship in moments of ambiguity and conflict provides insight into how ideals were pulled down into the daily lives of these groups and gained the potential to shape the groups' actions.

Speaking Collectively versus Individually

Compared to Interfaith members, who spent much of their time negotiating how they could speak collectively, members of the Patriots insisted on speaking as individuals even while presenting themselves as part of a broader group or movement. Yet these lines between individual and collective voice were blurry in practice and required the Patriots to occasionally rearticulate the limits of what they would do together as a group. This was particularly necessary when group members proposed new ideas that pushed these limits. This dynamic can be observed in a situation that transpired shortly after the 2010 elections.

On the Friday after Election Day, I headed to the small town where many of the Patriots lived for a Friday night "Pizza and Politics" discussion. The town's Republican Club had hosted a handful of these dinner conversations that fall, and although this was not specifically a Tea Party meeting, around half of the regular attendees were active in the Patriots and other area Tea Party groups. The others may not have considered themselves Tea Partiers, but they were generally supportive of the Tea Party's efforts.[15] In fact, the idea for these casual discussions was sparked in part by a desire to capitalize on local Tea Party energy by getting people more involved in town politics.

The meetings were held in the cozy side room of a pizzeria tucked along the edge of a wooded road. Pulling into the unpaved parking lot, I could see people had already arrived. Inside the building, the excitement was palpable. Participants in these dinners had spent the previous few months distributing lawn signs, volunteering in candidates' offices, and canvassing their neighborhoods, and now several of the candidates they had backed were headed to Washington and their state capital. Jamie was showing Linda one of the leftover campaign signs, from the supply that had been sent a few weeks earlier by the national organization FreedomWorks after Jamie had lobbied them to support one of the Patriots' favored candidates. He had already gotten a handful of people to sign it, and as I entered he handed me a pen. "Sign it! We're going to give it to him to hang in his new office in Washington!" I added my initials in cursive, small and toward the bottom of the sign.

Without being formalized, the theme of the discussion that night was very clearly "now what?" Now that the Republican Party, aided by a surge of Tea Party support, had swept back into power across the country, all eyes were on these newly minted activists to see what they would do next. Handing back the pen, I congratulated Jamie and posed this very question: "What's next?" He was smiling ear to ear. "Well, this sign . . . ," he explained almost breathlessly, "it's all part of a new plan. We're changing the way this whole thing works."

I asked what he meant and glanced at Linda, who was standing nearby. She shrugged and raised her eyebrows as if to say, "Hear him out." He explained that, in the past, when individuals were elected they went down to Washington alone. "Now, they will go with their team." I asked him what he meant, and he explained his plans for a new effort that would bring together Tea Party groups around the state. It would be nothing less than a "paradigm shift in the way we hold candidates accountable."

Jamie was a salesman by trade, and this speech had all the trappings of a rehearsed pitch. He had now gotten the attention of a few others who had been milling around before the meeting started, and he explained his plan. Basically, they would all come together and form a "legislative liaison team" for each of the candidates who had been elected at the national and state levels. They would meet with the candidates once a month and ask what they had done that month and what they needed from the team. The team would then report to each representative what it was seeing and feeling on the ground at home. He later explained this to me further in an interview:

> You either got a principled candidate in or we don't. But in any event, we have to watch 'em. We have people who made commitments to us, who told us stories when they were out on the stump. And now that we've put them into office, we have to watch them and make sure that they do what they said they were going to do. I kept thinking it through, and I said, "Well, our representative is one of us." . . . So I said our representative should not go to Washington by himself. He should go as a member of a team. We should be there to watch him and keep him from straying from the fold. And at the same time, we should support him—if they're bad-mouthing him in the newspaper, we should cover his back. If he isn't doing what he said he was going to do, we have to support him from our end. This becomes a combination of accountability and responsibility—accountability on the representative's part and accountability on the constituent's part. And notice I don't use the word *leader*, but I use the word *representative*. Because in our theory, we don't have elected leaders—we have elected representatives. So, we're teamed with our representative. . . . That's how we took it to the next step. What do you do after the election? You watch who you sent down there and make sure they do what they said they would do. And that's how the concept came about.

Back at the pizzeria, Jamie was getting excited listing the different ways they could work together—the Tea Party groups and their representatives— as a team. He explained, "Let's say he needs letters. He just has to say the word and we'll send letters to whoever he needs us to! If he has a hearing, or if he needs bodies in D.C. for something, he can turn to us. We will be the support he needs, to do what he needs to do!"

Up until this point, I had kept an eye on Linda, who had been nodding patiently. Although she was the founder and leader of the Patriots, she welcomed new ideas from participants and typically gave Jamie and the other more outspoken members of the group free reign to share their ideas at group meetings and rallies. But at this point, she interjected. In her no-nonsense tone, she corrected Jamie's comment that "we will be the support he needs." Instead, she said, "Not so much *supporting* as *saying,* "Don't forget." She looked skeptical, but Jamie barreled on: "Right, right, exactly. And if he does something we don't like, we will tell him."

For the next few weeks, I scanned Linda's email each morning for a mention of the new initiative and saw nothing. I asked around at the next few events, and no one knew anything about it. The holidays came, and the meetings stopped. I wondered if they would ever start again. Or had the group run its course?

In late January, I met with Linda at a diner near her home to hear her thoughts about the past year and the future of the group. I asked what had become of Jamie's idea. She explained that she had met with her "main people" shortly after the election. Jamie had been pushing his plan, and people did not want to do it. I asked whether they agreed with his premise that it was necessary to hold these elected officials accountable, and she said they did. The problem, she explained, was that this should be a "concerted effort of *two thousand* people, not *two.*" She elaborated: "[The idea] was to have two people represent a group of people, and speak for a group of people, without having a meeting to understand what that group of people is thinking. I couldn't do that. *I wouldn't do that.* I'd rather tell you, 'Here's what happened. Send an email.' It's much more effective if you are in an elected position, I would think, to get two thousand emails, letters, calls, opposed to meeting with two people that supposedly represent two thousand people."

Not only did she think Jamie's plan would be less effective than what they were currently doing, but she also thought the idea of selecting a handful of people to "represent" the interests of the entire group was incongruent with the group's vision of what it meant to be an active citizen. Group members were not supposed to just sit back while someone represented them—this kind of passivity was, after all, what many believed had led to the country's current troubles. Rather, members were each supposed to actively follow issues, develop informed positions, and communicate their preferences to their representatives.

As the group's leader, she encouraged practices that reinforced this vision. Even her role in the group reflected this ideal, as she explained: "I am nothing more than a mechanism of pertinent information. It's all I am. What they do with it, they do with it. Whatever I write, if it warrants something that sticks with them, they send an email. Or they show up. And I think that's much more effective than me going and meeting with [the congressman] and saying, 'Well, I'm speaking for all my people.' Well, no I'm not, because I'm not talking to all of them every single day! Some of them, I've never even spoken to at all. So I *can't*." Jamie's plan was, in short, incompatible with the logic that organized the Patriots' work together.

Although I had, at the time, been surprised to hear her say this, I understood her point. When Jamie first described his plan to me, I could not help but note its structural *similarity* to Interfaith's approach to accountability. Internally, it presupposed that a small number of individuals could earn the authority to speak on behalf of their entire community, just as Doris had at Interfaith's action involving conditions in her apartment building. Externally, the type of relationship his model envisioned existing between the teams and their representatives (not "leaders") was an ongoing give-and-take between partners, marked by mutual "accountability and responsibility." With mutual understanding, knowledge sharing, and partnership at the center of the team model, it resembled the kind of "listening community" that Interfaith sought to develop. While none of the Patriots, to my knowledge, drew a parallel between the team plan and the work of community organizations like Interfaith—whose tactics they tended to view with suspicion—it made sense in light of this congruence that they would view the plan as inappropriate.

But this was not the last I heard of the team plan. Like many of the Patriots, Jamie approached active citizenship with the same entrepreneurial spirit with which he ran his business. For members like him, the Patriots were one of many vehicles through which to pursue projects like these. Jamie took the idea to a neighboring Tea Party group, and they adopted the plan. It is noteworthy that this other Tea Party group also chose to endorse candidates, something the Patriots refused to do on principle, for essentially the same reasons they were uncomfortable with the team-based plan.

The fact that this Tea Party group embraced Jamie's plan confirms that the Patriots did not reject the idea because it was not "conservative"

enough—indeed, both groups embraced a similar set of conservative principles. Rather, it suggests that even within the same movement, different
local groups may be animated by subtly different visions of how citizens
should interact with one another and with government, or conversely, that
even within two groups sharing the same basic imaginary, the appropriateness of practices could be interpreted differently.

In the end, by choosing not to adopt the plan, the Patriots distinguished
their way of doing things from the methods of both this neighboring Tea
Party group and community organizations like Interfaith. Despite their
different ideological commitments, both Interfaith and the neighboring
Tea Party group viewed it as appropriate—even meaningful—to empower
a subset of leaders to speak on behalf of the group as a whole. In contrast,
the Patriots worried that empowering a subset of leaders who were just as
unaccountable to the group as their elected representatives risked undermining their newfound roles as active and informed citizens. By referencing their broader visions of active citizens' proper role within a democracy,
the Patriots interpreted the team plan as an inappropriate way to organize
their relationships to one another and with their elected officials, and they
did not pursue it.

Replacement versus Persuasion

Since their earliest days, the Patriots had viewed elections as a powerful
mechanism of accountability. This idea was straightforward: with enough
individuals mobilized they could replace any elected official who did not
properly represent their interests; and the very threat of replacement
would provide them with the necessary leverage to make demands upon
sitting representatives.[16] When determining whether a representative was
doing his or her job properly, members drew a distinction between *career
politicians*—viewed as out of touch and more interested in preserving
their status and power than serving their constituents—and *citizen politicians*, viewed as "people like us" who remained connected to their constituents' lives even if this meant bucking the party establishment. With
this in mind, the Patriots elected two of their own members to public
office during the 2010 election cycle while also supporting a variety of
other Tea Party candidates. The following year, Linda decided that she,

too, would put her "money where her mouth is," as she told me, and announced she was running for a local legislative seat. The group thought that by electing "people like them," they would ensure greater accountability; but they soon confronted the reality that the system could corrupt even those lawmakers who started out as "one of them."

Following that first successful election, the Patriots watched as these newly minted Tea Party politicians struggled to represent group members' values and interests. Some of the Patriots sought to understand the practical complexities of their representatives' new roles. Linda for example, adopted a "realist" position: "If you believe, at their core, they're trying to do the right thing, you gotta give 'em a little rope." But many in the group declared these politicians traitors to their cause and vowed to replace them at the next opportunity, just as they had replaced the previous officials whom they believed had not truly represented them—recall Gilbert's threat at the county budget hearing: "We'll remember in November."

This latter approach was more natural for a group of people who framed their relationships with elected officials in terms of a zero-sum battle between individual freedom and government control. Through this lens, an oppositional stance was necessary to avoid ceding too much power to those officials. Giving them "a little rope" could be dangerous. But a perpetual campaign of replacement required collective action, and this had proven difficult for this group as well. As Phil once explained to me, "When you want to work on a political campaign or work inside politics in any way, it requires that the group work together and throw their support behind a particular candidate." But, he went on to say, "with these guys, it's very difficult, because any form or any sign that somebody's trying to exert authority within the group, and people get squeamish and run."

In 2012, several members of the Patriots—including Jamie and Phil—pitched a transition to "Tea Party 3.0" as a solution to this dilemma. In their telling, Tea Party 1.0 had been all about education and distancing themselves from politics. Tea Party 2.0 had been focused on education, too, but it had also involved supporting candidates. Tea Party 3.0 would still involve participation in electoral politics, but they would be "getting in the trenches and trying to take over the Republican Party from the inside," as Phil put it. This was "about engaging in politics rather than distancing ourselves from it." But it was also quite individualized—as individuals (and sometimes without revealing their affiliation with the Tea Party) they would work to infiltrate their local Republican committees.

In the meantime, they would also continue to pursue individual tactics outside of party politics: blogging about what their representatives were doing, reading the news from multiple sources in order to reveal the truth, and speaking at public hearings. In different ways, each of these practices expressed their view that vigilance was a necessary (though not necessarily sufficient) ingredient in any recipe for accountability. These tactics were less directly confrontational than some of their earlier efforts and certainly less public and performative. (As Phil once explained to me, "The Tea Party is not dead. We're alive. We're just not in show business anymore. We don't need to make a show in public.")

These tactics were also more diffuse and potentially less effective. Yet these practices—of insider agitation and of vigilant critique—had the benefit of being consistent with the group's way of imagining what it meant to be an active citizen: they placed the responsibility to act on individuals, while acknowledging a role for cooperation and camaraderie; and they expressed an inherently oppositional relationship between individual freedom and government control. As a result, these practices were accepted as logical expressions of what it meant to be a patriot.

Counterintuitively, the Patriots' move away from a strategy of coordinated electoral replacement reflected an acknowledgment of the same limitations cited by Jeffrey Stout in his study of faith-based community organizing. In Stout's view, electoral accountability strategies are insufficient. "When used in isolation from the exercise of other political rights," he writes, "voting often provides too little accountability, too late."[17] He thus argues that groups must pursue accountability through other means, and he holds up as a model the accountability practices developed within the progressive faith-based community-organizing field.

Like the groups that Stout studied, Interfaith, too, viewed elections as insufficient mechanisms of accountability. Although the membership occasionally experimented with electoral strategies, these consisted primarily of "get out the vote" campaigns. Describing how they approached potential voters in their congregations, Nora once paraphrased their message: "It's time to vote. We don't care who. But it's time to vote." From afar, it may seem surprising that Interfaith's members did not emphasize their electoral power more. Their public accountability actions involved gathering large crowds of their neighbors and partners, and these could have been viewed as powerful displays of their potential electoral force. Yet they did not threaten coordinated electoral action to replace officials who did not do their bidding. This was in part due to restrictions imposed by their nonprofit tax status, but it also would have felt contrary to their vision of what it means to engage in active citizenship. Indeed, instead of threatening replacement, they typically sought to persuade decision makers by offering either information that could change their positions or moral arguments that could shift their priorities.

For example, during a group discussion about a local priest's discomfort with confrontational organizers, Rev. Fischer explained why he viewed Interfaith's style as different: "We don't go after politicians via confrontation," he explained, "because we know this only makes them dig [in] deeper. Our model is more human and thorough in knowledge and research." An older Catholic man in the group nodded then added, "Yes. More than confronting them, our model is about converting them."

This was an apt description of their process. During my time with the group, they met in almost equal numbers with Democrats and Republicans, seeking out conversations with anyone who had the power to influence the issues on which they were focused. Michael, an elderly Catholic man involved in the group's health-care working group, once explained when proposing that they set up a meeting with their newly elected Republican congressman: "It need not be a Democrats versus Republicans thing." Rather, they needed to "try and address him in terms of moral imperatives." There was some debate around the table concerning whether they would actually be able to influence the congressman's thinking. Someone noted that the congressman was not currently talking about health care as a moral issue. Still, Michael insisted that if they set up a meeting with him, and if "different denominations come together and talk to him about the moral argument, it will be harder for him to ignore us." One woman concurred: "He couldn't talk the same way in that context."

Nora interrupted at that point and said they probably shouldn't assume they would be able to "convince him," but that instead they could "neutralize him." She suggested, "We should just try to listen to him and build a relationship with him and try to understand that he is under a lot of pressure as a congressman." Helen took issue with this approach, suggesting they needed to be more forceful. "We need to use our power," she said. "We need to say this is a moral and social imperative; this is what we hear from your *constituents*." Her use of this term, which clearly referenced their electoral power, provoked a response from Michael. His voice now raised, he insisted that they should speak not simply as the congressman's "constituents" but rather as a "faith-based voice." Rev. Fischer nodded and said he would support him if he wanted to set up a meeting. Despite her protests, Helen agreed to attend the meeting. Nora told Michael to set it up and assured him that the working group would be there.

Viewed side by side, the two groups' discussions about electoral "replacement" as a strategy of accountability reveal how their imaginaries shaped the practices they viewed as most appropriate. In both cases, the groups were capable of mobilizing large numbers of voters to replace elected officials who were not representing their interests. The Patriots' disillusionment with this strategy and their shift toward other forms of individualized action (inside and outside of the party system) reflected a concern that a perpetual replacement strategy required collective action that would be difficult to square with their general resistance to internal authority. They deliberately chose an alternative path that allowed for both an oppositional stance and maximum individual autonomy.

Interfaith, too, viewed replacement as an insufficient strategy, but for quite a different reason. Threatening to replace a representative for not representing their interests would imply a narrower conceptualization of their relationship with their representatives than the one cultivated by Interfaith—a contract rather than a covenant. It also implied a narrower conceptualization of self-interest. As we saw in the case of Tanya's struggle to make sense of Interfaith's approach, they viewed each individual's self-interest as a starting point from which to seek the common good. As a result, they sought to draw elected officials into extended relationships through which they could work together, as partners, to determine where their varied interests and values intersected for the good of the community as a whole.

APPROPRIATENESS AND CULTURAL DIVERGENCE

Interfaith and the Patriots both sought to improve the relationships of accountability that undergird democratic life, yet they developed different styles of holding government accountable. The style each group adopted reflected their idealized vision of how active citizens ought to behave. In examining how the groups' democratic imaginaries influenced their styles of action, we have seen that these imaginaries were pulled down into the groups' discussions and debates; they were interpreted in the course of the groups' interactions; and ultimately they channeled the groups toward certain behaviors and away from other (seemingly plausible) options.

A close look at several moments in which each group struggled to determine the best course of action, and at differences in the ways that the groups confronted similar challenges, illuminates how this process works. These accounts reveal a key mechanism through which the groups' imaginaries shaped their choices about how to act and interact. In each case, the group was guided by considerations of what kind of action was *appropriate* for a "group like them" in light of how members understood their roles as active citizens.

Even after the groups had developed shared ideas about who they were and what it meant to be active citizens—when we might have expected their decisions about how to act to become automatic, habituated, or routine—moments regularly arose in which group members were prompted to artic- ulate reasons for pursuing one path versus another seemingly plausible path: for example, when more established group members articulated typi- cally unspoken reasons for the groups' actions in order to teach newer mem- bers "how they do things"; when new ideas were proposed that pushed the limits of what "groups like us" do; or when disappointing outcomes required group members to reevaluate why they had chosen a certain path. In each of these unsettled situations, group members referenced their abstract understandings of how citizens ought to relate to one another and to gov- ernment as justification for choosing one path over another. In such moments, these imaginaries served as moral compasses, helping the groups to navigate between alternative choices about how to work together.

For example, when members of Interfaith routinely insisted that it was their role as people of faith to be a moral voice and to treat their partners with civility, this led them to choose a style that was less confrontational than other styles available to them. This choice did not reflect their "progressive" political stance—after all, the other community-organizing network and local labor union they distanced themselves from shared many of their progressive policy goals. In spite of this policy agreement, Interfaith chose a different path, one that allowed them to live out their understanding of their role as prophetic voices in their community, which was tempered by a covenantal understanding of how to interact with one another and with elected officials. The fact that they chose this path over one that might have enhanced their immediate political impact also serves as evidence of the way in which appropriateness, more than simple efficacy, shaped and constrained their group actions.

Similarly, the Patriots' choice to pass on the team-based plan to hold their elected representatives accountable did not reflect their "conservative" political stance—after all, the plan was adopted by a neighboring Tea Party group that shared their conservative policy goals. Rather, the Patriots' choice reveals how group members' visions of how active citizens should behave shaped their interpretations of what kinds of practices were appropriate. The Patriots sought to cultivate active citizens capable of confronting their elected officials with knowledgeable demands and vigilantly holding them accountable for keeping the promises they have made. They made these demands as individual citizens, based on their own experiences, concerns, and interests, even as they also worked together to refine their skills as researchers, debaters, and public speakers. The proposed plan sought to transform this loose agglomeration of mutually supportive but autonomous individuals into a team that spoke with one voice. This was interpreted by Patriots members as inconsistent with their shared understanding of the nature of their relationships to one another and with their elected officials, and they passed on the idea.

Finally, an analysis of each group's stance toward replacing elected representatives who were not serving their interests demonstrates how members of both groups, in order to justify the choices they made, referenced their shared understandings of how citizens should interact with their elected officials. In the Patriots' case, the transition to Tea Party 3.0 was pitched explicitly as a means of respecting individual autonomy while also maintaining an oppositional relationship with government officials.

Meanwhile, when the Interfaith member explained that, "more than confronting them, our model is about converting them," this justified the group's strategy of pursuing long-term relationships with their representatives and of working through those relationships to persuade them to see issues differently. By explicitly referencing these ideals, members of the two groups were not only channeled toward decisions that reflected their imagined role as active citizens but also reassured that they were already on the right path.

As these varied examples show, the groups' choices about how to act and interact with others were filtered through considerations of what styles of action were appropriate for "groups like them" in light of their respective visions of how democracy worked and the proper role of active citizens within it. Knowing this helps us understand how two groups committed to a similar ideal of good citizenship could nonetheless develop divergent styles of putting that ideal into action. It also offers some insight into why groups like the Patriots and Interfaith view one another's tactics with suspicion, despite their shared desire to hold government accountable. If their approaches to accountability were reflections of their underlying democratic imaginaries, then disagreements over whether any given approach was appropriate was really a disagreement over more fundamental questions about how representative democracy ought to work and the proper role of citizens in it.

7 Conclusion

In my mind I often return to that urban church auditorium, that suburban hotel meeting room, and many rooms like them, where I heard people from very different social worlds mourning the death of the American dream. Their grief was real, as was their anger and their disappointment and their cynicism. But so was their hope. In gatherings like the ones discussed in chapter 1, people saw that their personal troubles were also their neighbors' troubles—to paraphrase the sociologist C. Wright Mills, they came to view these as public issues.[1] Unlike most Americans, whose anxiety paralyzed them, or who chose distraction over action, these individuals decided to join others to confront head-on the problems they believed the country was facing. They would try to change the way the system worked so that it better served people like them.

To be sure, members of Interfaith and the Patriots had dramatically *different* ideas about how their government could best serve people like them. But when we begin by situating these groups in a broader historical and political perspective, this allows us to look at them differently than we might if we viewed them exclusively in the context of contemporary political polarization. This broader perspective shifts our focus from the ends they sought—the policy demands that were often the most visible aspect of their efforts—to the means through which they made these demands. It also shifts our focus from their specific policy preferences to their concerns about the political process itself. Both Interfaith and the Patriots organized to more effectively insert their voices, values, and knowledge into this process while also critiquing and seeking to reform it. When we focus on this aspect of their work, surprising similarities between the groups become visible—similarities that set them apart from most other Americans. One of my primary goals in this book has been to illuminate these similarities.

In the context of economic crisis and rising discontent with government's responsiveness to ordinary citizens, these individuals set out to become active citizens. In so doing, participants in both groups tapped into one of several historically available models of what good citizenship looks like. In justifying their choice to become active citizens and distinguishing this choice from alternatives, participants in both of the groups drew on a *civil discourse* that valorized the qualities associated with active citizenship and a *civil religious discourse* that interpreted active participation in the American democratic project as sacred. In the process, members of both groups worked to reimagine how a democratic society ought to work and how active citizens like them could best enact their role within it.

This account of the parallels between these groups' efforts challenges some of our prevailing understandings of how conservative and progressive groups participate in American public life. Both of these groups embraced a contentious approach to exerting people power that is more typically associated with groups on the political left. Both groups also asserted that religion offers values, lessons, and notions of "the good" that can help solve the country's most pressing problems—a claim typically associated with groups on the political right. Focusing on these similarities destabilizes these kinds of assumptions and forces us to develop a fuller and more nuanced picture of the contemporary political landscape.

But there are also meaningful differences in how Interfaith and the Patriots engaged in active citizenship. Although they referenced a common model for their actions, the United States' complex political and religious heritage supplied them with a wide array of often-competing and contradictory stories, symbols, and ideas, as well as a large repertoire of tactics, organizational forms, and practices from which to draw in their efforts to put this ideal into action. They ultimately drew on different clusters of these ideas, symbols, and practices, and as a result their shared ideal of active citizenship took two different forms in practice. Explaining the nature and source of this divergence has been my second major goal in this book.

Throughout, I have sought to describe the groups' efforts as evenhandedly as possible, and to heed Michael Schudson's warning not to judge such efforts against any single model of how political participation *ought* to work.[2] Schudson's work, after all, highlights the fact that active citizenship is only one of many ways for Americans to enact the role of citizen. This book builds on this observation: it demonstrates that active citizenship itself takes a variety of forms today, each reflecting a different practical understanding of what it means to be a good citizen in a democracy. Moreover, it shows that the groups themselves were aware of the existence of these varied styles, and worked diligently to frame their respective styles, and the democratic ideals underlying them, as more authentically American than other alternatives.

IMAGINARIES IN ACTION AND INTERACTION

Regardless of where one stands on this issue, the comparison of these two groups refines our understanding of how broadly shared political ideas and ideals are brought to life in different ways by actual groups of citizens. When demonstrating how this complex process worked in this case, I have paid particular attention, first, to the role of group *narratives* in the development of divergent imaginaries, and second, to a key mechanism through which these imaginaries shaped and constrained the groups' styles of action and interaction—namely, via group deliberations about what kinds of practices were most *appropriate* for a group like them.

Narratives: Putting Imaginaries in Motion

As the men and women I studied worked to fulfill their roles as active citizens, they took inspiration from other men and women in history, each of whom, through hard work and bravery, had challenged the country to live up to the democratic promise on which it had been founded. Studying these models from the past was an important way in which members of the two groups became informed about how citizens could become involved in political life. And as these examples were referenced in the course of each group's efforts, they coalesced into shared narratives of active citizenship. Yet the groups' narratives took meaningfully different forms. Although they each supplied group members with exemplary models of how active citizens should interact with their fellow citizens, with government, and with God, they featured different historical exemplars, emphasized different pivotal events in history, and linked these through different plotlines.

Moreover, as chapter 3 shows, the clusters of narrative elements that each group gravitated toward were not selected at random. Members of these groups tended to draw on the stories and symbols that were most prominent in the broader political, religious, and media subcultures in which they were embedded. This was because these elements were more familiar to them owing to this exposure, but also because gatekeepers sometimes policed the perceived appropriation of "their" heroes and stories by rival subcultures. The resulting narratives that each group assembled supplied the groups with different ideal-typical models of active citizenship—the prophet and the patriot.

By providing models of how active citizens in history acted and interacted with others in various contexts, these narratives helped the groups to collectively imagine what it would look like for them to carry forward this tradition of active citizenship. When the groups referenced these shared narratives in the course of their work together, this facilitated a process through which these understandings were refined and through which new group members were introduced to them. These narratives thus helped group members collectively define who they were, who they were not, and what they were doing together. They put the groups' imaginaries in motion.[3]

Appropriateness: Channeling Action and Interaction

When we keep these different narratives in mind, a close look at the groups' religious and political practices, discussed in chapters 4 and 5, reveals not only that each group developed a distinctive style of active citizenship but also that these styles reflected their respective ways of imagining how active citizens should act and interact with others. Understanding precisely how their imaginaries influenced their styles required attention to the process through which these imaginaries were pulled down into the daily lives of these groups and interpreted in the course of their work together. Through this process, as described in chapter 6, the groups' divergent imaginaries channeled participants toward certain practices and away from others.

Chapter 6 also specifies a key mechanism through which this worked in these cases. In each situation described, the groups were guided, more and less explicitly, by their understanding of what kind of action was *appropriate*—not only for the context in which they were acting but also in light of how a "group like theirs" should ideally act. It was these perceptions of appropriateness, more than evaluations of effectiveness or ideological motivations, that consistently channeled the groups toward their respective styles of active citizenship. In the day-to-day lives of the groups, this was most visible when group members explicitly referenced their abstract understandings of how citizens ought to relate to one another, to government, or to God as justification for choosing one style of action over another. In these instances, their imaginaries operated as moral compasses, helping them navigate between alternative choices about how to work together.

This sometimes involved measuring themselves against their ideal model of active citizenship, and sometimes involved distinguishing themselves from other groups that were engaging in styles they viewed as inconsistent with their ideal model. In cases where the groups engaged in this kind of boundary work with other groups, it is noteworthy that these other groups often shared their ideological commitments and policy goals. What they did *not* share was the same vision of citizens' ideal relationship with one another, with government, and with God.

Their choice to distance themselves from these potential allies highlights the extent to which these groups were not *exclusively* focused on short-term political victories (although they were also focused on these). They had also organized in order to reimagine how American politics ought to work. By developing group cultures and practices that reflected their ideal visions of democracy and citizenship, Interfaith and the Patriots each prefigured the kind of politics they sought to bring about through their action.

CULTURAL BARRIERS TO POLITICAL COOPERATION

Understanding this process not only advances our understanding of the complex cultural underpinnings of political action but also helps to resolve a political question that I considered frequently during my fieldwork: If these groups are so similar, why don't they work together? In chapter 1, I recounted the familiar refrain I heard while crisscrossing the state conducting fieldwork for this book: "I worked hard and followed the rules my whole life, and now I have nothing to show for it. What do I do now?" I also recounted thinking that if there was ever an opportunity for working and middle-class Americans to come together in shared grief, this was the time.

Of course, I was cognizant that these groups would disagree on most questions of policy; but they had similar critiques of the policy-making process and of the political system itself. The forms their action took also shared a common history and were developed in response to shared political challenges and, as a result, had certain structural features in common. The sociologist Pierre Bourdieu argued that this kind of homology between groups could become the basis for unlikely political alliances.[4] And indeed, political life is replete with strange bedfellows who join forces on one shared project only to face off on another.

Would it be so different for these groups to team up to demand greater government accountability and responsiveness to citizens? My curiosity about whether this was possible deepened as the groups' similarities came into clearer focus. But gradually, so too did my understanding of why it was unlikely that groups like the Patriots and Interfaith could ever work together.

The reason has little to do with differences in their policy goals, although these were substantial. Rather, it was the very thing that they shared—their commitment to active citizenship—that ultimately prevented them from viewing one another as potential allies. Although both groups sought to reassert the role of ordinary citizens' voices, values, and knowledge in political life, they did so in profoundly different ways. And these differences were not random; they reflected different readings of America's past, present, and future and different understandings of how ordinary citizens should interact with one another and with government.

These divergent democratic imaginaries filtered the groups' perceptions of what kinds of organizational forms, cultural practices, and political tactics were appropriate in any given situation. This led them not only to develop different styles of active citizenship but also to view alternative choices as inappropriate, undemocratic, and even un-American. This made it difficult for them to simply view one another's style as a different, equally legitimate expression of the same shared ideal—instead, they viewed one another's style as a potential threat to democracy itself.

Despite the fact that certain common features may have been visible to an observer like me, these groups inhabited very different interpretive worlds. The notion that groups would be able to overcome such a meaningful cultural barrier in order to pursue shared goals underestimates the moral salience of these interpretive differences.

FAITH IN THE AMERICAN DEMOCRATIC PROJECT

Americans are not linked to one another by blood or by creed. They are not necessarily bound by shared customs, norms, or even language. Nor do all Americans share common memories of the country's past or expectations of its future. Yet when people identify as Americans, they reference more than a legal status; they speak as part of a political "people." To declare oneself part of the American people is to claim a set of political and social rights as a citizen of the most powerful democratic nation in the world and to embed oneself in a community of other Americans, to whom one acknowledges certain moral and political obligations.

This political community is *real*—in the sense that hundreds of millions of real individuals call themselves Americans, carry U.S. passports, and reside on U.S. soil. But it is also *imagined*. As Benedict Anderson argues in his classic study of nationalism: "All communities larger than primordial villages of face-to-face contact (and perhaps even these) are imagined. Communities are to be distinguished, not by their falsity/genuineness, but *by the style in which they are imagined*" (emphasis added).[5]

We should expect that just as Americans represent a variety of races, ethnicities, religions, cultural heritages, and so on, so too would they have a variety of ways of imagining what it means to be part of the American people. In the words of the political scientist Rogers M. Smith, they will tell many different "stories of peoplehood."[6] And indeed, we have seen that Interfaith and the Patriots did tell different stories of American peoplehood. Moreover, when they set out to enact their roles in the ongoing story of America, the divergent ways in which they imagined what it meant to be part of the American people channeled them toward different styles of action.

Despite these differences, however, members of both groups were unwavering in their faith in the American democratic project itself. And this may be the most significant feature of American political culture that this book illuminates—even groups who viewed one another as opponents recognized the same set of stakes in the fight. This finding underscores the observation by the historian Stephen Prothero that "the nation rests not on agreement about its core ideas and values, but on a willingness to continue to debate them." And this debate is never settled. Indeed, he notes, "in every generation, the nation must be imagined anew."[7]

Interfaith, the Patriots, and countless groups like them are participants in this ongoing project of reimagining the nation; but it is not quite accurate to say they reimagine it *anew*. When these groups tell stories about America that emphasize the pivotal activities of active citizens, they are drawing from a deep reservoir of stories, symbols, and ideals that circulate in American political culture—the historical residue of two and a half centuries of efforts by Americans to bring democracy to life through their vigilant critique of the political system.

Some readers will likely be troubled by the fact that from this common well of culture and history, groups could assemble such different understandings of the country's past, present, and future. Surely, they will argue, one is right and one is wrong. Those on the political left will be quick to point to inaccuracies in the Patriots' historical knowledge and understanding of how the contemporary political process works; those on the political right will do the same to Interfaith. And both camps will be partly right. As the historian Jill Lepore and the journalist E. J. Dionne Jr. both argue, most stories of America are historically inaccurate to some degree.[8] Rogers M. Smith's transnational analysis goes further, suggesting that no stories of peoplehood are complete or universally shared.[9] This is particularly true in societies as diverse as the United States. These stories are ever changing, perennially contested, and unavoidably incomplete.

The instability of the American story may also cause concern among those who seek to locate the broadly shared ideas and ideals that *all* Americans share. When the sociologist Robert Bellah wrote his now classic 1967 essay about the American civil religion, this was described less as a *religion* per se than as a unifying *story* to which all Americans could subscribe, despite their myriad religious and political differences. In the years that followed, however, Bellah himself was among the first to sound the alarm warning that the civil religion could no longer hold the nation together amid growing cultural atomization and fragmentation.[10] More recently, other scholars have registered concern that the emergence of competing, and seemingly irreconcilable, ideas about the meaning of American citizenship and of America's place in the world could spell trouble for democracy itself.[11]

This is a genuine concern, and one that feels even more urgent as divisions between citizens appear to deepen. Yet it is unclear whether, in any era of American history, there was a broad cultural consensus about these questions. Indeed, sociologists of religion N.J. Demerath III and Rhys H. Williams suggest that groups and subcultures have always referenced different (even contradictory) stories of American democracy.[12] This more conflictual view of U.S. political culture is consistent with a large body of historical scholarship documenting the ways in which American politics have always been marked by competition between "multiple traditions." Indeed, residues of these varied political traditions continue to be felt symbolically, rhetorically, and institutionally in American political life today.[13]

Unfortunately, much of the research on these competing traditions has been based on public opinion research or on the rhetoric of political elites, leaving us with only a surface-level understanding of how these traditions are brought to life and contested by actual groups of citizens. This book begins to fill this gap by illustrating that these competing visions of American citizenship and democracy do not passively circulate through American political thought; they are actively carried and put into practice by groups like Interfaith and Patriots.

VARIETIES OF ACTIVE CITIZENSHIP: A BLESSING AND A CURSE

People will surely disagree about whether these groups' visions of active citizenship are good or bad for American democracy, but this does not change the fact that the aggregated efforts of groups like these actually *comprise* America's complex democratic tradition, for better or for worse. This tradition is living—it is not merely a set of abstract principles enshrined in law; it is hundreds of millions of citizens trying (and often failing) to put these principles into practice. It is improvisational; it is messy; it often produces outcomes that are inconsistent with large groups of Americans' values.

American democracy, as we have seen, also means profoundly different things to different people. The complexity of this tradition is both a blessing and a curse. On one hand, the fact that it is possible for groups to weave together such different stories of citizenship has generated perpetual disagreement over what it means to be a good citizen. And because much of this disagreement is based, not on facts, but on choices about which aspects of the country's heritage to emphasize, and on how stories are interpreted, this disagreement has proven nearly impossible to resolve.

At the same time, however, these different ways of imagining the nation—however partial and imperfect—also play a powerful role in political life by embedding a diverse array of citizens in structures of meaning that encourage political commitment, help people interpret changing political realities, and enable them to chart courses toward alternative futures. As a result, they facilitate citizen involvement in political life. If one accepts the view that widespread citizen participation is necessary for a functioning democracy, then one must welcome the participation of even those citizens with whom one disagrees.

Although this will inevitably generate conflict, conflict may not necessarily be such a bad thing. Rather than calling for a return to a mythical past in which all Americans embraced a single vision of democracy and citizenship, it is worth considering Rogers M. Smith's alternative vision of democratic flourishing. The "Madisonian" solution he proposes embraces the "inescapable realities of the always-continuing, always-competitive politics of people-making."[14] Put differently, as long as multiple groups cultivate and enact different stories of America, and no single story becomes dominant, then citizens can productively interrogate their respective benefits and drawbacks.

It may be tempting to silence those groups whose visions of American peoplehood seem especially problematic. But our judgments about which stories are most troubling will surely differ, and silencing one's fellow citizens contradicts widely shared democratic values. Alternatively, if groups are encouraged to bring competing narratives—even those perceived as extreme and troubling—into public view, then citizens have the opportunity to evaluate them side by side and deliberate about their merits and dangers.

It is my hope that this book enables its readers to do just this. By stepping outside of these two groups' interpretive worlds, I have sought to describe, as evenhandedly as possible, how they each imagined American democracy and their role within it. I have also shown how their respective visions of democracy translated into different ways of practicing active citizenship. It is ultimately up to readers to consider which of these stories, if either, aligns with their own ways of imagining the nation, and how they too might transform their ideals into action.

Methodological Notes

STUDYING AND COMPARING CITIZEN
GROUPS ETHNOGRAPHICALLY

This appendix elaborates on the descriptions, provided in chapter 1, of the fieldwork, the groups, and the methods I employed when conducting the research for this book. In addition, it includes a more extended discussion of a key challenge of conducting multisite comparative ethnography across the political divide—namely, how I evaluated and managed my position in relation to the two groups.

FIELDWORK, GROUPS, AND METHODS

The preceding chapters draw primarily on data collected through ethnographic fieldwork with Interfaith and the Patriots between 2010 and 2012. During this time, I produced more than a thousand typed pages of detailed field notes and collected thousands of pages of print and digital materials (e.g., flyers, newsletters, training materials, and online communications) that circulated within the two groups during this period. I also conducted fifty interviews with participants in the two groups, including repeated interviews with selected core members in order to gain insights into how they were navigating changes their group faced over the course of the fieldwork. In addition, during the three years after I left the field, I continued to follow up with selected participants in both groups, receiving regular updates in person, by email, and by phone, and observing their activities both online and off. Together, these data are the basis for the material presented. Below, I present more specific details about my fieldwork with each group.

Patriots

I began spending time with the Patriots toward the end of their first year of activity. They had gained momentum rapidly, swept forward by the excitement of participating in what quickly became a national Tea Party movement. In the wake of this momentum and early electoral victories, the group swelled in size and regularly turned out large crowds at rallies, meetings, and protests. But group members' hopeful spirit was tested time and again as they confronted evidence that "politics as usual" endured. During the time I spent with the Patriots, the group alternated between bursts of enthusiastic activity and periods of dormancy.[1]

I introduced myself to group members as a researcher interested in grassroots citizen activism. Because Linda was in the process of completing her bachelor's degree—having returned to school after raising her five kids—she was particularly supportive of this research. Most of the Patriots knew I was from "the city" and affiliated with a university many associated with "liberals." Whenever asked, I told them that my personal politics were to the left of theirs, but that I was there with an open mind to learn about the issues that concerned them and spurred them to action. Most responded that they were open to people of all political stripes who sought to be informed participants in the political process. With few exceptions, they welcomed me into their activities, and I developed friendly and mutually respectful relationships with them.

During this time, I attended the majority of their meetings and rallies, as well as occasional social gatherings. In addition, I attended candidate meet and greets and debates sponsored by area Tea Party groups; spent a weekend with volunteers staffing the group's informational tent at a local flea market; accompanied group members to a local shooting range for "some good old American Pistol/ Rifle Shooting" and a group discussion about gun rights; volunteered alongside group members at the campaign headquarters of a popular Tea Party–backed candidate for statewide office; joined the early risers among them to pass out their group newspaper to morning train commuters; and traveled with them to Glenn Beck's Restoring Honor Rally in Washington, D.C.

In addition, I attended meetings of other community groups with which Patriots members cross-pollinated: the local Republican Club's Friday night "Pizza and Politics" discussions, a meeting of a local taxpayers' watchdog group, and a regular gathering of veterans. I also followed several of my key contacts in the Patriots to their activities with other local Tea Party groups, since some were involved in several area groups. Observing the interactions between these groups proved instructive.

Overall, my role in the group was generally that of a low-level participant who did not take on a leadership position. This generally involved immersing myself in the group's online communications and media worlds and regularly attending group meetings, rallies, and other activities. Beyond merely being present, I also occasionally took on more specific tasks like carrying supplies or signs, or running errands with other group members. This position offered opportunities for close observation of group dynamics and interactions while also providing some insight into the experience of participating in the group.

My field notes are supplemented by material drawn from the group's extensive body of electronic communications, which I systematically collected during my time with them. Many of the Patriots posted regularly on social networking platforms like Meetup, Facebook, and Twitter and received email communications from national organizations supporting Tea Party activism—the Tea Party Patriots and FreedomWorks, for example. I, too, plugged into most of these outlets during my time with the Patriots. At the height of their activity, I received twenty to thirty emails on average per day from different local and national groups, and the databasing software that I used to collect web content captured nearly that many blogs and comments posted daily by Tea Partiers I knew personally.

Most significant to the internal life of the group, however, was a daily email called the *Must Know News*, which is discussed in chapter 2. Each edition was written by Linda but crafted with the input of group members who contacted her about their concerns each day. This daily news digest can thus be seen as a crystallization of the groups' collective sentiments, and it is an invaluable source of insight into the group's culture and understanding of issues at any given moment. Over the course of fieldwork, I systematically collected 726 editions (nearly every edition) spanning the period from October 14, 2009, to January 11, 2013.

Although thousands of people immersed themselves in this online community, the group's face-to-face activities drew smaller crowds: local rallies could draw several hundred people; between twenty-five and seventy-five people attended most group meetings and activities. Of these, around ten were considered core members who, along with Linda and her husband, steered the group's major strategic decisions. These included many of the individuals in this book, such as Gilbert, Jamie, Phil, and Cam, among others.

Interfaith

I also draw on data collected through ethnographic fieldwork with Interfaith, a faith-based community-organizing coalition affiliated with the PICO National Network. During the period in which I conducted fieldwork, PICO as a whole was enjoying increasing prominence, having played a pivotal role in pressing for the reauthorization of the children's health insurance program in 2009. As a result, they had a seat at the table in ongoing national debates about health-care reform, immigration, and bank accountability, and they were eager to provide this platform to their local leaders while also showcasing their grassroots strength to national decision-makers. For Interfaith members, it was a time of excitement and activity interspersed with periodic lulls, during which the group assessed whether their limited resources and membership base were sufficient to support their activity levels and future needs.[2]

In an introductory meeting with Nora, Interfaith's executive director, I explained that I had become interested in PICO's work during a previous research project and wanted to understand how the local organizing process worked on the ground. Just as I did with the Patriots, I introduced myself to group members as a researcher interested in grassroots citizen activism and explained that I was there with an open mind to learn about the issues that concerned them and spurred them to action. Similarly, I shared my own political views whenever asked. They were patient and supportive of my research; some were even excited that their typically low-profile efforts were being chronicled. As with the Patriots, I developed friendly and mutually respectful relationships with them.

During this time, I attended a majority of their groupwide activities, including organizing and leadership training sessions, quarterly meetings, the annual general assembly, and most of their public accountability actions. However, these groupwide events constituted only a portion of the group's overall activities. Because Interfaith organized primarily around issues facing individual congregations or neighborhoods, much of its activity occurred within smaller groups of volunteer leaders within these congregations or neighborhoods. These smaller groups were called local organizing committees or social justice ministries or teams. On occasion, a cluster of neighboring congregations and other local organizations joined forces and formed a working group focused on a shared concern.

While I was conducting fieldwork, a group of predominantly white, middle-class leaders in the neighborhoods of Riverside and Hillside worked on issues related to health-care affordability and access, while groups of predominantly black (African American and Caribbean) low- and middle-income leaders in Westside worked on issues related to immigration, economic justice, housing, and bank accountability. Toward the end of my fieldwork, a majority-Latino congregation also became involved in Interfaith's work, focusing on health care and immigration.

I became a regular participant in the working group focused on health-care affordability and access. For around eighteen months, ten to fifteen core members of this working group met in Riverside one to two times per month. The working group included leaders from Catholic, Lutheran (Evangelical Lutheran Church in America), and Jewish congregations and a local faith-based hospital. Participants were religiously diverse, but the large majority (including me) were white, middle-class professionals. Although Interfaith's membership as a whole was quite diverse, this subset of the group shared many demographic characteristics with the Patriots. Having exposure to this relatively privileged subset of Interfaith's overall membership proved a helpful means of evaluating (and eventually ruling out) the possibility that the groups were simply motivated by different material interests.

During the meetings of this working group, I participated in much the same way as the other participants and was often assigned the role of notetaker or given research assignments. I also attended and played minor roles in "research actions" (information-gathering meetings) with state and local elected officials and other stakeholders in the local health system, and traveled with Interfaith leaders to actions where they worked alongside leaders from other PICO coalitions from around the country. The health-care working group included many of the individuals in this book, including Nora, Robert, Rev. Fischer, Tanya, and Helen, among others.

Although much of my time was focused on the health-care issue, I also closely followed the group's other localized activities through observations of public actions organized by the other congregations and working groups, interviews with key participants, and regular discussions with Nora, the staff organizers, and the clergy. These interactions, in addition to my regular participation in coalition-wide activities, enabled me to develop a broader set of relationships, including with several other individuals in this book, such as Father O'Donnell, Farah, Doris, and Raquel, among others.

Finally, I accompanied Interfaith's staff organizers to two congregations that were in the early stages of organizing. On these occasions, the organizers conducted training sessions on key aspects of Interfaith's organizing model, sometimes with my assistance. One of these congregations subsequently became more active, while the other stalled in its progress. Observing this process offered insights not only into how the group's organizing model and philosophy were presented to outsiders but also into how newcomers were incorporated into their efforts. Overall, my position in the group offered opportunities for close observation of group dynamics and interactions, as well as enabled insight into the experience of participating in the group.

Representativeness of Groups

Although the Patriots considered themselves part of the national assemblage of groups known as the Tea Party movement, and although they were generally comparable to other Tea Party groups demographically and in terms of their policy attitudes, no single group can be considered representative of the movement as a whole.[3] In their study of the national Tea Party movement, Theda Skocpol and Vanessa Williamson highlight meaningful variation across local Tea Party groups.[4] Likely among the most significant sources of this variation was the political and economic context in which groups operated. For example, although Tea Party activity in the country was observed primarily in "red" states, the Patriots operated in a state that traditionally voted Democratic.[5] The feeling of political marginalization that this generated was compounded by the economic position of their suburban and rural communities in relation to the urban center of the state, which not only is a liberal stronghold but also has thrived economically even as the rest of the state has been weakened by decades of deindustrialization. The resultant perception of an imbalance in power between the city and the rest of the state fuels resentments that permeate the statewide political landscape and provides context for aspects of the Patriots' talk and practices that may not be shared by Tea Party groups operating in different contexts.

Similarly, although Interfaith was part of the broader faith-based community-organizing field, no single coalition is representative of this field as a whole. Still, in contrast to the internal variation found within the Tea Party movement, most of the coalitions that comprise this field employ similar organizing models that share historical and institutional roots. This is not to suggest they employ these models in identical ways, but rather that they share a common set of tools with which to build their group cultures. Coalitions differ more significantly in their demographic compositions and in the political and economic contexts in which they operate. In demographic terms, Interfaith was slightly above the national average of all FBCO coalitions nationwide in terms of its religious, racial, and income diversity, and below average in terms of its educational diversity.[6]

With regard to community context, Interfaith was working to build power in one of the most densely populated and diverse cities in the nation, one that has a large, established civil society in which new groups were constantly emerging. This contrasts sharply to some of PICO's most established groups, which operate in cities where the PICO affiliates are among the major grassroots players on the political scene.[7] This meant Interfaith not only faced more competition for decision makers' time and attention but also had to engage in broader coalition building. With very limited staff and resources, they sought to balance these demands with the more fundamental work of developing leaders within their member congregations. Taken together, these factors provide context for the group's talk and practices, inflecting their efforts in ways that may not be shared by FBCO coalitions operating in different contexts.

Although neither the Patriots nor Interfaith is perfectly representative of its respective national movement, the comparison still offers insights into the similarities and differences between Tea Party activism and faith-based community organizing. As discussed in chapter 1, this is useful insofar as these two movements have never before been systematically compared to one another. It is also a rare example of an ethnographic comparison of conservative and progressive movements.

More generally, we can also view these groups as two cases of active citizenship. Dozens of grassroots groups and civic organizations dedicated to active citizenship emerge every year in most cities.[8] Of course, no two groups could be representative of this field as a whole, and indeed there are features of Interfaith and the Patriots—like their use of religious discourses and practices—that are not shared by other groups engaged in active citizenship. Still, the general findings of this book offer insight into this broader field of activity. By offering a detailed analysis of these two groups, this study allows us to more precisely understand the relationship between how groups imagine and practice active citizenship in the United States today.

ETHNOGRAPHY ACROSS THE POLITICAL DIVIDE: A SYMMETRICAL APPROACH

As discussed in chapter 1, the collection and analysis of data about these two groups were carried out as neutrally and symmetrically as possible. In practice, this meant suspending judgment about what motivated participants in each group, how they defined themselves and understood their actions, and how they situated their efforts in relation to others. It also meant applying the same basic analytic strategy to both groups while making every effort not to squeeze both cases into an explanatory framework that fit one better than the other.

In addition to applying a symmetrical approach to the analysis, I also sought to maintain a relatively symmetrical position in relation to each group during the fieldwork itself. This task is complicated for all multisite comparative researchers, but it is particularly challenging when conducting research in politically dissimilar or opposing groups.[9] Political affinity with the people one studies can enable a researcher to achieve access to and rapport with, as well as gain the trust of, his or her research subjects. Alternatively, lack of political affinity can impede access, rapport, and trust.[10] Studying two groups with which one has differing degrees of political affinity can create unique challenges with regard to one's relationships to research subjects.

By extension, this could also impede one's ability to communicate authoritative knowledge about one's research site. After all, ethnographers often emphasize their *closeness* to research sites as signals of access, as evidence of the depth of their knowledge, and as the basis of their authority to make empirical claims.[11] To be close goes beyond what the sociologist Gary Alan Fine refers to as becoming "an *expected* participant in group life, and not an *ethnographic tourist*, appearing when convenient."[12] After all, this is a principle of most good ethnography. Many ethnographers also highlight the fact that they have achieved intimacy with research subjects, transgressed the boundary between a stranger and a friend, and perhaps most significantly, aligned their personal interests with those of their subjects.[13]

This emphasis on closeness, however, largely presumes closeness to one group of actors (whether they are studied within one bounded place or followed through multiple geographic and institutional spaces over time). The question is whether it is also crucial for multisite comparative research. To the extent that being close to one's research subjects has implications for the knowledge that one is able to produce and communicate about each site, this would suggest that comparative researchers should seek to achieve equal degrees of closeness to each group they study, or *symmetrical closeness*. This presents a unique challenge to those who engage in multisite ethnography, particularly across the political divide. When researchers have different degrees of political affinity with their research subjects, questions inevitably emerge about whether they are closer to one group than another and, more acutely, whether this will meaningfully influence their analysis.

The reality, however, is that focusing exclusively on political affinity with one's research subjects ignores other sources of potential affinity that can help secure access to, rapport with, and the trust of research subjects and, by extension, the authority to make claims about them. Indeed, throughout this research, it proved useful to reflect on my position in relation to research subjects along multiple axes, including but not limited to political affinity. One's relationship to research subjects along each axis could be defined in terms of closeness/distance, insider/outsider, or similarity/difference, depending on which is relevant in each case.

These axes included group membership (how easy or difficult was it to become a member and/or feel like part of each group?), demographic characteristics (how similar or different was I, in terms of my race, gender, age, and socioeconomic position, to other members of each group?), religious identity (to what extent did I share religious values, beliefs, or practices with members of each group?), political affinity (to what extent did I share each group's political goals?), and other amorphous factors (to what extent did I develop a friendly rapport with members of each group?).

For example, with regard to group membership, while people familiar with my research often assumed it was more difficult to gain access to the Patriots than to Interfaith, the Patriots' openness to newcomers and frequent online communications about events and activities helped me gain entry to their group relatively easily. Membership in the Patriots was informal, defined more by showing up than signing up. By reading Linda's daily email and regularly attending events, I was quickly able to follow conversations, recognize references, and generally feel "in the flow" of group life. This feeling deepened as I developed relationships with people in the group, who informed me of less widely advertised events and filled me in on conversations and situations that I missed. The barrier to entry for newcomers seeking to participate in the Patriots' activities was thus significantly lower than it was for Interfaith, in which formal membership was required and members could join only through their congregations. Despite the fact that Interfaith leaders welcomed my presence as a researcher, inconsistent communications from the group sometimes created the feeling that I was out of the loop, especially early in my fieldwork. It was only after developing a network of relationships with group members that I was able to overcome this initial barrier.

This asymmetrical feeling regarding group membership helped balance my asymmetrical political affinity with the two groups. And this is only one example. Overall, my position in relation to each group on each axis of identity varied, and I experienced different degrees of insider-ness, closeness, and sameness in relation to each group in different ways. The bottom line is that I was not truly an "insider" in either group. My position in relation to both groups was more akin to what Paul Lichterman calls an "insider-outsider," or to Georg Simmel's notion of a "stranger," whose position "does not simply involve passivity and detachment; it is a particular structure composed of distance and nearness, indifference and involvement."[14]

Although this position did not involve symmetrical closeness per se, it did allow me to maintain a relatively balanced position overall in relation to each group without compromising access to, rapport with, or the trust of participants. In fact, it may even have permitted me to gain insights that a pure insider would not have gained, either because an insider would have taken for granted certain aspects of group life that I took note of, or because group members may have been less willing to explain things to an insider than to someone with relative distance from their social world.[15]

In the end, this position proved invaluable to my analysis of these groups. After all, as discussed in chapter 7, members of these groups operated within different interpretive worlds, which shaped their perceptions of what kinds of information were credible, their perceptions of their relationships with people outside of their groups, and their perceptions of what practices were meaningful and appropriate. During fieldwork, I commonly caught myself being pulled into one interpretive world or another. Whether I had been with the Patriots or Interfaith, I would often arrive at home after an extended period of time spent with them and announce that I had heard something about a political figure or issue, only to find that it was not true, or more often, that it was not the whole story. I was sucked in and then yanked out each time I moved between these groups or to and from my "real" life.

I existed for several years in this liminal space—embedded in multiple interpretive worlds but immersed fully in none. The experience challenged many of my own political assumptions and has permanently altered my political outlook. But it also enabled me to trace the understandings outlined in this book. It is my hope that this book provides readers with a similar kind of destabilizing experience, and that this helps them gain a deeper understanding of American political life today.

Notes

ONE. INTRODUCTION

1. With the exception of references to public figures, the names of individuals, groups, and places are pseudonyms. In certain cases, selected details have been withheld or altered to protect individuals' privacy. Excerpts of conversations and details of interactions are drawn from extensive field notes, transcripts of interviews and selected events, and print and electronic materials collected during ethnographic fieldwork between 2010 and 2012 and follow-up observations and conversations during the following three years. When conversations were not recorded verbatim, I have reconstructed them as faithfully as possible from detailed field notes. See the appendix for more details about the fieldwork, data, and analysis.

2. The other national organizing networks are Gamaliel, the Industrial Areas Foundation, and National People's Action. Regional networks include the DART (Direct Action and Research Training) Center in the Southeast and Midwest, the Ohio Organizing Collaborative, and the Inter-Valley Project in New England. In addition to *faith-based* community organizing, the terms *broad-based, congregation-based,* and *institution-based* refer to organizing models with similar historical and institutional roots.

3. "Obamacare" was the name many Americans used to describe President Obama's health-care reform bill, which was officially called the Affordable Care Act and was signed into law on March 23, 2010.

4. This perception, communicated through populist rhetoric on the political left and right, is supported by evidence that the U.S. government is more responsive to economic and political elites than to ordinary Americans (e.g., Gilens 2014).

5. Several scholars examine moral and political disagreement within American society, including Luker (1984), Ginsburg (1998), Klatch (1999), and Lakoff (2002). Hunter (1991) argues that a steep uptick in this disagreement has culminated in a "culture war" (see also Wuthnow 1988), yet others question whether there has been a significant increase in polarization among the public (see DiMaggio et al. 1996; Fiorina et al. 2005; Greeley and Hout 2006).

6. Much sociological research attributes political action to the instrumental *ends* that individuals or groups seek. Scholars have, however, increasingly called for theories of political action that apply regardless of actors' ends. Efforts in this vein include work on repertoires of contention (e.g., Tilly and Tarrow 2007), deliberation (e.g., Jacobs et al. 2009), and populist politics (e.g., Jansen 2011; Calhoun 2012), all of which are aimed at illuminating the *means* through which politics is practiced, independent of the ends sought.

7. In 2011, Beck left *Fox News* and founded his own multimedia news platform.

8. Alinsky 1946:46.

9. As reported in *Politico*, "Employees of [former House Majority Leader Dick] Armey's FreedomWorks group have been studying and using Alinsky's methods . . . since before he got hot, as an alternative to traditional conservative organizational tactics that focused on influencing elites and intellectuals. And FreedomWorks' organizers utilized and spread the Alinsky gospel as they traveled the country last year helping newly engaged tea party activists set up their own groups" (Vogel 2010).

10. See Schlozman et al. 2012.

11. McAdam 1986.

12. According to a 2016 Pew Research Center analysis, the voter turnout rate for the 2012 presidential election in the United States was 53.6 percent, far lower than turnout rates for comparable elections in other OECD countries, including Belgium (87.2 percent), Turkey (84.3 percent), and Sweden (82.6 percent), and only slightly higher than for Switzerland (38.6 percent), the OECD country with the lowest turnout (Desilver 2016).

13. Prothero 2012:1, 2.

14. Schudson 1998, 2006.

15. Schudson 1998:6.

16. Schudson 2006:592.

17. Schudson 2006:592.

18. Schudson 1998.

19. Schudson 1998:147.

20. Schudson 1998:147.
21. Schudson 1998:147.
22. Schudson 1998:187.
23. Schudson 1998:6.
24. Taylor 2007:3.
25. Chaves (1994) defines secularization as declining religious authority and argues that it is necessary to independently examine the nature and extent of this decline at the individual, organizational, and societal levels. As an example, he notes that the United States is "a society in which rather uniformly high societal-level secularization coexists with substantial internal variation on individual-level secularization" (761). See also Casanova 1994; Wuthnow 1994; Yamane 2000.
26. See Herberg (1955) on U.S. religious life in the early twentieth-century. The 1965 Immigration and Naturalization Act, also known as the Hart-Cellar Act, replaced national-origins quotas with a system that prioritized family reunification, skilled workers, and political refugees.
27. According to the Pew Research Center's 2014 "U.S. Religious Landscape Survey," 70.6 percent of Americans identify as Christian and 1.9 percent identify as Jewish. See Wuthnow (2005) on the implications of religious diversity for Americans' religious understandings.
28. According to the Pew Research Center's 2014 "U.S. Religious Landscape Survey," 22.8 percent of all Americans, and 36 percent of respondents aged eighteen to twenty-nine, identify as atheist, agnostic, or nothing in particular.
29. See Hout and Fischer 2002; Masci 2015.
30. Hunter (1991) acknowledges that not all liberal groups are *secular*, per se, but highlights their *secularist* visions of public life.
31. Casanova (1994) demonstrates that religious groups are "going public" around the world, despite significant changes to the religious landscapes in which they operate. For additional discussions of liberal/progressive religious organizations involved in advocacy and activism, see Hertzke (1988), Hofrenning (1995), Wuthnow and Evans (2002), Fowler et al. (2014), Braunstein et al. (forthcoming). On why religious activism is typically viewed as conservative despite the widespread presence of liberal/progressive religious groups, see Braunstein et al. (forthcoming).
32. See Audi and Wolterstorff 1997; Habermas 2006, 2008. Scholars also argue that certain religious institutions, values, and practices laid the groundwork for the historical development of democratic public expression and continue to foster democratic participation today. See Zaret 1992; Weithman 2002; Calhoun 2008.
33. See Bellah et al. 1985; Wuthnow 2011.
34. For example, Casanova 1994; Stout 2010; Yukich 2013.
35. See Eliasoph and Lichterman 2003; Lichterman and Eliasoph 2014.

36. See Wood 1999, 2002; Eliasoph and Lichterman 2003; Wilde 2004; Perrin 2006; Blee 2012; Leondar-Wright 2014; Lichterman and Eliasoph 2014.

37. The strategy of comparison employed in this case is consistent with a most-different research design, which involves the comparison of cases that maximize difference along most known axes of comparison yet share a common "outcome"—in this case, the groups' engagement in "active citizenship." The selection of the cases themselves followed what Glaser and Strauss (1967) call "theoretical sampling." Lichterman (2008: 89) applies a similar logic to his selection of two cases that are "conceptually comparable" but which "maximize variation" on factors of conceptual interest.

38. There are two main benefits of ethnographic comparison of dissimilar groups. Empirically rich ethnographic data on each group enables detailed *within-case* analyses and comparisons. But because each group also serves as a foil to the other, *across-case* comparisons are also used to further sharpen the within-case insights. Theoretically, similarities in the patterns found across both groups suggest more generalizable patterns at work. Lichterman and Eliasoph (2014) further elaborate these benefits. In this vein, it could also be fruitful to compare *multiple* cases, as a handful of recent studies have done, albeit by relying on either quantitative methods or team-based field research (Perrin 2006; Blee 2012; Baiocchi et al. 2014).

39. For example, Boyte 1989; Hart 2001; Osterman 2002; Wood 2002. Although Warren (2001) and Stout (2010) briefly consider how FBCOs compare to more conservative grassroots efforts, this is not central to their analyses.

40. See Rosenthal and Trost 2012; Skocpol and Williamson 2012; Parker and Barreto 2013; Fetner and King 2014; McVeigh et al. 2014; Deckman 2016.

41. See Alterman et al. 2011; Dovi 2011; Friedersdorf 2011; Gitlin 2011; NPR Staff 2011.

42. Skocpol and Williamson (2012:90–92) conducted a systematic count of active Tea Party groups during spring–winter 2011 and found more than eight hundred regularly meeting local groups, some of which claimed more than five hundred members.

43. Although few local Tea Party groups considered themselves formally affiliated with a single national organization, there were nonetheless a variety of national organizations seeking to speak on their behalf, as detailed in Zernike (2010a), and Skocpol and Williamson (2012). These groups provided some organizational support and training to local groups but did not dictate their day-to-day activities.

44. A 2011 census of FBCO coalitions operating nationwide found that this field as a whole represented over 5 million people, up from around 2 million in 2001. Contextualizing these figures, the authors of the 2011 census report note, "Associations incorporating such a high proportion of citizens are rare in American history; those that have done so have profoundly shaped society during challenging times" (Wood 2002; Wood et al. 2012).

45. This is not to say there has been no research on these groups. In the past decade, the FBCO field has received increasing attention from scholars (e.g., Hart 2001; Warren 2001; Osterman 2002; Wood 2002; Swarts 2008; Bretherton 2010, 2015; Stout 2010; Day et al. 2013; Wood and Fulton 2015) and practitioners (Jacobsen 2001; Chambers and Cowan 2003; Gecan 2004; Whitman 2007).

46. See Wood and Fulton 2015.

47. Because FBCOs occupy this niche position, Braunstein et al. (2014) refer to them as "politically oriented civic organizations." This same label could be applied to many local Tea Party groups.

48. See Skocpol et al. 2000.

49. A handful of excellent studies comparing groups on opposite sides of the political spectrum are exceptions (e.g., Luker 1984; Klatch 1999; Ginsburg 1998; Fetner 2008; Massengill 2013).

50. This issue is rooted not only in the ways that researchers *explain* political action but also in the *organization* of research itself. For example, social movement researchers ask questions about which characteristics unite "conservative movements," yet it is telling that there is no category of "progressive movements"—movements are simply assumed to be progressive unless stated otherwise (McAdam et al. 2005; Blee and Creasap 2010). This results in the sorting of movements into different categories for analysis based on their position on the ideological spectrum and, by extension, different theoretical explanations for their action.

51. See Baiocchi et al. 2014. See also Summers-Effler 2010; Blee 2012.

52. Alexander and Smith (1993) and Alexander (2006) examine the structure and use of civil discourse (also called the "discourse of civil society").

53. Williams and Alexander (1994) and Gorski (forthcoming) show that various groups draw on civil religious discourse to justify and lend meaning to their political actions.

54. Stout (2010:100) refers to this as a "moral concept of a citizen," which can "outstrip the corresponding legal category." This meaning differs from Glenn's (2002) concept of substantive citizenship, for which legal citizenship is a necessary, albeit insufficient, precondition.

55. See Volokh (2015) on public debates about how to describe the American political system.

TWO. BECOMING ACTIVE CITIZENS

1. Much of the written work that was circulated within the group, including early editions of this newspaper, did not include individual attributions of authorship. When material was borrowed from publicly available sources, I was

often able to identify the source through online searches. But there were many instances when it was unclear if things had been written by group members (and if so, by whom) or borrowed from other sources.

2. This mantra is listed as rule 5 of Kibbe's *Rules for Patriots* (a reference to Saul Alinsky's *Rules for Radicals*), which states, "When a lawmaker heads to your state capital or Washington, D.C., they are instantly surrounded by special interests, well-organized and well-funded national groups who have a stake in how policy is set. So if you aren't the ones showing up in your lawmaker's office, on the phone, and in the mailbox, the only ones who are showing up are the entrenched special interest groups that don't necessarily have your best interests in mind." On the connection to Alinsky's book, Kibbe writes, "To America's Founders and the Sons of Liberty, who won our freedom; and to Saul Alinsky, whose rules we expropriate to win it back." See http://rulesforpatriots.fwsites.org/rules-for-patriots/.

3. See DeYoung et al. 2004; Emerson 2006.

4. Evidence suggests that internally diverse groups have more strategic capacity and, thus, greater political efficacy (Ganz 2000, 2009; Warren 2001); and political organizations that reflect the diversity of the communities they represent possess greater political legitimacy (McCarthy 1995; Parekh 2002; Chambers 2003).

5. Schudson 2006:592.

6. See Alexander and Smith 1993; Alexander 2006.

7. See Schlozman et al. 2012.

8. Schumpeter (1942) views this as citizens' primary role in a representative democracy.

9. Representative democracy is a compromise between elite control and direct control by citizens. Individual citizens relinquish some of their authority over decision making and allow elected representatives to act "on the basis of their enlightened knowledge and wisdom, on their deeper moral commitment to democracy and its long-term health," according to Schlozman et al. (2012:105). This system works as long as representatives' goals are aligned with those of their constituents and citizens believe their representatives have their best interests at heart. When these conditions are not met (or are not perceived to be met), the system loses its legitimacy.

10. Mansbridge (2003:515) distinguishes between "anticipatory representation" (in which "representatives focus on what they think their constituents will approve at the next election, not on what they promised to do at the last election") and "promissory representation" (in which representatives "made promises to constituents [during the previous election], which they then kept or failed to keep"). To these election-centric concepts of representation, she also adds "gyroscopic representation" (in which "the representative looks within, as a basis for action, to conceptions of interest, 'common sense,' and principles derived in part from the representatives' own background").

11. See Lessig 2011.

12. Stout 2010:70.

13. Skocpol (2003) argues that the professionalization of advocacy has transformed ordinary citizens from active participants to names on a mailing list. More recently, social networking platforms have become a major channel for casual political engagement (see Smith 2013). Contributing money to political campaigns and candidates is an increasingly common, albeit relatively inactive, form of political participation (Schlozman et al. 2012). Finally, Americans engage in charitable giving and volunteer work at high levels, yet this work is often individualized, depoliticized, and disconnected from broader efforts to reform social and political systems (Wuthnow 1991; Eliasoph 1998).

14. Alexander 2006; see also Alexander and Smith 1993.

15. Alexander 2006:57–59.

16. See Bellah 1967.

17. While this is not a religious narrative per se, Bellah (1967) observed that it has a distinctly religious *structure*, which appeals to citizens of a nation that is highly religious despite also being (even in its earliest days) sensitive to public displays of sectarianism.

18. Gorski (forthcoming) builds on Bellah's (1975:3) formulation of civil religion as a narrative that the American people draw upon to "interpret its historical experience in the light of transcendent reality." But he distinguishes between what he views as the authentic "American civil religion" and religious nationalism. While his subsequent distinction between prophetic religion and religious nationalism is invaluable, I conceptualize both, along with civic republicanism, as strands of a multifaceted civil religious discourse that ordinary citizens can draw upon in practice. Because movements use civil religious symbols and stories in complex ways that do not necessarily map onto the "ideal-typical" traditions that Gorski delineates (e.g., Williams and Alexander 1994), this broader conceptualization enables me to demonstrate how each group references various elements of this discourse across different contexts.

THREE. NARRATIVES OF ACTIVE CITIZENSHIP

1. Bellah (1967) identified three "times of trial": when Americans faced defining questions about how they would handle independence, slavery, and their role as the world's leader. I use this term in a more open-ended sense, as any moment when Americans feel that the future of the country is at stake.

2. This phrase, found in the preamble to the Constitution ("We the people of the United States, in order to form a more perfect union . . ."), was more recently used as the title of President Obama's March 18, 2008, speech on the role of race in his life, his campaign, and the country's history.

3. Dionne (2012) and Lepore (2010) point to inaccuracies in the historical narratives embraced by Tea Party groups and, more broadly, by contemporary

conservatives. Yet they also acknowledge that *most* narratives of American history are partial and distorted, reflecting the political interests and perspectives of the tellers and the moments in which they are being told. Smith (2003) places contestation over "stories of peoplehood" in broader historical and political perspective.

4. This is a reference to Ayn Rand's novel *Atlas Shrugged*, which has become a key cultural reference for contemporary libertarians.

5. The term *Founding Father* is used most broadly to describe those men who were instrumental in the country's fight for independence. When defined in this way, some of the Sons of Liberty, including Samuel Adams and Patrick Henry, as well as influential authors like Thomas Paine, are counted among them. Historians in recent decades have sought to further broaden the category of founders to include several Founding Mothers (Norton 1980). Narrower uses of this term reference only a handful of key figures from this period, with an emphasis on those who signed the Declaration of Independence or took part in drafting the Constitution. This group typically includes John Adams, Benjamin Franklin, Alexander Hamilton, John Jay, Thomas Jefferson, James Madison, and George Washington (Morris 1973). While the Patriots occasionally referenced the broader set of Founding Fathers, they mainly focused on those men who were involved in the drafting of the founding documents.

6. See Liptak (2010) and Zietlow (2012) on the constitutional philosophies that have been embraced and popularized by the Tea Party movement.

7. Crapanzano (2001) traces parallels between religious and political-legal literalism in American society from an anthropological perspective. Approaching the issue from a legal perspective, Smith and Tuttle (2011:693) argue that constitutional originalism and biblical literalism "share a core commitment to the idea that their relevant texts have a timeless, fixed meaning that is readily ascertainable. In addition, both interpretive approaches are in significant part projects of restoration; both are deeply concerned about the loss of constraint that results from interpretation that is untethered to text; both have a strong, self-consciously populist impulse and an equally strong and self-conscious disdain for elite opinion, with respect to both interpretive norms and cultural values; and both maintain that all other approaches to their relevant texts are fundamentally illegitimate because they breach a duty of fidelity."

8. See Hooper 2010.

9. See Dionne 2012:38.

10. Wilentz (2010) writes of *The 5,000 Year Leap:* "By the time Skousen died, in 2006, he was little remembered outside the ranks of the furthest-right Mormons. Then, in 2009, Glenn Beck began touting his work. . . . After Beck put the book in the first spot on his required-reading list—and wrote an enthusiastic new introduction for its reissue—it shot to the top of the Amazon best-seller list. In the first half of 2009, it sold more than two hundred and fifty thousand cop-

ies. Local branches of the Tea Party Patriots, the United American Tea Party, and other groups across the country have since organized study groups around it." See also Dionne 2012.

11. Here, the Patriots were tapping into a perspective that has been gaining adherents within conservative circles since the 1950s, according to Wood (1988), who observes, "We Americans attribute to the revolutionary generation and to the creation of the Constitution a sacred, quasi-religious character. . . . Many Americans believe that there at the 'Founding' some permanent truths about politics were established, and that we depart from them at our peril."

12. In June 2009, the *Chicago Tribune* posted the cartoon online with the caption "This is a 1934 Chicago Tribune political cartoon that many say rings true in today's political and economic climate. What do you think?" See www .chicagotribune.com/lifestyles/health/sns-pod-1934-cartoon-pic-photo.html.

13. See Kruse (2015) for a history of how religious conservatives, corporate opponents of big government, and anticommunists became allied in the wake of the New Deal and the Cold War.

14. During the 2016 election season, a partisan disagreement emerged about how to refer to the terrorist organizations Al Qaeda and ISIS. Republican presidential candidates criticized President Obama for his unwillingness to refer to these groups as "radical Islamic terrorists," while Obama insisted that using this term legitimized the terrorists' claim to represent Islam (Greenberg 2015).

15. See Walzer 1985.

16. Smith 2003.

17. Taylor 2004:23. By examining how imaginaries are enacted by groups of ordinary citizens and how they animate contemporary civic life, I extend previous work on social imaginaries that has focused on macrohistorical shifts in these understandings, and on the cultural and institutional conditions under which they emerge in elite discourse and eventually permeate entire societies. See Gaonkar 2002; Anderson 2006.

18. These narratives are thus *collective* versions of what Somers calls "ontological narratives" (1994:618), in which social actors define who they are, what they are doing, where they have been, and where they are going. Whereas individual ontological narratives are typically based on biographical time, collective versions of these narratives embed groups in historical time. In this sense, they are rooted in "public narratives" (1994:619). The ability of narratives to "locate" actors in time is also discussed by Hadden and Lester (1978). See also Hunt and Benford 1994; Tilly 2002; Polletta 2006.

19. Two qualities that enable stories to carry different meanings for and facilitate communication between different groups of political actors are the ambiguity of their symbols and metaphors and their openness to interpretation. See Nepstad (2001), Stone (2002), and Polletta (2006) for examples of how this works in different kinds of political settings.

20. Although collective identities are often viewed in terms of membership in preexisting categories (like race, gender, or class), a large body of research finds that collective actors do not simply exist; *they are made.* Collective identities are constructed through a variety of group practices, referred to as "identity work." See Snow and Anderson 1987; Fantasia 1988; Gamson 1992; Calhoun 1994; Schwalbe and Mason-Schrock 1996; Bernstein 1997, 2008; Polletta and Jasper 2001; Reger et al. 2008. When storytelling practices are involved, this is referred to as "narrative identity work" (see Hunt and Benford 1994; Somers 1994; Tilly 2002; Polletta 2006).

21. See Gamson 1992.

22. See Alexander and Smith 1993; Alexander 2006.

23. Brubaker 2004:47, 44.

24. See Lichterman 2005. See also Perrin 2006; Glaeser 2011.

25. In this way, their narrative structurally resembles the jeremiads associated with conservative Christian elites like Jerry Falwell, which directed blame outward at "evil" forces, from "Gentiles" to secular humanists to international foes; but also occasionally accused American Christians of being too passive in responding to moral decay, a response that parallels the Patriots' self-approbation for their past political complacency (Gorski forthcoming).

26. See Norton 1980; Manseau 2015.

27. Deckman (2016) underscores the surprising progressivism inherent in the Tea Party movement's elevation of women leaders at every level of their movement.

28. This archive can be conceptualized as a kind of "cultural repertoire"—the available set of political and religious symbols that are recognizable or familiar to members of a society, and on which public actors draw when framing their activities. See Williams 1995; Jasper 1997.

29. Gorski (forthcoming) refers to these clusters of texts, characters, and historical narratives as "traditions." Although scholars of American political culture emphasize important distinctions between these traditions, ordinary citizens are likely to mix elements from various traditions they encounter.

30. Whitman (2007) and Stout (2010) explicitly situate faith-based community organizing in a historical lineage that includes several of these past movements.

31. See Dionne 2012:41.

32. *The Glenn Beck Program* (Premiere Radio Networks), MediaMatters for America, May 26, 2010, http://mediamatters.org/video/2010/05/26/beck-says-his-8-28-rally-will-reclaim-the-civil/165327.

33. See Montopoli 2010.

34. See Baiocchi et al. 2014. More generally, on the ways future-oriented thinking can shape action, see Emirbayer and Mische 1998; Mische 2009; Gibson 2011; Blee 2012; Frye 2012; Tavory and Eliasoph 2013.

35. See Meyer 2006.

36. See Gorski forthcoming.

37. Gorski (forthcoming) argues that in the Hebrew prophetic tradition "time is spiral." See also Walzer 1985.

38. Dionne 2016:1.

39. This experience is akin to what McVeigh (2009) calls "power devaluation," a process that can, under certain conditions, spur relatively advantaged people to engage in collective action.

40. See Smith 2003; Lepore 2010.

FOUR. PUTTING FAITH INTO ACTION

1. See Casanova 1994; Chaves 1994; Taylor 2007.

2. See the Pew Research Center's 2014 "U.S. Religious Landscape Survey."

3. Klassen and Bender (2010:12) highlight the complexities of conceptualizing "pluralism" and call for greater attention to "religious interactions as they take place in the world." They note that existing academic discussions of pluralism fail to "adequately acknowledge the great diversity (and sometimes conflict) within particular religious traditions or the ways in which the political projects of pluralism (whether religious or otherwise) hinge on exclusions and occlusions of various religious and political actors."

4. See Braunstein et al. 2014. Percentages are based on the religious composition of Interfaith's board of directors, which was composed of representatives from each of Interfaith's member congregations. No board members were conservative Protestant or "other." Meanwhile, the organization overrepresented religious minorities, like Jews and Muslims, who represented approximately 1.5 percent and 1.1 percent of the U.S. population, respectively, based on the 2012 General Social Survey (Smith et al. 2012).

5. One lobbyist for a local hospital was involved in the health-care working group; and one woman involved in local education activism became an "adopted" member of the group.

6. These groups are generally absent from such efforts. See Wood et al. 2012.

7. See also Yukich forthcoming.

8. See Wood et al. 2012.

9. See Swartz 2012; Steensland and Goff 2014.

10. Bean (2014) identifies cultural forces that encourage members of evangelical congregations to identify as conservatives (and often, Republicans) despite the fact that some report liberal or progressive attitudes on some issues. Yukich and Braunstein (2015) show that although *individuals* of various faith traditions, including evangelicals, participate in interfaith political work, *organizations* that officially speak on behalf of religious communities are often bound by

their stakeholders to engage in religious boundary maintenance that complicates interfaith work. These mechanisms may prevent evangelical congregations from officially participating in FBCOs that involve interfaith cooperation.

11. One respondent who identified as Baptist and one who identified as born-again Christian were counted as Evangelical Protestant; two who identified as Episcopalian were counted as mainline Protestant.

12. See Jones and Cox 2010.

13. See Khan 2011; see also Hagerty 2010.

14. Beck's language here can be viewed as civil religious, in that it avoids sectarian specificity, "ties together understandings of God's will with national history, and projects a mandate for rightly-guided action onto all members of the national community" (Williams and Alexander 1994:4).

15. This line of questioning closely echoes Beck's (2010) discussions about this issue: "You've heard Barack Obama say that his 'individual salvation depends on collective salvation.' What does that mean?"

16. See Beck 2010.

17. See Herberg (1955) and Alexander (2006) on the acceptance of Catholics and Jews as "American" after facing nativist sentiments as newcomers.

18. This was according to ACT's website in October 2010.

19. Many religious practitioners, as well as much research on prayer to date, conceptualize prayer in these ways. Yet more recent research has expanded our understanding of the public and communicative dimensions of prayer. Ladd and Spilka (2002) find prayers can have inward, outward, and upward dimensions, with the outward aspects focused on establishing "human–human connections." Focusing on this outward dimension, Wuthnow (2008) argues that spoken prayers can function as ways of communicating with others. Warren (2001) and Braunstein et al. (2014) show how this works in political groups.

20. See Braunstein et al. (2014) for an extended discussion and analysis of these prayer practices.

21. His paraphrasing blended different translations. According to a translation commonly used by Catholics, the New Revised Standard Version, this psalm is titled "The blessedness of unity" and begins, "How very good and pleasant it is when kindred live together in unity!" In the New American Bible (Revised Edition) translation, this psalm is titled "A vision of a blessed community" and begins, "How good and how pleasant it is, when brothers dwell together as one!"

22. For examples, see Braunstein et al. 2014.

23. Diaz-Edelman (forthcoming) refers to practices like these as part of a "multicultural activist etiquette," which socially diverse activist organizations use to promote equality and security among participants.

24. This is similar to the kind of commonplace talk about "safe" religious topics that Bender (2003:24) observed among volunteers at a nonprofit service organization.

25. See Wood 1988.

26. Kruse 2015.

27. This concern is articulated by the "Million Windows" Campaign, a project of the Congressional Prayer Caucus Foundation, which seeks to reaffirm the centrality of phrases like "In God We Trust" in American public life (http://ingodwetrust.com/about-the-cause/). Linda circulated information about this campaign to her email list.

28. See Kaskowitz 2013.

29. See Dionne 2012.

30. Within many Protestant denominations, the doctrine of *sola scriptura*—meaning "by scripture alone"—refers to the belief that the Bible, as the word of God, is the supreme authority on all questions of religious doctrine and practice.

31. See Crapanzano (2001) and Smith and Tuttle (2011) on the historical and cultural parallels between biblical literalism and political-legal literalism in American society; Gorski (forthcoming) on the development of a hermeneutic of suspicion among American conservatives; and Williams (2009) on evangelicals' antielitism.

32. Within Protestant Christianity, the doctrine of the "priesthood of all believers" asserts that all believers have direct access to God without requiring religious leaders as intermediaries. I am indebted to Daniel Winchester for suggesting this phrase.

33. See Braunstein et al. forthcoming.

34. See Dionne et al. 2014; Braunstein et al. forthcoming.

FIVE. HOLDING GOVERNMENT ACCOUNTABLE

1. See www.whitehouse.gov/21stcenturygov/actions/first-principles.

2. This was the headline used on a virtual "comment box" through which citizens were invited to submit their ideas for improving government during President Obama's transition to the White House (http://change.gov/agenda/ethics_agenda/).

3. See Clemens (1993) and Tilly (1993) on how organizational forms vary within the collective-action field.

4. Gamson 1992:6.

5. See Fischer (1990) for an account of experts' growing authority over politics and policy making.

6. See Habermas (1987), Fischer (1990), and Turner (2001) for critical perspectives on this question.

7. See Schudson 1998.

8. This idea can be traced to Alexis de Tocqueville's (2003) observations about the effects of civic participation on citizens, and has been developed

further by political scientists interested in how these "schools" work in practice (Mansbridge 1999; Warren 2000; Talpin 2011).

9. While this kind of knowledge-work is most commonly associated with civic organizations, it has also been central to more explicitly politicized efforts as well (Evans and Boyte 1992; Polletta 1999). Projects ranging from late nineteenth-century populism to mid-twentieth-century feminism cultivated participants' capacity to challenge hegemonic knowledge and the authority of experts (Goodwyn 1976; Collins 2000).

10. See Sampson et al. 2005.

11. The significance of this reference to Psalm 133 is discussed in chapter 4.

12. Stout 2010:100.

13. This was a meeting of a smaller, neighboring Tea Party group whose membership overlapped significantly with that of the Patriots, and which was taken over after the departure of its founders by two active members of the Patriots. As a result, I treat this group as an extension of the Patriots.

14. Bastiat's *The Law* (1850) and Hayek's *Road to Serfdom* (1944) were widely read and discussed within the movement nationally (Zernike 2010b). Phil once gave me a copy of *The Law* as a gift, explaining he had a box of them for just that purpose.

15. Glenn Beck's multimedia news platform.

16. See Gorski forthcoming; see also Crapanzano 2001; Williams 2009.

17. See Morales 2012.

18. See Skocpol and Williamson 2012:202.

19. See Mansbridge 1999; Warren 2000; Tocqueville 2003; Talpin 2011.

20. Participatory democracy is "an organizational form in which decision-making is decentralized, nonhierarchical, and consensus-oriented. It can be contrasted with bureaucracy, in which decision-making is centralized, hierarchical, and based on a formal division of labor, as well as with majority vote" (Polletta 2013). This organizational style also tends to reflect a rejection of authority. See Polletta (2002) on participatory democracy within American social movements.

21. Williams 1995:130–131. See also Bellah 1975; Gorski forthcoming.

22. See Williams 1995.

23. Williams 1995:133. See also Gorski forthcoming.

24. Williams 1995:133.

25. Witte 1987:592. According to Puritan thought, the civil ruler is a vessel representing God's authority on earth. Even so, the relationship between civil authorities and the people is to be marked by mutual accountability.

SIX. STYLES OF ACTIVE CITIZENSHIP

1. See Clemens 1993; Tilly 1993; Williams 1995; Jasper 1997; Tilly and Tarrow 2007.

2. This finding is consistent with recent research challenging the assumption that political ideologies are coherent cultural schemas motivating action. Rather, this work suggests political ideologies are better understood as (1) complex cultural traditions that contain varied, evolving, and sometimes contradictory ideas that actors pragmatically draw upon to justify action, or (2) group identities that shape action insofar as individuals behave according to shifting ideas about "what conservatives do" or "what progressives do." See Fine and Sandstrom 1993; Gross et al. 2011; Lichterman 2012, 2013.

3. See Goffman 1959.

4. This is akin to Clemens's (1993:775) observation that political actors often ask, "What kind of group are we? and What do groups like us do?" when selecting organizational styles.

5. This is a collective version of what Brubaker (2004) calls "situated subjectivity."

6. See Vaisey 2009.

7. Bourdieu 1984; see also Calhoun 2003; Brubaker 2004. On how this relates to recent research on human cognition, see Vaisey (2009).

8. Participants do not necessarily develop common *motivations* for acting; rather, groups tend to develop shared *justifications* for their work before they move forward together. These can take the form of frames, collective identities, or narratives and are constructed through ongoing cultural work. See Snow et al. 1986; Polletta and Jasper 2001; Polletta 2006; Reger et al. 2008.

9. Swidler 1986:278.

10. Eliasoph and Lichterman 2003; Lichterman and Eliasoph 2014.

11. Blee 2012.

12. According to Blee, true "turning points"—when groups "consider options that were previously dismissed as unthinkable"—are quite rare (2012:40). But the frequency with which groups will still face "unsettled" situations likely depends on the size and structure of a group. The small size, organizational flexibility, and voluntary nature of groups like Interfaith and the Patriots, compared to those of large bureaucratic organizations, for example, may prompt more frequent demands to revisit and rearticulate organizational choices.

13. Eliasoph and Lichterman (2003) observe that interactions or proposals that breach the unspoken norms of a group force group members to rearticulate those norms.

14. It is also in such moments that the influence of imaginaries on group behavior becomes most *visible*. I cannot rule out the possibility that these imaginaries did not also influence group behavior through less visible mechanisms—for example, by shaping each individual's unconscious cultural schema. This is a limitation of the data and methods used in this study. Although observations of group interactions and interviews with participants offer significant insight into how group members debate and justify collective activities, they cannot be used

to discern the unconscious motivations of individuals (see Vaisey [2009] for a critique of interview methods on these grounds).

15. Several members of this local Republican Club attended social events hosted by the Patriots, including the group's election night parties and their one-year anniversary party later that year.

16. See Mansbridge 2003.

17. Stout 2010:70.

SEVEN. CONCLUSION

1. Mills (2000:5) advanced "the idea that the individual can understand his own experience and gauge his own fate only by locating himself within his period, that he can know his own chances in life only by becoming aware of those of all individuals in his circumstances. In many ways it is a terrible lesson; in many ways a magnificent one."

2. Schudson 1998.

3. Lichterman and Cefai (2006:403) note that narratives "put shared representations in movement."

4. Bourdieu (1991) made this argument most notably to explain the context in which intellectuals and workers became political allies, arguing this was rooted in their homologous positions of subordination within their respective fields. One could argue that, because groups like Interfaith and the Patriots operate within the same political field, this theory would not apply to them. But Bourdieu leaves open the possibility that groups occupying structurally similar positions within any field could forge political alliances on this basis (Swartz 1997).

5. Anderson 2006:6.

6. Smith 2003.

7. Prothero 2012:1, 2; see also Lepore 2010, 2012.

8. Lepore 2010; Dionne 2012.

9. Smith 2003.

10. Bellah 1967, 1975.

11. See Wuthnow 1988; Hunter 1991.

12. Demerath and Williams 1985.

13. See Morone 1990; Schudson 1998; Stears 2007; Gorski forthcoming. Recent work also highlights the racialized and gendered dimensions of contests over the meaning of citizenship (Glenn 2002; Bloemraad 2006; Fox 2012).

14. Smith 2003:158, 185. In *Federalist #10*, James Madison proposed managing dangerous factions by multiplying the number of all factions rather than abolishing the dangerous ones.

APPENDIX

1. It is not uncommon for movements to experience ebbs and flows in their activity levels. See Taylor 1989; Whittier 1997.

2. They relied primarily on grant funding and staff support from PICO, in addition to dues from member congregations, but often faced funding shortages. Many groups face such constraints in addition to other challenges and are thus short-lived. As community organizers working broadly in the tradition of Saul Alinsky commonly quip, "All organizing is reorganizing" (Osterman 2002:70; Gecan 2004).

3. See Zernike and Thee-Brenan 2010; Williamson et al. 2011; Skocpol and Williamson 2012.

4. Skocpol and Williamson 2012.

5. See Skocpol and Williamson's map of nationwide Tea Party activity (2012:91).

6. See Braunstein et al. 2014.

7. See Wood 2002.

8. See Blee 2012.

9. A review of several comparative ethnographies of two or more civic or political groups reveals that researchers employed various strategies to position themselves symmetrically in relation to each of the groups they studied (see Wood 2002; Lichterman 2005, 2008; Summers-Effler 2010; Baiocchi et al. 2014; Bean 2014). Yet these studies offer only limited insight into the challenges of studying politically dissimilar or opposing groups ethnographically. One exception is Ginsburg (1998).

10. Blee (2007:121) notes, "Far-right groups tend to regard academics as untrustworthy or hostile and generally are determined to prevent entree to their groups or members," and "scholarly access to the far right also is limited because academics tend to have few, if any, personal contacts through whom they can gain entrance to secretive rightist groups or who can vouch for them to less secretive ones." This is not to say, however, that ethnographers are unable to study people from whom they differ politically (e.g., Ginsburg 1998; Shapira 2013).

11. These assumptions ignore critiques of a close and/or "insider" relationship. See Merton 1972.

12. Fine 2003:53.

13. For example, see Duneier 1999; Black 2010; Goffman 2014.

14. Simmel 1950:404; Lichterman 2008:88.

15. See Merton 1972; Lichterman 2008.

References

Alexander, Jeffrey C. 2006. *The Civil Sphere*. New York: Oxford University Press.

Alexander, Jeffrey C., and Philip Smith. 1993. "The Discourse of American Civil Society: A New Proposal for Cultural Studies." *Theory and Society* 22(2):151–207.

Alinsky, Saul. 1946. *Reveille for Radicals*. New York: Vintage Books.

Alterman, Eric, James Antle, Ayesha Kazmi, Sally Kohn, Doug Guetzloe, Frances Fox Piven, and Douglas Rushkoff. 2011. "Occupy Wall Street and the Tea Party Compared." *The Guardian*, October 7. www.guardian.co.uk/commentisfree/cifamerica/2011/oct/07/occupy-wall-street-tea-party.

Anderson, Benedict. 2006. *Imagined Communities: Reflections on the Origin and Spread of Nationalism*. New ed. London: Verso.

Audi, Robert, and Nicholas Wolterstorff. 1997. *Religion in the Public Square: The Place of Religious Convictions in Political Debate*. Lanham, MD: Rowman and Littlefield.

Baiocchi, Gianpaolo, Elizabeth A. Bennett, Alissa Cordner, Peter Taylor Klein, and Stephanie Savell. 2014. *The Civic Imagination: Making a Difference in American Political Life*. Boulder, CO: Paradigm.

Bean, Lydia. 2014. *The Politics of Evangelical Identity: Local Churches and Partisan Divides in the United States and Canada*. Princeton, NJ: Princeton University Press.

Beck, Glenn. 2010. "Glenn Beck: Liberation Theology and Social Justice." *Glenn Beck* blog, July 13. www.glennbeck.com/content/articles/article/198/42891/.

Bellah, Robert N. 1967. "Civil Religion in America." *Daedalus* 96(1):1–21.

———. 1975. *The Broken Covenant: American Civil Religion in Time of Trial.* Chicago: University of Chicago Press.

Bellah, Robert N., Richard Madsen, William M. Sullivan, Ann Swidler, and Steven M. Tipton. 1985. *Habits of the Heart: Individualism and Commitment in American Life.* Berkeley: University of California Press.

Bender, Courtney. 2003. *Heaven's Kitchen: Living Religion at God's Love We Deliver.* Chicago: University of Chicago Press.

Bernstein, Mary. 1997. "Celebration and Suppression: The Strategic Uses of Identity by the Lesbian and Gay Movement." *American Journal of Sociology* 103(3):531–565.

———. 2008. "The Analytic Dimensions of Identity: A Political Identity Framework." In *Identity Work in Social Movements,* edited by Jo Reger, Daniel J. Myers, and Rachel L. Einwohner, 277–301. Minneapolis: University of Minnesota Press.

Black, Timothy. 2010. *When a Heart Turns Rock Solid: The Lives of Three Puerto Rican Brothers on and off the Streets.* New York: Vintage Books.

Blee, Kathleen M. 2007. "Ethnographies of the Far Right." *Journal of Contemporary Ethnography* 36(2):119–128.

———. 2012. *Democracy in the Making: How Activist Groups Form.* New York: Oxford University Press.

Blee, Kathleen M., and Kimberly A. Creasap. 2010. "Conservative and Right-Wing Movements." *Annual Review of Sociology* 36:269–286.

Bloemraad, Irene. 2006. *Becoming a Citizen: Incorporating Immigrants and Refugees in the United States and Canada.* Berkeley: University of California Press.

Bourdieu, Pierre. 1984. *Distinction: A Social Critique of the Judgement of Taste.* Cambridge, MA: Harvard University Press.

———. 1991. *Language and Symbolic Power.* Cambridge, MA: Harvard University Press.

Boyte, Harry C. 1989. *Commonwealth: A Return to Citizen Politics.* New York: Free Press.

Braunstein, Ruth. 2011. "Who Are 'We the People'?" *Contexts* 10(2):72–73.

———. 2014. "Who Are 'We the People'? Multidimensional Identity Work in the Tea Party." In *Understanding the Tea Party Movement,* edited by Nella Van Dyke and David S. Meyer, 149–173. Burlington, VT: Ashgate.

Braunstein, Ruth, Todd Nicholas Fuist, and Rhys H. Williams. Forthcoming. *Religion and Progressive Activism: New Stories about Faith and Politics.* New York: NYU Press.

Braunstein, Ruth, Brad R. Fulton, and Richard L. Wood. 2014. "The Role of Bridging Cultural Practices in Racially and Socioeconomically Diverse Civic Organizations." *American Sociological Review* 79(4):705–725.

Bretherton, Luke. 2010. *Christianity and Contemporary Politics: The Conditions and Possibilities of Faithful Witness.* Chichester, U.K.: Wiley-Blackwell.

———. 2015. *Resurrecting Democracy: Faith, Citizenship, and the Politics of a Common Life.* New York: Cambridge University Press.

Brubaker, Rogers. 2004. *Ethnicity without Groups.* Cambridge, MA: Harvard University Press.

Calhoun, Craig J. 1994. *Social Theory and the Politics of Identity.* Oxford, U.K.: Blackwell.

———. 2003. "The Variability of Belonging: A Reply to Rogers Brubaker." *Ethnicities* 3(4):558–568.

———. 2008. "'Recognizing' Religion." *Immanent Frame.* http://blogs.ssrc.org/tif/2008/03/24/recognizing-religion/.

———. 2012. *The Roots of Radicalism: Tradition, the Public Sphere, and Early Nineteenth-Century Social Movements.* Chicago: University of Chicago Press.

Casanova, José. 1994. *Public Religions in the Modern World.* Chicago: University of Chicago Press.

Chambers, Edward T., and Michael A. Cowan. 2003. *Roots for Radicals: Organizing for Power, Action, and Justice.* New York: Continuum.

Chambers, Simone. 2003. "Deliberative Democratic Theory." *Annual Review of Political Science* 6:307–326.

Chaves, Mark. 1994. "Secularization as Declining Religious Authority." *Social Forces* 72(3):749–774.

Clemens, Elisabeth S. 1993. "Organizational Repertoires and Institutional Change: Women's Groups and the Transformation of U.S. Politics, 1890–1920." *American Journal of Sociology* 98(4):755–798.

Collins, Patricia Hill. 2000. *Black Feminist Thought: Knowledge, Consciousness, and the Politics of Empowerment.* New York: Routledge.

Crapanzano, Vincent. 2001. *Serving the Word: Literalism in America from the Pulpit to the Bench.* New York: New Press.

Day, Katie, Esther McIntosh, and William Storrar, eds. 2013. *Yours the Power: Faith-Based Organizing in the USA.* Leiden, Netherlands: Brill.

Deckman, Melissa. 2016. *Tea Party Women: Mama Grizzlies, Grassroots Leaders, and the Changing Face of the American Right.* New York: NYU Press.

Demerath, N.J., III, and Rhys H. Williams. 1985. "Civil Religion in an Uncivil Society." *Annals of the American Academy of Political and Social Science* 480:154–166.

Desilver, Drew. 2016. "U.S. Voter Turnout Trails Most Developed Countries." Fact-Tank: News in the Numbers. Pew Research Center, August 2. www.pewresearch.org/fact-tank/2016/08/02/u-s-voter-turnout-trails-most-developed-countries/.

DeYoung, Curtiss Paul, Michael O. Emerson, George Yancey, and Karen Chai Kim. 2004. *United by Faith: The Multiracial Congregation as an Answer to the Problem of Race.* New York: Oxford University Press.

Diaz-Edelman, Mia. Forthcoming. "Activist Etiquette in the Multicultural Immigrant Rights Movement." In *Religion and Progressive Activism: New Stories about Faith and Politics,* edited by Ruth Braunstein, Todd Nicholas Fuist, and Rhys H. Williams. New York: NYU Press.

DiMaggio, Paul, John Evans, and Bethany Bryson. 1996. "Have Americans' Social Attitudes Become More Polarized?" *American Journal of Sociology* 102(3):690–755.

Dionne, E. J., Jr. 2012. *Our Divided Political Heart: The Battle for the American Idea in an Age of Discontent.* New York: Bloomsbury.

———. 2016. *Why the Right Went Wrong: Conservatism—from Goldwater to the Tea Party and Beyond.* New York: Simon and Schuster.

Dionne, E. J., Jr., William A. Galston, Korin Davis, and Ross Tilchen. 2014. *Faith in Equality: Economic Justice and the Future of Religious Progressives.* Washington, DC: Brookings.

Dovi, Chris. 2011. "Can Occupy and the Tea Party Team Up?" *Salon,* December 7. www.salon.com/2011/12/07/can_occupy_and_the_tea_party_team_up/.

Duneier, Mitchell. 1999. *Sidewalk.* New York: Farrar, Straus and Giroux.

Eliasoph, Nina. 1998. *Avoiding Politics: How Americans Produce Apathy in Everyday Life.* Cambridge: Cambridge University Press.

Eliasoph, Nina, and Paul Lichterman. 2003. "Culture in Interaction." *American Journal of Sociology* 108(4):735–794.

Emerson, Michael O. 2006. *People of the Dream: Multiracial Congregations in the United States.* Princeton, NJ: Princeton University Press.

Emirbayer, Mustafa, and Ann Mische. 1998. "What Is Agency?" *American Journal of Sociology* 103(4):962–1023.

Evans, Sara M., and Harry C. Boyte. 1992. *Free Spaces: The Sources of Democratic Change in America.* Chicago: University of Chicago Press.

Fantasia, Rick. 1988. *Cultures of Solidarity: Consciousness, Action, and Contemporary American Workers.* Berkeley: University of California Press.

Fetner, Tina. 2008. *How the Religious Right Shaped Lesbian and Gay Activism.* Minneapolis: University of Minnesota Press.

Fetner, Tina, and Brayden G. King. 2014. "Three-Layer Movements, Resources, and the Tea Party." In *Understanding the Tea Party Movement,* edited by Nella Van Dyke and David S. Meyer, 35–54. Burlington, VT: Ashgate.

Fine, Gary Alan. 2003. "Towards a Peopled Ethnography: Developing Theory from Group Life." *Ethnography* 4(1):41–60.

Fine, Gary Alan, and Kent Sandstrom. 1993. "Ideology in Action: A Pragmatic Approach to a Contested Concept." *Sociological Theory* 11(1):21–38.

Fiorina, Morris P., Samuel J. Abrams, and Jeremy Pope. 2005. *Culture War? The Myth of a Polarized America*. New York: Pearson Longman.

Fischer, Frank. 1990. *Technocracy and the Politics of Expertise*. Newbury Park, CA: Sage.

Fowler, Robert Booth, Allen D. Hertzke, Laura R. Olson, and Kevin R. den Dulk. 2014. *Religion and Politics in America: Faith, Culture, and Strategic Choices*. 5th ed. Boulder, CO: Westview Press.

Fox, Cybelle. 2012. *Three Worlds of Relief: Race, Immigration, and the American Welfare State from the Progressive Era to the New Deal*. Princeton, NJ: Princeton University Press.

Friedersdorf, Conor. 2011. "Why the Tea Party and Occupy Wall Street Should Cooperate." *The Atlantic*, October 11. www.theatlantic.com/politics/archive/2011/10/why-the-tea-party-and-occupy-wall-street-should-cooperate/246413/.

Frye, Margaret. 2012. "Bright Futures in Malawi's New Dawn: Educational Aspirations as Assertions of Identity." *American Journal of Sociology* 117(6):1565–1624.

Gamson, William A. 1992. *Talking Politics*. Cambridge: Cambridge University Press.

Ganz, Marshall. 2000. "Resources and Resourcefulness: Strategic Capacity in the Unionization of California Agriculture, 1959–1966." *American Journal of Sociology* 105(4):1003–1062.

———. 2009. *Why David Sometimes Wins: Leadership, Organization, and Strategy in the California Farm Worker Movement*. New York: Oxford University Press.

Gaonkar, Dilip Parameshwar. 2002. "Toward New Imaginaries: An Introduction." *Public Culture* 14(1):1–19.

Gecan, Michael. 2004. *Going Public: An Organizer's Guide to Citizen Action*. New York: Anchor Books.

Gibson, David R. 2011. "Speaking of the Future: Contentious Narration during the Cuban Missile Crisis." *Qualitative Sociology* 34(4):503–522.

Gilens, Martin. 2014. *Affluence and Influence: Economic Inequality and Political Power in America*. Princeton, NJ: Princeton University Press.

Ginsburg, Faye D. 1998. *Contested Lives: The Abortion Debate in an American Community*. 2nd ed. Berkeley: University of California Press.

Gitlin, Todd. 2011. "The Left Declares Its Independence." *New York Times*, October 8. www.nytimes.com/2011/10/09/opinion/sunday/occupy-wall-street-and-the-tea-party.html.

Glaeser, Andreas. 2011. *Political Epistemics: The Secret Police, the Opposition, and the End of East German Socialism*. Chicago: University of Chicago Press.

Glaser, Barney G. and Anselm L. Strauss. 1967. *The Discovery of Grounded Theory: Strategies for Qualitative Research*. Chicago: Transaction.

Glenn, Evelyn Nakano. 2002. *Unequal Freedom: How Race and Gender Shaped American Citizenship and Labor*. Cambridge, MA: Harvard University Press.

Goffman, Alice. 2014. *On the Run: Fugitive Life in an American City*. Chicago: University of Chicago Press.

Goffman, Erving. 1959. *The Presentation of Self in Everyday Life*. Garden City, NY: Doubleday.

Goodwyn, Lawrence. 1976. *Democratic Promise: The Populist Moment in America*. New York: Oxford University Press.

Gorski, Philip. Forthcoming. *American Covenant: A History of Civil Religion from the Puritans to the Present*. Princeton, NJ: Princeton University Press.

Greeley, Andrew M., and Michael Hout. 2006. *The Truth about Conservative Christians: What They Think and What They Believe*. Chicago: University of Chicago Press.

Greenberg, Jon. 2015. "War of Words: The Fight over 'Radical Islamic Terrorism.'" *PolitiFact*, December 11. http://politifact.com/truth-o-meter/article/2015/dec/11/war-words-fight-over-radical-islamic-terrorism/.

Gross, Neil, Thomas Medvetz, and Rupert Russell. 2011. "The Contemporary American Conservative Movement." *Annual Review of Sociology* 37:325–354.

Habermas, Jürgen. 1987. *The Theory of Communicative Action*. Vol. 2. Boston: Beacon Press.

———. 2006. "Religion in the Public Sphere." *European Journal of Philosophy* 14(1):1–25.

———. 2008. "Notes on Post-Secular Society." *New Perspectives Quarterly* 25(4):17–29.

Hadden, Stuart C., and Marilyn Lester. 1978. "Talking Identity: The Production of 'Self' in Interaction." *Human Studies* 1(1):331–356.

Hagerty, Barbara Bradley. 2010. "The Tea Party's Tension: Religion's Role in Politics." *NPR*, September 30. www.npr.org/2010/09/30/130238835/the-tea-partys-tension-religions-role-in-politics.

Hart, Stephen. 2001. *Cultural Dilemmas of Progressive Politics: Styles of Engagement among Grassroots Activists*. Chicago: University of Chicago Press.

Herberg, Will. 1955. *Protestant-Catholic-Jew: An Essay in American Religious Sociology*. Garden City, NY: Doubleday.

Hertzke, Allen D. 1988. *Representing God in Washington: The Role of Religious Lobbies in the American Polity*. Knoxville: University of Tennessee Press.

Hofrenning, Daniel J. B. 1995. *In Washington but Not of It: The Prophetic Politics of Religious Lobbyists*. Philadelphia, PA: Temple University Press.

Hooper, Molly K. 2010. "Constitution Is This Year's Big Best-Seller." *The Hill*, May 21. http://thehill.com/homenews/administration/99099-constitution-is-this-years-big-best-seller.

Hout, Michael, and Claude S. Fischer. 2002. "Why More Americans Have No Religious Preference: Politics and Generations." *American Sociological Review* 67(2):165–190.

Hunt, Scott A., and Robert D. Benford. 1994. "Identity Talk in the Peace and Justice Movement." *Journal of Contemporary Ethnography* 22(4): 488–517.

Hunter, James Davison. 1991. *Culture Wars: The Struggle to Define America*. New York: Basic Books.

Jacobs, Lawrence R., Fay Lomax Cook, and Michael X. Delli Carpini. 2009. *Talking Together: Public Deliberation and Political Participation in America*. Chicago: University of Chicago Press.

Jacobsen, Dennis A. 2001. *Doing Justice: Congregations and Community Organizing*. Minneapolis, MN: Fortress Press.

Jansen, Robert S. 2011. "Populist Mobilization: A New Theoretical Approach to Populism." *Sociological Theory* 29(2):75–96.

Jasper, James M. 1997. *The Art of Moral Protest*. Chicago: University of Chicago Press.

Jones, Robert P., and Daniel Cox. 2010. "Religion and the Tea Party in the 2010 Election: An Analysis of the Third Biennial American Values Survey." Washington, DC: PRRI. www.prri.org/research/religion-tea-party-2010/.

Kaskowitz, Sheryl. 2013. *God Bless America: The Surprising History of an Iconic Song*. New York: Oxford University Press.

Khan, Huma. 2011. "Is the Tea Party a Religious Movement? 'Anthem' Invokes God, Judgment Day." *ABC News*, October 18. http://abcnews.go.com/blogs/politics/2011/10/is-the-tea-party-a-religious-movement-anthem-invokes-god-judgment-day/.

Klassen, Pamela E., and Courtney Bender. 2010. "Introduction: Habits of Pluralism." In *After Pluralism: Reimagining Religious Engagement*, edited by Courtney Bender and Pamela E. Klassen, 1–30. New York: Columbia University Press.

Klatch, Rebecca E. 1999. *A Generation Divided: The New Left, the New Right, and the 1960s*. Berkeley: University of California Press.

Kruse, Kevin M. 2015. *One Nation under God: How Corporate America Invented Christian America*. New York: Basic Books.

Ladd, Kevin L., and Bernard Spilka. 2002. "Inward, Outward, and Upward: Cognitive Aspects of Prayer." *Journal for the Scientific Study of Religion* 41(3):475–484.

Lakoff, George. 2002. *Moral Politics: How Liberals and Conservatives Think*. Chicago: University of Chicago Press.

Leondar-Wright, Betsy. 2014. *Missing Class: Strengthening Social Movement Groups by Seeing Class Cultures.* Ithaca, NY: Cornell University Press.

Lepore, Jill. 2010. *The Whites of Their Eyes: The Tea Party's Revolution and the Battle over American History.* Princeton, NJ: Princeton University Press.

———. 2012. *The Story of America: Essays on Origins.* Princeton, NJ: Princeton University Press.

Lessig, Lawrence. 2011. *Republic, Lost: How Money Corrupts Congress—and a Plan to Stop It.* New York: Twelve Books.

Lichterman, Paul. 2005. *Elusive Togetherness: Church Groups Trying to Bridge America's Divisions.* Princeton, NJ: Princeton University Press.

———. 2008. "Religion and the Construction of Civic Identity." *American Sociological Review* 73(1):83–104.

———. 2012. "Religion in Public Action: From Actors to Settings." *Sociological Theory* 30(1):15–36.

———. 2013. "Studying Public Religion: Beyond the Beliefs-Driven Actor." In *Religion on the Edge: De-centering and Re-centering the Sociology of Religion,* edited by Courtney Bender, Wendy Cadge, Peggy Levitt, and David Smilde, 115–136. New York: Oxford University Press.

Lichterman, Paul, and Daniel Cefai. 2006. "The Idea of Political Culture." In the *Oxford Handbook of Contextual Political Analysis,* edited by Robert E. Goodin and Charles Tilly, 392–416. Oxford, U.K.: Oxford University Press.

Lichterman, Paul, and Nina Eliasoph. 2014. "Civic Action." *American Journal of Sociology* 120(3):798–863.

Liptak, Adam. 2010. "Tea-ing Up the Constitution: The Tea Party and the Constitution." *New York Times,* March 13. www.nytimes.com/2010/03/14/weekinreview/14liptak.html.

Luker, Kristin. 1984. *Abortion and the Politics of Motherhood.* Berkeley: University of California Press.

Mansbridge, Jane. 1999. "On the Idea That Participation Makes Better Citizens." In *Citizen Competence and Democratic Institutions,* edited by Stephen L. Elkin and Karol Edward Soltan, 291–325. University Park: Penn State Press.

———. 2003. "Rethinking Representation." *American Political Science Review* 97(4):515–528.

Manseau, Peter. 2015. *One Nation, under Gods: A New American History.* New York: Little, Brown.

Masci, David. 2015. "Q&A: A Look at What's Driving the Changes Seen in Our Religious Landscape Study." Pew Research Center, May 27. www.pewresearch.org/fact-tank/2015/05/27/qa-a-look-at-whats-driving-the-changes-seen-in-our-religious-landscape-study/.

Massengill, Rebekah Peeples. 2013. *Wal-Mart Wars: Moral Populism in the Twenty-First Century.* New York: NYU Press.

McAdam, Doug. 1986. "Recruitment to High-Risk Activism: The Case of Freedom Summer." *American Journal of Sociology* 92(1):64–90.

McAdam, Doug, Robert J. Sampson, Simon Weffer, and Heather MacIndoe. 2005. "'There Will Be Fighting in the Streets': The Distorting Lens of Social Movement Theory." *Mobilization: An International Quarterly* 10(1):1–18.

McCarthy, Thomas. 1995. "Legitimacy and Diversity: Dialectical Reflections on Analytical Distinctions." *Cardozo Law Review* 17:1083–1125.

McVeigh, Rory. 2009. *The Rise of the Ku Klux Klan: Right-Wing Movements and National Politics*. Minneapolis: University of Minnesota Press.

McVeigh, Rory, Kraig Beyerlein, Burrel Vann, and Priyamvada Trivedi. 2014. "Educational Segregation, Tea Party Organizations, and Battles over Distributive Justice." *American Sociological Review* 79(4):630–652.

Merton, Robert K. 1972. "Insiders and Outsiders: A Chapter in the Sociology of Knowledge." *American Journal of Sociology* 78(1):9–47.

Meyer, David S. 2006. "Claiming Credit: Stories of Movement Influence as Outcomes." *Mobilization: An International Quarterly* 11(3):281–298.

Mills, C. Wright. 2000. *The Sociological Imagination*. New York: Oxford University Press.

Mische, Ann. 2009. "Projects and Possibilities: Researching Futures in Action." *Sociological Forum* 24(3):694–704.

Montopoli, Brian. 2010. "Al Sharpton: Glenn Beck Trying to 'Hijack' Civil Rights Movement." *CBS News Online*, August 28. www.cbsnews.com/news/al-sharpton-glenn-beck-trying-to-hijack-civil-rights-movement/.

Morales, Lymari. 2012. "U.S. Distrust in Media Hits New High." Gallup. September 21. www.gallup.com/poll/157589/distrust-media-hits-new-high.aspx.

Morone, James A. 1990. *The Democratic Wish: Popular Participation and the Limits of American Government*. New York: Basic Books.

Morris, Richard B. 1973. *Seven Who Shaped Our Destiny: The Founding Fathers as Revolutionaries*. New York: Harper and Row.

Nepstad, Sharon Erickson. 2001. "Creating Transnational Solidarity: The Use of Narrative in the U.S.-Central America Peace Movement." *Mobilization: An International Quarterly* 6(1):21–36.

Neuhaus, Richard John. 1984. *The Naked Public Square: Religion and Democracy in America*. Grand Rapids: W. B. Eerdmans.

Norton, Mary Beth. 1980. *Liberty's Daughters: The Revolutionary Experience of American Women, 1750–1800*. Ithaca, NY: Cornell University Press.

NPR Staff. 2011. "Occupy Wall Street, Tea Party: United in Distrust." *NPR*, October 22. www.npr.org/2011/10/22/141619672/finding-common-ground-between-two-movements.

Osterman, Paul. 2002. *Gathering Power: The Future of Progressive Politics in America*. Boston: Beacon Press.

Parekh, Bhikhu C. 2002. *Rethinking Multiculturalism: Cultural Diversity and Political Theory.* Cambridge, MA: Harvard University Press.

Parker, Christopher S. and Matt A. Barreto. 2013. *Change They Can't Believe In: The Tea Party and Reactionary Politics in America.* Princeton, NJ: Princeton University Press.

Perrin, Andrew J. 2006. *Citizen Speak: The Democratic Imagination in American Life.* Chicago: University of Chicago Press.

Pew Research Center. 2014. "U.S. Religious Landscape Survey." www.pewforum.org/religious-landscape-study/.

Polletta, Francesca. 1999. "'Free Spaces' in Collective Action." *Theory and Society* 28(1):1–38.

———. 2002. *Freedom Is an Endless Meeting: Democracy in American Social Movements.* Chicago: University of Chicago Press.

———. 2006. *It Was Like a Fever: Storytelling in Protest and Politics.* Chicago: University of Chicago Press.

———. 2013. "Participatory Democracy in Social Movements." In *The Wiley-Blackwell Encyclopedia of Social and Political Movements,* edited by David Snow, Donatella Della Porta, Bert Klandermans, and Doug McAdam. Wiley Online Library, http://onlinelibrary.wiley.com/doi/10.1002/9780470674871.wbespm442/abstract.

Polletta, Francesca, and James M. Jasper. 2001. "Collective Identity and Social Movements." *Annual Review of Sociology* 27:283–305.

Prothero, Stephen. 2012. *The American Bible: How Our Words Unite, Divide, and Define a Nation.* New York: HarperOne.

Reger, Jo, Daniel J. Myers, and Rachel L. Einwohner. 2008. *Identity Work in Social Movements.* Minneapolis: University of Minnesota Press.

Rosenthal, Lawrence, and Christine Trost. 2012. *Steep: The Precipitous Rise of the Tea Party.* Berkeley: University of California Press.

Sampson, Robert J., Doug McAdam, Heather MacIndoe, and Simón Weffer-Elizondo. 2005. "Civil Society Reconsidered: The Durable Nature and Community Structure of Collective Civic Action." *American Journal of Sociology* 111(3):673–714.

Schlozman, Kay Lehman, Sidney Verba, and Henry E. Brady. 2012. *The Unheavenly Chorus: Unequal Political Voice and the Broken Promise of American Democracy.* Princeton, NJ: Princeton University Press.

Schudson, Michael. 1998. *The Good Citizen: A History of American Civic Life.* New York: Free Press.

———. 2006. "The Varieties of Civic Experience." *Citizenship Studies* 10(5):591–606.

Schumpeter, Joseph A. 1942. *Capitalism, Socialism and Democracy.* New York: Harper and Brothers.

Schwalbe, Michael L., and Douglas Mason-Schrock. 1996. "Identity Work as Group Process." *Advances in Group Processes* 13:113–147.

Shapira, Harel. 2013. *Waiting for José: The Minutemen's Pursuit of America.* Princeton, NJ: Princeton University Press.

Simmel, Georg. 1950. *The Sociology of Georg Simmel.* Translated by Kurt H. Wolff. New York: Free Press.

Skocpol, Theda. 2003. *Diminished Democracy: From Membership to Management in American Civic Life.* Norman: University of Oklahoma Press.

Skocpol, Theda, Marshall Ganz, and Ziad Munson. 2000. "A Nation of Organizers: The Institutional Origins of Civic Voluntarism in the United States." *American Political Science Review* 94(3):527–546.

Skocpol, Theda, and Vanessa Williamson. 2012. *The Tea Party and the Remaking of Republican Conservatism.* New York: Oxford University Press.

Smith, Aaron. 2013. "Civic Engagement in the Digital Age." Pew Research Center's Internet and American Life Project. http://pewinternet.org/Reports/2013/Civic-Engagement.aspx.

Smith, Peter J., and Robert W. Tuttle. 2011. "Biblical Literalism and Constitutional Originalism." *Notre Dame Law Review* 86(2):693–763.

Smith, Rogers M. 2003. *Stories of Peoplehood: The Politics and Morals of Political Membership.* Cambridge: Cambridge University Press.

Smith, Tom W., Peter Marsden, Michael Hout, and Jibum Kim. 2012. *General Social Surveys, 1972–2012: Cumulative Codebook.* Chicago: National Opinion Research Center.

Snow, David A., and Leon Anderson. 1987. "Identity Work among the Homeless: The Verbal Construction and Avowal of Personal Identities." *American Journal of Sociology* 92(6):1336–1371.

Snow, David A., E. Burke Rochford Jr., Steven K. Worden, and Robert D. Benford. 1986. "Frame Alignment Processes, Micromobilization, and Movement Participation." *American Sociological Review* 51(4):464–481.

Somers, Margaret R. 1994. "The Narrative Constitution of Identity: A Relational and Network Approach." *Theory and Society* 23(5):605–649.

Stears, Marc. 2007. "The Liberal Tradition and the Politics of Exclusion." *Annual Review of Political Science* 10:85–101.

Steensland, Brian, and Philip Goff. 2014. *The New Evangelical Social Engagement.* New York: Oxford University Press.

Stone, Deborah A. 2002. *Policy Paradox: The Art of Political Decision Making.* Rev. ed. New York: Norton.

Stout, Jeffrey. 2010. *Blessed Are the Organized: Grassroots Democracy in America.* Princeton, NJ: Princeton University Press.

Summers-Effler, Erika. 2010. *Laughing Saints and Righteous Heroes: Emotional Rhythms in Social Movement Groups.* Chicago: University of Chicago Press.

Swarts, Heidi J. 2008. *Organizing Urban America: Secular and Faith-Based Progressive Movements*. Minneapolis: University of Minnesota Press.

Swartz, David. 1997. *Culture and Power: The Sociology of Pierre Bourdieu*. Chicago: University of Chicago Press.

Swartz, David R. 2012. *Moral Minority: The Evangelical Left in an Age of Conservatism*. Philadelphia: University of Pennsylvania Press.

Swidler, Ann. 1986. "Culture in Action: Symbols and Strategies." *American Sociological Review* 51(2):273–286.

Talpin, Julien. 2011. *Schools of Democracy: How Ordinary Citizens (Sometimes) Become Competent in Participatory Budgeting Institutions*. Colchester, U.K.: ECPR Press.

Tavory, Iddo, and Nina Eliasoph. 2013. "Coordinating Futures: Toward a Theory of Anticipation." *American Journal of Sociology* 118(4):908–942.

Taylor, Charles. 2004. *Modern Social Imaginaries*. Durham, NC: Duke University Press.

———. 2007. *A Secular Age*. Cambridge, MA: Harvard University Press.

Taylor, Verta. 1989. "Social Movement Continuity: The Women's Movement in Abeyance." *American Sociological Review* 54(5):761–775.

Tilly, Charles. 1993. "Contentious Repertoires in Great Britain, 1758–1834." *Social Science History* 17(2):253–280.

———. 2002. *Stories, Identities, and Political Change*. Lanham, MD: Rowman and Littlefield.

Tilly, Charles, and Sidney G. Tarrow. 2007. *Contentious Politics*. Boulder, CO: Paradigm.

Tocqueville, Alexis de. 2003. *Democracy in America*. London: Penguin Classics.

Turner, Stephen. 2001. "What Is the Problem with Experts?" *Social Studies of Science* 31(1):123–149.

Vaisey, Stephen. 2009. "Motivation and Justification: A Dual-Process Model of Culture in Action." *American Journal of Sociology* 114(6):1675–1715.

Vogel, Kenneth P. 2010. "The Right Loves to Hate—and Imitate—Saul Alinsky." *Politico*, March 22. www.politico.com/story/2010/03/right-loves-to-hate-imitate-alinsky-034751.

Volokh, Eugene. 2015. "Is the United States of America a Republic or a Democracy?" *Washington Post*, May 13. www.washingtonpost.com/news/volokh-conspiracy/wp/2015/05/13/is-the-united-states-of-america-a-republic-or-a-democracy/.

Walzer, Michael. 1985. *Exodus and Revolution*. New York: Basic Books.

Warren, Mark E. 2000. *Democracy and Association*. Princeton, NJ: Princeton University Press.

Warren, Mark R. 2001. *Dry Bones Rattling: Community Building to Revitalize American Democracy*. Princeton, NJ: Princeton University Press.

Weithman, Paul J. 2002. *Religion and the Obligations of Citizenship.* Cambridge: Cambridge University Press.

Whitman, Gordon. 2007. "Beyond Advocacy: The History and Vision of the PICO Network." *Social Policy* (Winter 2007):50–59.

Whittier, Nancy. 1997. "Political Generations, Micro-Cohorts, and the Transformation of Social Movements." *American Sociological Review* 62(5):760–778.

Wilde, Melissa J. 2004. "How Culture Mattered at Vatican II: Collegiality Trumps Authority in the Council's Social Movement Organizations." *American Sociological Review* 69(4):576–602.

Wilentz, Sean. 2010. "Confounding Fathers." *New Yorker,* October 18. www.newyorker.com/magazine/2010/10/18/confounding-fathers.

Williams, Rhys H. 1995. "Constructing the Public Good: Social Movements and Cultural Resources." *Social Problems* 42(1):124–144.

———. 1999. "Visions of the Good Society and the Religious Roots of American Political Culture." *Sociology of Religion* 60(1):1–34.

———. 2009. "Politicized Evangelicalism and Secular Elites: Creating a Moral Other." In *Evangelicals and Democracy in America,* edited by Steven Brint and Jean Reith Schroedel, 143–178. New York: Russell Sage Foundation.

Williams, Rhys H., and Susan M. Alexander. 1994. "Religious Rhetoric in American Populism: Civil Religion as Movement Ideology." *Journal for the Scientific Study of Religion* 33(1):1–15.

Williamson, Vanessa, Theda Skocpol, and John Coggin. 2011. "The Tea Party and the Remaking of Republican Conservatism." *Perspectives on Politics* 9(1):25–43.

Witte, John, Jr. 1987. "Blest Be the Ties That Bind: Covenant and Community in Puritan Thought." *Emory Law Journal* 36:579–601.

Wood, Gordon S. 1988. "The Fundamentalists and the Constitution." *New York Review of Books,* February 18. www.nybooks.com/articles/1988/02/18/the-fundamentalists-and-the-constitution/.

Wood, Richard L. 1999. "Religious Culture and Political Action." *Sociological Theory* 17(3):307–332.

———. 2002. *Faith in Action: Religion, Race, and Democratic Organizing in America.* Chicago: University of Chicago Press.

Wood, Richard L., and Brad R. Fulton. 2015. *A Shared Future: Faith-Based Organizing for Racial Equity and Ethical Democracy.* Chicago: University of Chicago Press.

Wood, Richard L., Brad R. Fulton, and Kathryn Partridge. 2012. "Building Bridges, Building Power: Developments in Institution-Based Community Organizing." Boulder, CO: Interfaith Funders.

Wuthnow, Robert. 1988. *The Restructuring of American Religion: Society and Faith since World War II.* Princeton, NJ: Princeton University Press.

————. 1991. *Acts of Compassion: Caring for Others and Helping Ourselves.* Princeton, NJ: Princeton University Press.

————. 1994. *Producing the Sacred: An Essay on Public Religion.* Urbana: University of Illinois Press.

————. 2005. *America and the Challenges of Religious Diversity.* Princeton, NJ: Princeton University Press.

————. 2008. "Prayer, Cognition, and Culture." *Poetics* 36(5–6):333–337.

————. 2011. "Taking Talk Seriously: Religious Discourse as Social Practice." *Journal for the Scientific Study of Religion* 50(1):1–21.

Wuthnow, Robert, and John H. Evans. 2002. *The Quiet Hand of God.* Berkeley: University of California Press.

Yamane, David. 2000. "Naked Public Square or Crumbling Wall of Separation? Evidence from Legislative Hearings in Wisconsin." *Review of Religious Research* 42(2):175–192.

Yukich, Grace. 2013. *One Family under God: Immigration Politics and Progressive Religion in America.* New York: Oxford University Press.

————. Forthcoming. "Progressive Activism among Buddhists, Hindus, and Muslims in the U.S." In *Religion and Progressive Activism: New Stories about Faith and Politics,* edited by Ruth Braunstein, Todd Nicholas Fuist, and Rhys H. Williams. New York: NYU Press.

Yukich, Grace, and Ruth Braunstein. 2014. "Encounters at the Religious Edge: Variation in Religious Expression across Interfaith Advocacy and Social Movement Settings." *Journal for the Scientific Study of Religion* 53(4):791–807.

Zaret, David. 1992. "Religion, Science, and Printing in the Public Spheres in Seventeenth-Century England." In *Habermas and the Public Sphere,* edited by Craig J. Calhoun, 212–235. Cambridge, MA: MIT Press.

Zernike, Kate. 2010a. *Boiling Mad: Inside Tea Party America.* New York: Henry Holt.

————. 2010b. "Movement of the Moment Looks to Long-Ago Texts." *New York Times,* October 1. www.nytimes.com/2010/10/02/us/politics/02teaparty .html.

Zernike, Kate, and Megan Thee-Brenan. 2010. "Poll Finds Tea Party Backers Wealthier and More Educated." *New York Times,* April 14. www.nytimes .com/2010/04/15/us/politics/15poll.html.

Zietlow, Rebecca E. 2012. "Popular Originalism? The Tea Party Movement and Constitutional Theory." *Florida Law Review* 64(2):483–511.

Index

Abraham, 68, 69
academics: discussions of pluralism, 211n3; and far-right groups, 217n10; and FBCOs, 22, 146; and Occupy movement, 21
accountability: active citizenship and, 35, 49, 82, 157; appropriate practices, 176–78; and becoming informed, 139–142; and common good, 162; frame development, 147tab.1; goals of, 144–47; of government, 3, 13, 19, 24, 118–121; individual accountability actions, 151; listening/speaking, 127–130; mutual accountability, 149, 150, 168, 170–71; organizing for collective action, 67, 122–24, 135–37; and patriotism, 137–39; pressure tactics, 130–35, 142–44, 147tab.1; public accountability actions, 99–100, 122–24, 126–27, 164–66; and public officials, 50, 124–27, 160–61; and public worship spaces, 149; replacement vs. persuasion strategies, 171–75; and representative democracy, 5, 49–50, 168–69; styles, 99, 122, 144–47, 147–151, 147tab.1, 148fig.1. *See also* government accountability
action: Alinsky on, 8; appropriate practices, 11, 25, 153–56, 176–78; biographical availability for, 9; channeling of, 157, 182–85; and civil discourse, 51; distraction and, 10; divergent styles of, 19–21, 114–15; engagement as, 34; narratives, 24, 181–82; organizing public action, 8; and patriotism, 79; political action, 45; and political ideologies, 215n2; as prophetic voices, 53; public accountability actions, 99–100, 122–24, 164–66; public actions, 8, 43–45, 47, 70; social action, 38–39, 45, 67, 72. *See also* collective action; faith into action; interactions; political action
active citizenship, 7, 9, 11, 204n37; awareness and, 37–47; change in, 14–15; and civil discourse, 24; civility vs. confrontation, 157–162, 177–78; and civil religious discourse, 24; collective vs. individual voice, 166–171; comparative perspective of, 21–23, 26; contractual model of, 25, 149; covenantal model of, 148, 149, 150; divergence of, 19–21; and group cultural processes, 20, 24; historical context, 47–54; *Informed Citizen*, 28–37; listening, 37–47; narratives of, 11, 24; patriot model of, 24; political context, 47–54; prophetic voice, 37–47; prophet model of, 24; and public projection of values, 19; and religious institutions, 203n32; replacement vs. persuasion, 171–78; rise of, 13–16; role of, 24; self-interest vs. common good, 162–66;

233

active citizenship *(continued)*
    shared vision of, 7, 9, 11; styles of, 12, 19,
    24, 25, 152–178; substantive citizenship,
    205n54; varieties of, 187–88
Adams, John, 208n5
Adams, Samuel, 208n5
advocacy organizations: early, 14; passive
    activities, 10, 50; professionalization of,
    207n13
Affordable Care Act (Obamacare), 3, 6, 30,
    31, 61, 141, 160, 164, 201n3
agnostics, 17, 93, 203n28
Alexander, Jeffrey C., 51, 205nn52
Alexander, Susan, 205nn53
Alinsky, Saul, 8, 9, 19, 159, 202n9, 206n2,
    217n2
anger, 42, 161, 179
anticipatory representation, 49, 206n10
antidemocratic shift, 17, 18, 116
anxiety, 3, 7, 96, 179
appropriate practices: changing nature of,
    49; and channeling, 182–85; and cultural
    divergence, 176–78; and founding docu-
    ments, 110; and group perceptions, 11,
    12, 25, 175, 181; and historical figures, 60,
    78; interpretation of, 170–71, 199; judg-
    ments of, 153–56; and religious values,
    83, 114
Armey, Dick, 59, 202n9
atheism/atheists, 17, 64, 92, 93, 108, 112, 113,
    203n28
Atlas Shrugged (Rand), 57, 58, 208n4
authority: challenges to, 214n9; of citizens,
    32; civil authority, 214n24; earned
    authority, 128, 170; God's authority,
    214n24; rejection of, 137–39, 172, 214n20;
    and religion, 16, 52

Bastiat, Frédéric, 138, 214n14
Bean, Lydia, 211n10
Beck, Glenn: and collective salvation,
    212nn14–15; influence of, 9, 63, 78, 105–7,
    110, 202n7; Left response to, 140; and
    nonreligious, 112; Restoring Honor Rally
    (Washington, D.C.), 7, 78, 90–97, 192; and
    Skousen, 208n10
behavior, influences on group, 70, 153–56,
    161–62, 176, 215n14
belief(s): differences in, 114; in government,
    4; in media, 141; and nonreligious, 107,
    113, 115; religious, 18, 19, 83, 93, 116; and
    religious minorities, 98; and research
    methodology, 198; and secularization, 16;

and *sola scriptura* doctrine, 213n30;
    standing up for, 144
Bellah, Robert N., 52–53, 187, 207n1,
    207nn16–18
Bender, Courtney, 211n3, 212n24
Berry, Wendell, 71
biblical literalism, 61, 110–11, 208n7, 213n30
blame, 32, 42, 47, 51–52, 75, 210n25
Blee, Kathleen M., 155, 215n12
Bourdieu, Pierre, 154, 184, 216n4
Brubaker, Rogers, 74, 215n5
Buddhism, 17, 83, 88–89, 91, 92, 96

Casanova, José, 203n31
Catholic(s): confrontational relationships,
    160, 174; Day as, 69, 76; diversity and, 17,
    66, 123; Interfaith and, 2, 84–87, 99, 157;
    Muslim comparison, 96; and research
    methodology, 194; and social justice,
    38–40, 148; and Tea Party activism, 92
Cefai, Daniel, 216n3
Chaves, Mark, 203n25
Chavez, Cesar, 68, 69, 70, 76
Chicago Tribune political cartoon, 64, 209n12
Christianity: identifying with, 203n27; and
    religious diversity, 17, 83; and seculariza-
    tion, 97. *See also* Catholicism/Catholics;
    Protestantism/Protestants
Christian Right. *See* conservative religious
    groups
citizens: moral concept of, 205n54; substantive
    concept of, 205n54; use of term, 26–27
citizenship. *See* active citizenship, citizens
civil discourse, 24, 51, 52, 54, 180, 205n52
civility, 157–162, 177–78
civil religious discourse, 24, 53, 180, 205n53,
    207n17–18, 212n14
Clemens, Elisabeth S., 215n4
collective action: appropriate practices,
    153–56; and compromise, 67; and putting
    faith into action, 115; frames, 120; indi-
    vidual action vs., 135–37, 147tab.1; organ-
    izing for, 121, 122–24, 145; and power
    devaluation, 211n39; and replacement
    strategy, 172, 175
collective identities, 73, 210n20, 215n8; as
    active citizens, 73, 74–78; and appropriate
    practices, 153–56; and democratic imagi-
    naries, 149, 166–171; and narratives, 149,
    215n8; situated intersubjectivity, 74, 153;
    situated subjectivity, 74, 215n5
collective vs. individual voice, 25, 166–171,
    212n15

volunteering, 7, 51, 69, 167, 192, 194, 207n13
voter turnout, 10, 15, 173, 175, 202n12

waking up, 6, 23, 28, 33, 51, 53
Wall Street, 5
Washington, George, 208n5
Whitman, Gordon, 210n30
Wilentz, Sean, 208n10
Williams, Rhys H., 148, 149, 187, 205n53,
    210n28, 213n31

Williamson, Vanessa, 195, 204n42
women: citizenship of, 15; feminism, 214n9;
    role of, 75, 76; in Tea Party movement, 9,
    210n27
Wood, Gordon S., 209n11
Wood, Richard L., 204nn36, 39, 44,
    205nn45-46, 211nn6,8, 217nn7,9
Wuthnow, Robert, 212n19

Yukich, Grace, 211n10